Tanner
"Boy Orphan"

Sixteen-Years-Plus Memories of A Home I'm Proud To Have Had

By Fred Tanner

Edited by Perry Lefeavers
G. William "Bill" Adkins

Special Technical Assistance
Jean Lewis Beacham
John McMahon
Amy Higgins Feltz
Wanda Tillett Tanner

Special Thanks to
Kristie Loiacono
Alex Peel
At Trafford Publishing Company

Note for Librarians: a cataloguing record for this book that includes Dewey Decimal Classification and US Library of Congress numbers is available from the Library and Archives of Canada. The complete cataloguing record can be obtained from their online database at:
www.collectionscanada.ca/amicus/index-e.html
ISBN 1-4120-5387-0
Printed in Victoria, BC, Canada

TRAFFORD

Offices in Canada, USA, Ireland, UK and Spain
This book was published on-demand in cooperation with Trafford Publishing. On-demand publishing is a unique process and service of making a book available for retail sale to the public taking advantage of on-demand manufacturing and Internet marketing. On-demand publishing includes promotions, retail sales, manufacturing, order fulfilment, accounting and collecting royalties on behalf of the author.
Book sales for North America and international:
Trafford Publishing, 6E–2333 Government St.,
Victoria, BC v8t 4p4 CANADA
phone 250 383 6864 (toll-free 1 888 232 4444)
fax 250 383 6804; email to orders@trafford.com
Book sales in Europe:
Trafford Publishing (uk) Ltd., Enterprise House, Wistaston Road Business Centre,
Wistaston Road, Crewe, Cheshire cw2 7rp UNITED KINGDOM
phone 01270 251 396 (local rate 0845 230 9601)
facsimile 01270 254 983; orders.uk@trafford.com
Order online at:
www.trafford.com/robots/05-0282.html

10 9 8 7 6 5 4 3 2

This book is dedicated to all adults who care for and about children and especially for those who gave me a chance at life through sacrifice of their own.

A special thanks to all friends of The Methodist Children's Home in Winston-Salem for caring when so many of us were in need of a home.

About The Author

Fred was born just a year before the Japanese forced the United States into World War Two. He was born into the typical poor Appalachian mountain family. The early death of his mother forced the decision on his desperate family to let his sister and him grow up in an orphanage or home for children. At the orphanage Fred survived the many hardships other children suffered of family separation from entering at such an early age. His life at the home would be nurtured and guided by some of the nation's best and devoted caregivers. There were many trying times in his growing years as he was a very spirited lad. Fred was slightly smaller than many of the boys his age but there was no smallness in his heart. Competition was a matter of survival during all of his youthful years. With much forgiveness, devoted staff members helped set his style in life. He learned from the adults everything they were willing to teach him. (Being all boy, sometimes not always in his studies though.) He learned to work hard early in his youth, and that hard work ethic would be noticed by all that knew him in his lifelong career in the United States Coast Guard. Fred's learning experiences in his youth of making things better would be carried with him into his career. He feels that these experiences actually saved his life and that of his fellow crewmembers on many occasions. Fred loved his orphan home and wished every child could have a year with the experiences he lived with and with having over four hundred brothers and sisters to learn to live with.

Preface

Hello, My name is Fred. This is my story about my life, as an orphan boy, growing up in an orphanage. Don't feel sorry for me as I had a warm bed, food to eat and a better chance at life by growing up in this home for children. As my story is told, one must understand that no real harm, I believe, was ever intended to any child in the orphanage, but strong discipline, peer pressure, hard work, rough play and accidents were a matter of fact. One must also understand that, in this era, the type of punishment noted in my story was accepted by society. Personal affection was not a requirement but a welcomed experience at times when our caregivers had the time and kindness to share some with us. Usually punishment was administered to those that required punishment to modify their behavior, and a lot of us boys needed a taste of it once in a while. I believe a little punishment, when needed, helped a lot of boys break the habit of bad behavior before they became men. Your question might be: "Were they bad boys or good boys or were they just mischievous boys?" In our time, my thoughts were that we were mischievous and always looking for some relief in our attempt to be accepted by the other boys, find happiness any way possible or just seeking enjoyment. To keep control of four hundred plus children, there had to be a little fear incentive to help remind us of where we stood in the chain of life. With thirty boys growing up in one cottage and one Home Mother to manage them all, early discipline was important. Good moral character was demanded of us all.

My story will express the many challenges we boys and girls experienced as we grew into young adults. Some of the boys would push well beyond the limits of the rules we were expected to follow. Along with the discipline that we received, you will see caring, love and real concern about our upbringing. We experienced most of the growing pains and love just like children in regular family homes. We were loved; we felt love; we gave love and sometimes we experienced the hurt of love in our learning to try to be normal children.

The Methodist churches of Western North Carolina and the many individual contributors around the state and nation made this Children's Home possible for so many needy children. One could never vision what this Children's Home has grown into from its humble beginning. It started from just four old wooden buildings from Davis School, a discontinued military academy, and developed into a crown jewel of many nice buildings for so many needy children to make their home. Thousands of people up and down the economic ladder made all of this possible. Those who made it well in life had the greatness of giving shelter to needy children. Those who had less gave what they could and altogether made it possible for myself, my sister and many hundreds of other children to have a chance at life and a place to grow up in a Christian environment. It also took many devoted adults, many who had previously grown up at this wonderful place, and gave their entire adult lives to the needs of less fortunate boys and girls.

As you read my story you will see that we had a lot of room to play as children and a lot of chances to learn self-responsibility along with it. We made mistakes and as you will see, we were not perfect little angels. We were forgiven often after some correcting! With four hundred plus children there to care for at any one time, we boys pushed the limits of our freedom. The girls were even more restricted. There is humor that you may not understand. There is hard work. There is sadness. There is happiness. This was a place where, in our imaginations, we could be cowboys, Indian Chiefs, preachers, pilots, soldiers, sailors, sports heroes, doctors, nurses, engineers, teachers or just about anything we wanted to be. As we grew up we would become those people in real life. The Children's Home kids would grow up and become prominent citizens in just about every corner of the country. There was love, sadness and happiness, but most importantly this was a place provided for us where children like myself who had no other place to live could

go and grow into useful citizens. We have so many people
to thank for that.

Chapter One

My story begins in the Appalachian Mountains of Western
North Carolina, some of the most beautiful land in all of our
great country. The rivers, lakes and streams are blessed with
good fish stocks. The trees and vegetation look as though they
were planted especially for this place. My people, along with
most people of the mountains were very poor in terms of
wealth but very rich in practical survival skills. I guess you
could say we were "Culturally Rich" in mountain culture.
Many people today collect the items made by our mountain
people from hundreds of years ago. Mountain lore and music
have become a treasure for studies and museums. This was
just a simple way of life for my family as it was for most all
peaceful mountain people.

I was born in a small cabin near the town of
Hayesville, North Carolina, on the edge of the Nantahala
National Forest in Cherokee country. The cabin, which sat
on the bank of Hyatt's Mill Creek just above the point
where the creek merged into the Hiawassee River, is no
longer there. My Uncle Roy tells me that it burned down
after I had left the area to go to the orphanage. I often

wondered what it would have been like to live there in the mountains. Would my future have taken a different path? Would I have clung to my ancestors' natural ways or would I have ventured into the modern lifestyle? In my lifetime I would experience both lifestyles, finding richness in both! I have strong feelings in my heart for the mountains and the mountain people, and I have learned to love other places like the rivers and oceans in different parts of the world as well.

I have an older sister named Charlena that some people call "Charlie". Neither one of us was given a middle name. Some folks, just kidding with us, say that our family was so poor that Mom and Dad could not afford to give us a middle name.

Lula Bell (Ledford) Tanner
with hound pup.

Though my mother's name was Lula Bell, everyone called her "Bell". Her maiden name was Ledford, a prominent name from the early settlers in the area.

Charlie Jackson Tanner

My dad Charlie Jackson Tanner grew up across the
state line, on a farm in the mountains near Young Harris,
Georgia. Some of my family lived in Hiawassee, Georgia.

My parents came from very patriotic families. A lot of
the men served this great country whenever there was a
need for their services all the way back to the war for our
independence. I'm told my mother was part Cherokee from
some generations back and had quite a spirit. I've listened
to stories, from older family members, about my mother.
She didn't fear much of anything. She would work right
alongside my dad and stand up to anyone who threatened
her family.

I am glad that I inherited my parents' strength and
pride to be able to face my life's complicated journey. I
found myself to be quite spirited and a little stubborn as I
was growing up. My grandmother on my dad's side of the
family ruled the roost at their farm. "So I'm told!" Every one
of the children in Grandma Nannie Gibson Tanner's house
had better pull their share of the workload. Later on as a
young boy, on visits to the mountains, I only remember
seeing my Grandma Tanner a couple of times. One of
those times she was running around making sure that
everything was going, as she wanted.   She would cook big
meals for their large family every day. There was a large

3

wood-burning stove in the kitchen and the kitchen is where everyone would eat at a big table. I don't think that there is a place anywhere in the country where you could buy a meal in a restaurant that tasted as good as the ones we ate at Grandma's house.

Some members of Tanner family with hunting rifles

After supper the men would sit on the front porch chewing their tobacco and challenging each other with their long rifles. Uncle Ed was the best shot with his German Rifle. He could knock a crow out of a tree from a couple of hundred yards away. He wore thick glasses, but he could shoot better than any of the other boys. Several of my uncles had served in the war and knew how to shoot very well. Of course there was a little of that clear stuff in a jar that worked up their bravery and bragging rights after they had taken a couple of swigs. Grandma would get on them if they took to many swigs of that recipe.

4

Grandma Nannie Gibson Tanner

Grandma was proud of her boys that were in the military. She loved Uncle Aude and wore his Army insignia on her lapel. She was proud that her boys helped win the war and saved our country from the Japanese and the Nazis. She was proud of all of her children, all twelve of them, no matter what their line of work.

There was an old outhouse, a two holer, about twenty paces from Grandma's front porch and an old log cabin behind the main house. When we youngsters would go back to the mountains for a visit we would sleep in the loft of that cabin. There were a couple of mattresses up there and we would cover ourselves with quilts to keep warm at night. We could see through the cracks in the boards covering the sides of the cabin.

Grandma's house was in a beautiful spot halfway to the top of the mountain and the road coming up to the farm crossed a wide creek with rocks piled up to drive across. As long as there was no heavy rain, the cars and trucks could manage to cross the creek safely though the road was rutted out and packed hard from years of traffic.

There was a lot of pastureland for the cows to graze and woods as far as you could see.

All of grandma's children helped out on the farm so there was plenty to eat for the large family. Granddad and his sons would go hunting and bring in fresh meat from time to time. Once in a while one of the girls would go with them.

Willa Mae, Sally, Grandpa Elbert, Ed, Baby Charlena, Grandma Nannie Tanner

Sometimes Aunt Louella would take my sister and me to the mountains to visit Grandma's place. During one of our visits we found Grandma sick in bed. She could no longer manage to do the chores that she had always done. Even though she was in bed she would still try to tell everyone what needed to be done and how to do it correctly. She was a tough woman, and I never heard her complain once about how she was hurting. She was still chewing her tobacco while in bed and aiming her spit towards the fireplace across the room. She would spit without missing a word while talking to us. All she wanted to do was hold her grandchildren. She wanted us with her all the time. I had to get out around the farm and see what was going on. That visit would be the last time that I would see my Grandma and Grandpa Tanner. My dad became familiar with hard work early in his boyhood. After he left home and married my mother, he worked very hard trying to care for his family. He dragged logs off the mountain with a mule and did just about any work that could be found. Jobs were hard to come by in those years and, if you could get one, there was very little pay.   My dad also worked on a dairy farm with my uncle Roy. They worked for Doc Killian, our local country doctor. Doc Killian looked after most of the families in that part of the country. Just about everyone was poor, so Doc Killian would accept a chicken or vegetables as payment for his services. There was a lot of trading for services in those times.

As I grew older in life I would also understand just what an impact Doc Killian's decisions would have on my life. Doc Killian delivered my sister and me in our tiny little cabin.

From time to time I would go back to visit with my Uncle Roy and he would tell me about what had happened in those years before I could remember. He told me that he and my dad palled around when they were young, and he told me of all the mischief and fun they had. He also told me about their going further up in the mountains to go hunting, about the mules, old cars and trucks that they used to get around on the mountains. He would take me to some of the most beautiful spots that I have ever been fortunate enough to see in my whole life. I could just sit there for hours and listen to the brooks gurgle as the cold water trickled across the rocks. The mountain laurel and the moss covered the banks of the brooks and the temperature was cool in the shade of the overhanging branches. We could get away from everything just a short distance from his home.

One day my Uncle Roy drove me to the cemetery where my mom and dad were buried. On the way to the cemetery we passed through an area named Jack Rabbit on the other side of Chatuge Lake from where we were born. He said that my mom and dad had lived in Jack Rabbit for a while. Uncle Roy showed me the cemetery at the Philadelphia Baptist Church where my mother and father were buried. The church and cemetery were right on the edge of the lake. It was a beautiful sight looking out across the lake. He said, "This is where your mother is buried," and pointed to the gravesite. He pointed down to a big rock and said, "The big rock is your mother's grave, and the smaller rock is where your Aunt Ruth is buried." My dad's grave had a nice head stone but mom's grave only had a rock for a marker. That just didn't seem right for my mother not to have a real headstone to mark her burial site. I asked Uncle Roy to show my wife Wanda and me the way to the "headstone-making place." I said, "We will put a headstone on my mother's grave before the large rock has a chance of being moved." That big rock had been there, marking my mother's grave, all of my life. Even though I never remembered her I had great concern of losing my mother for a second time.

Uncle Roy showed me where the Ledford cemetery was located. He showed me Granddaddy Ledford's gravesite. There was a rock at his grave, just as there was at my mother's grave. Granddaddy's grave did have one of those metal markers that were placed in the ground next to the rock! Boy, what a history of my mother's side of the family in this one cemetery. The Historical Society has since put brass markers on many of the gravesites where my ancestors made their mark in American history. I felt even more proud to be carrying on a part of American history as part of this patriotic community and patriotic family.

Uncle Roy told me that one night my dad was at the old store just down the road and two men jumped him. A lot of people were moving all over the country at that time looking for work to support their families. There were jobs in the area at the different dams being built by the TVA. He said that word reached my mother at home of what was taking place at the old store. He said my mom grabbed a double bit axe from the chopping block and took off towards the store. A double bit axe is an axe with a cutting edge on both sides. He further stated that my dad put up a good fight, but the two men were just too much for my dad to fend off. By the time my mom arrived at the store my dad was just about beaten to death by the two men. Some folks said that she walked into that store swinging that double bit axe and that she put one of the men to "eating soup for the rest of his life" with one swing of that axe. Both of the men ran out the door and never turned around to look back while they were within sight of that old country store. The men were never seen in that part of the country again. She kept close reigns on my dad after that little incident. I think it made my dad more of a family man after he recovered, although his family man behavior may have been influenced by the fear of my mother. She was a small lady, but was fierce in the protection of her family.

One day my mom and Aunt Lizzy (Uncle Roy's wife) went fishing up on the river. My mom and Aunt Lizzy went everywhere together and did all sorts of girl things. I mean that was "country girl" things, mind you! My mother and Aunt Lizzy loved to fish. They would try to catch trout to help feed the family. They would pick berries to make jams and pies for their families. They fished for a while and then decided to walk down the road to where some men were digging up an old cemetery. The men were moving bodies higher up on the mountain, above the water level of the new dam being built. There was a large tent set up at the site and the bodies were placed inside. Inside the tent masked men were preparing the bodies for reburial. Well, being the curious woman my mother was, she decided to go inside the tent and take a look at the bodies and caskets. Aunt Lizzy begged her not to go inside of that tent, but she couldn't stop my mom. My mom just had to see all of those bodies and what was going on in there. It was just her nature. Many of the old wooden caskets had long since rotted away so there was nothing left but bodies and bones covered in sheets by the men. Back in those years bodies were not embalmed to preserve them and kill diseases as bodies are today.

I was just one year old when my mother became ill with tuberculosis. She had contracted tuberculosis while being in that tent with all of those bodies. Tuberculosis was a deadly disease back in those years, with no medicine to treat the disease. Many people were sent to

sanatoriums. There they would lie in bed for long periods
of time in hopes of surviving the horrible disease. My
mother became sick while I was still nursing. Doc Killian
tried everything he could to persuade my mother to go to
the sanatorium and try to get well. He did get her to go to
the old Catholic Hospital in Murphy, about twenty miles
from our cabin. After all of the doctors evaluated my
mother's condition, they decided to plan an operation.
Well, my mother heard of what the doctors' plans were and
she had to get back to her children. She wasn't going to
have any operation so she decided to get out of that
hospital and go home to her family. She was in a room on
the second floor of the hospital. She opened the window
and pushed out the screen and jumped to the ground
below. Nobody was going to keep her from being with her
children. She walked the entire distance from Murphy to
her tiny cabin home. That was nearly twenty miles and
she walked it while being so sick that she could hardly
stand up. Doc Killian knew that my mother would never
leave her children as long as she had a breath left in her
body. He said it was all for the best that mom didn't go
through with the operation because she had the worst kind
of tuberculosis. He called it "Galloping Tuberculosis."
Mom died shortly after she had contracted the disease.

My sister, Charlena, became the woman of the cabin.
She helped feed me, bathe me and change my diapers. She
was five years old but watched after her little brother like a
mother hen watching her chick. My dad was devastated by
my mother's death and he couldn't hold himself together
for a while. He couldn't find a way to ease the pain as he
was consumed by the loss of our mother. My sister and I
needed a father at home, but my dad had to go to work to
provide the very minimum essentials for us to survive.

In later years my sister told me what it was like living
there in the cabin and what had happened. Our home was
heated with a wood-burning stove. It had a flat top that we
used for cooking. Mom would have Charlena bring in the
wood and keep the stove loaded. We often cooked beans
and meat all day on that stove. Charlena told me I had
just come into their lives and she just loved me so much.

She said that I never was much of a crying baby. She
stated that she was barely big enough to pick me up and
carry me around the cabin, but Mom had taught her how
to help care for me. She learned to change my diapers and
bathe me. We were fed real food very early in life like
mashed potatoes, fruit etc. She said that she has always
tried to block out as much of her memories of those times
because they were so sad and painful for her. She has
never gotten over it.

Our mother was a small and very kind person to
everyone. She would cook and jar things such as beans
and tomatoes in the summer. She would make things out
of washed out flour sacks. Our window curtains were
made from flour sacks. Charlena remembers the curtains
blowing when the wind would blow and the snow blowing
inside around the windows in the wintertime. Charlena's
dresses were made from flour sacks and so were my shirts.
My sister would help mom wash out the diapers and do the
other wash in an old outdoor wash pot. They would build a
fire around the wash pot to heat the water. Mom would
use a long stick to stir the clothes in the pot. Doc Killian
would come by and take me around on his house calls
when he went visiting his patients. "He loved that little
Freddy," Charlena said. Dr. Killian understood the pain
that this family was having to endure and he and his family
did all that was possible to ease the suffering.

Charlena first remembers our mother being sick when
mom told her that she was so tired and that she would
have to lie down. Mom told Charlena that she would have
to take care of me and that Doc Killian would be coming by
soon. It wasn't long until Doc Killian came to check on
mom. Doc Killian, Dad, Uncle Roy and Aunt Lizzy went out
on the porch. They all talked among themselves. Then my
dad told Charlena to take me out of the house for some
fresh air. Charlena never knew what transpired. She says
that from that day forward everything was a terrible
nightmare. They moved a bed onto the enclosed front
porch and put our mother in it. After that we only saw
mom when we needed her. She was so weak. Five-year-old
Charlena had to take care of me. Our dad had to go to

work. Sometimes he would be gone for two or three days at a time.

Grandma Ledford, Fred and Charlena

Grandma Ledford, Aunt Lizzy and Mrs. Ora would help look after us children. Charlena remembers putting potatoes on the stove to cook. Some people brought in cans and jars of food for us to eat. Mom would often tell Charlena to take her little brother out for fresh air. So she would take me down by the river. She would carry a rope with her and tie me to a big rock. Dad had taught her to tie the rope up under my arms so that I couldn't crawl into the river. She carried me to some blackberry bushes located nearby and we ate some blackberries. She would grab a green apple off of the tree for us to carry home and eat. She says those were really green and sour apples. Charlena said she wouldn't let her little brother eat but a little of the sour apples for fear that he would become sick with a stomachache.

Mom was getting worse and she was no longer able to nurse me. She would stay in bed all day and just tell Charlena what needed to be done. One day early in the morning Doc Killian came by to check on mom. Charlena heard Doc say to dad, "there is nothing we can do for Bell now." Doc told dad that they could send her to the TB Sanatorium. Dad replied that mom would not go and leave her children. Dad then asked Doc Killian not to tell Charlena, as it would kill her to know. Dad said that Freddy wouldn't understand. After hearing all of this, Charlena ran out the door crying with me in hand. Dad went running after us. He caught up with us and he sat Charlena down on a chopping block where we split our firewood. My sister then remembered that she was crying and that I was holding my hands on her knees. She said that I was crying because she was crying. Dad told her that she may not understand but that mom would not be with us much longer. Charlena said that she knew it was going to be soon. Dad put me on the bed next to mom and put Charlena on the other side of her. Mom told Charlena that she loved her and that she would have to look after Freddy. Mom told her that she wanted the two of us to go to a big home and get an education. Mom said to never let anybody separate us. Grandma Ledford would help look after the children all that she could.

Doc Killian sensed that my dad would no longer be able to care for my sister and myself. Dad had to work at construction and he was away from home for several days at a time. Doc, his daughter (Mrs. Ora Mae McGlamery) and Uncle Roy tried to come up with a solution to make things better for my sister and myself. They found that everyone in our extended family was having a difficult time just taking care of their own children. Grandpa Tanner was raising twelve children. Uncle Roy was struggling just as my dad was. World War II, which began when the Japanese bombed Pearl Harbor, made everything tight for all families. I had some family members who engaged in the art of moonshining, but Doc Killian would have nothing to do with sending us to any of them. There were other members of my family leaving to fight the war in Europe and the Pacific.

13

Front: Charles, Edward, Back: Uncle Roy,
Blonde Dell, Aunt Lizzy

Blonde, Edward, Thelma

Ora Mae

Doc Killian and Mrs. McGlamery decided to contact
"Pop" Woosley, the superintendent at The Methodist
Children's Home in Winston-Salem, to see if "Pop" had
room for two more children. "Pop" Woosley agreed to take
us, but that didn't mean that my dad and my Uncle Roy
were ready to send their kin that far away from home.
After many longs weeks of despair, my dad finally agreed
that the orphanage would be the best place for my sister
and me. So Doc Killian made the call to "Pop"Woosley and
"Pop" drove all the way to our home from Winston-Salem, a
distance of almost three hundred miles of crooked

14

mountainous roads. After our family's long and sad good-bye, "Pop" took us with him to live at The Methodist Children's Home in Winston-Salem. That was Valentines Day, February 14, 1943. "Pop" Woosley would become a father figure to me for as long as I would know him.

This Children's Home, which would become my home for the next 16 plus years of my life, was founded on the site of the vacated Davis Military Academy. With four wooden buildings salvaged from the Academy and with tremendous help from the Masonic Temple, the Home opened its doors to needy children on 13 September 1909 and has continuously grown in it's capability to care for children. While I would be living there the average number of resident children would exceed four hundred.

"Pop" Woosley loved us all.

Boy was I lucky that "Pop" came after me to give me a home. By the time I arrived at the Children's Home, many more buildings had been added. There was an infirmary with a nurse. There was a school with individual grade

15

classrooms that we children could attend through the eighth grade. The old wooden cottages had long since been torn down and new brick cottages built in their place. We had a large farm where we grew corn, grain and hay to feed the many cattle and other farm animals. We also had a smaller truck farm where we grew vegetables for all of us children to eat. We even had a swimming pool for the older children and a wading pool for the babies. There was a mother in every cottage and each mother would have about thirty children.

When my sister Charlena and I arrived at the Children's Home, we didn't go directly to a cottage with all of the other children but to the infirmary where we stayed for awhile with Miss Annie Smith, the campus nurse. In later years, Miss Smith would tell me about when I first came to the orphanage and how she and some of the older orphan girls who helped her would take care of me. She said they put me in a little baby bed and looked after me all day. She said that she and the older girls took turns carrying me around with them as they walked up and down the halls of the infirmary. Not long after we arrived at the infirmary, Miss Smith thought my sister was healthy enough to join the other children that were in her age group. Charlena went to the Smith Cottage to join twenty-five or so other little six and seven year old girls. I stayed at the infirmary for a while longer. I was just over two years old at this time and had been nursing from my mother until she became ill.

Miss Annie Smith our nurse

Miss Smith wanted to be sure that I was healthy before I moved in with the other children at the Baby Cottage. Finally I was considered well enough to join the other babies and my new home became the Baby Cottage, also known as the Reynolds Cottage.

Fred And Charlena
New home new clothes

My earliest memories begin sometime about this age.
Before this time, I don't remember anybody. I don't
remember my mother or father or where I came from. I
didn't know what I was doing at this place. There were a
lot of other babies in this place where I lived. Things were
very confusing to me. I sort of felt that I needed to be near
a mother and that's when things got very confusing. There
were a lot of mothers at the Children's Home. Not having
any memory of my parents or my short life prior to this
time, I'm sure that made it a little easier for me to be at the
orphanage than it did for my sister. It was very hard on my
sister not being with her little brother, whom she had
grown accustomed to caring for and protecting. For several
years I felt like it was quite some time between visits from
my sister. Visiting at that age was almost out of the
question. We were too small to walk to the other cottage by
ourselves. The children pretty much stayed with the group
in their own cottage until they were a little older.

When I began to remember, those life events would stay with me forever in my memories. You see, I woke up one day and discovered that I was in an orphanage. Maybe I did not understand at the time what an orphanage was, but I realized that I had about thirty brothers and sisters in this cottage. Wow! What a big house; everything was a zillion times bigger than I was! At first I crawled up and down the steps or one of the older girls would carry me. I remember being scared of the steps especially the long steps going down into the basement playroom. I finally learned to walk up and down those giant steps, but I always held on to the rail and put one foot down and then the other on the same step.

All of the children had to be helped with the essentials of everyday care from feeding, to use of the privy, to bathing and being put to bed. Oh, and I must not forget the diapers that had to be changed for a few of the younger ones. I found out that there was one real grown up lady there at the cottage (known later as the home mother).

Miss Harbour reading the bible to the children

Her name was Miss Eva Harbour. There was also about a half dozen not all grown up ladies there. These not all grown up ladies, as I soon found out, were more orphan sisters of mine who helped with the children's everyday care. This is why I was so confused because, at the time, I didn't know which one was my mother. I guess there was not much difference in Miss Harbour and the almost grown up girl's age than that of my real mother. All of the girls would all pick us up and hold us and care for us so I just didn't understand. As long as they were good to me, they could all be my mother, even though I thought there should be one mother to call my own. The girls lived in the same building but had their own almost grown up lady area to live. They would wake us up in the morning, dress us, feed us breakfast and take us out to play. In good weather the girls would let us play outdoors in the big yard. The yard had a fence all the way around so that the children would not walk into the road. We would walk down to the fence that was next to Reynolda Road and watch people driving by in their cars. We would wave to people riding by. Sometimes some of them would see us and would be kind enough to wave back. Once in a while an older person would be walking by on the sidewalk. Sometimes they would stop and talk to us. The older girls kept a close eye on us and saw to it that we would be safe and that we would mind our manners. Once in a while colored folks would walk by our cottage. They sure looked different to us. They would stop and talk just like the white folks would. They were all very kind to us. We were taught to call them "FRIEND" by the older girls.

There was a big spacious sand box with room for a lot of kids to play. We had lots of toys to play with. There were balls, hobbyhorses, tricycles and all kinds of fun things. On bad weather days we would play inside the very large playroom. There were wooden boxes all the way around the walls of the playroom. The boxes were all built together and each box had a lid. When the lid was down we could sit on the boxes. We called them junk boxes! This is where each child could keep their own toys or most of the year, toy parts. A lot of the time the almost grown up ladies would teach us how to play group games. A lot of the time we could play on our own. It seemed that all of our days were spent playing, eating or sleeping.

This seemed to be the best opportunity to explore and see what this place and this world was all about. This is when I sensed that my bottom end was there for a reason other than sitting on. I found out quickly who was in charge of my new home and why the all grown up lady was there. At times when we would be playing outside we would throw sand in one another's eyes. We would get in a tussle over a toy or get near the fence that had tall cut grass and poison ivy growing near it. At this time the older sisters would discipline us by making us stand or sit somewhere without being allowed to play. Sometimes there were a few of us that needed a little more attention than that and we were taken to the home mother. The home mother had a way of getting our unruliness under control. She would use the backside of a hairbrush to give us a few Rat-Tat-Tats on the bottom end. That usually gave us the right message to mend our ways. Many times after I had received my Rat-Tats on my bottom end I would try to pull my cheeks around to look and see what was stinging and how many red marks were on my behind. While waiting for our Rat -Tats on the buttocks, the fear began to build within us of just how bad it was going to be and that waiting would be worse than the Rat-Tat-Tats! On many other occasions I found that, along with the discipline, there was lots of caring and love given by the older sisters and Miss Harbour, our home mother. I seemed to always be the adventurer that received a lot of love, along with a great deal of the other! Oh boy, learning this new world was sinking in on both ends!

I remember the old soaps we were bathed with back during World War II. It certainly wasn't pleasant to get that kind of soap in your eyes. I experienced how kind the older girls were to us when we would get soap in our eyes. When a soap bar became small from use, it was placed into a gallon jar with a little water. Saving soap was something everyone did back then. As the soap melted in the jar it became almost like a slimy jelly. You could just reach into the jar and dip a hand full out to put on a bath cloth. The older girls had several small tubs that were used for bathing purposes. I liked getting dirty while playing but I never liked getting a bath! After the girls would finish with one baby, they would rinse the small tubs out and start all over with another baby until all of us were bathed. Getting sand in our eyes also happened often, as we spent a lot of time playing in the sand box. One day I was playing around our wooden junk boxes and accidentally jammed a large splinter under my right little fingernail. Boy, that was what you would call real pain. I had to go to the infirmary and let Miss Smith take the splinter out. All of the time while being in such pain one of the older girls stayed with me to give me comfort. I would cry and she would hug me, just like an almost grown up mother. My fingernail still has never grown back to normal. Sometimes I feel it was meant to be that way to remind me of the pain and then the love from such wonderful almost grown up sisters who treated me as if they were my real mothers. I would begin developing a special kind of love and respect for these older orphan sisters who cared so much for my happiness and well-being. Most all of the girls were very loving and gave their own kind affection to us little ones.

Some of the older girls that cared for us little ones still come back to our annual Children's Home reunion every spring. I get a kick out of the stories that they tell about when I first came to the Children's Home and lived with them at the Baby Cottage. There was a girl named Joyce (Leonard) Maness that I see from time to time at the homecoming reunion. Once she explained to me why and how things were done that I didn't understand. Joyce made birthday cakes for the children on their birthday. I remember the cakes with flowers on top for the decoration. She explained to me that during the war, a lot of things were just not available and especially not at the Children's Home. She said that we children had to be watched carefully because we would try to eat the flowers off the cake. Joyce says that she was experienced in parenthood, when that time came for her, from the experiences that she had while helping us little ones. She said that when we were very tiny, we couldn't wait to be held by one of the girls. When one of the children would get down from their arms, another child was ready to get into them. Joyce helped Miss Johnie Harrington, the lady in charge of the kitchen, with the cooking and the dishwashing. Another of the older girls was Mary "Mickey" (Doster) Duff. She always told me how much she loved all of the little babies that she helped while she worked and lived at the Baby Cottage. Each time I saw her, she had something nice to say to me. "Mickey" died in March 2002. Then there was Bobbie (Bowles) Hutto. At homecomings she always gives me a big hug and says, "You were the prettiest baby when you were at the Baby Cottage." She even says this in front of all the big boys that I wanted to always impress while I was growing up. Faye Davis was another one of the older girls who always talks of the babies she helped tend at the Baby Cottage.

Baby Cottage children 1943-44
Fred top row far right

My brother orphan Roy Byrd and I really liked to check out the playroom territory to see what was available for us to explore. The older girls would find us in the coal bin, laundry room or some other unusual place to play. They were not too happy when they would find us in the coal bin, black as tar, and have to bathe us and change our clothes. One day we started climbing up onto the wooden coat rack. The coat rack had enough coat hooks so that each child could hang his or her coat when they came in from outdoors. It just happened to be that some of the tips from the coat hooks were broken off. Roy and I were trying to climb on the coat rack when all of a sudden I slipped and fell. As I fell one of the coat hooks caught me in the mouth, and I was just hanging there like a fish on a hook. My feet would not reach the ground, and I was squirming to get myself free. Of all the hooks that I could have been snagged by, I had to hit one with a broken tip. The coat hook went through my tongue and into the roof of my mouth. I was trying to scream as loud as I could, even with that big coat hook stuck in the roof of my mouth. Finally, one of the older girls ran over and lifted me off that coat hook. I didn't know what would kill me first, the wound or the hugging all the way to the hospital by the girls. Well the doctors at the Baptist Hospital in Winston-Salem repaired my mouth and it wasn't long after that, that "young Freddy" was running wide open again. I look back on that painful event and sometimes just break out laughing. To me, that sort of thing was the beginning of what we call "Orphan Humor!" This type incident seemed to happen to me all too frequently over the next sixteen plus years that I would live at the orphanage.

Life would go on at the baby cottage and there would be many more enjoyable days of playing, loving care and Rat-Tat-Tats! There was Christmas, Thanksgiving, Easter and other holiday seasons to learn about and enjoy. There were lots of other girls and boys to play with and learn from. Friendships would developed that literally would last a lifetime. As time passed by we would become more used to where we were living and, although not understanding why things were as they were, we would be happy a lot of the time as we played with each other and grew up together.

Christmas was a wonderful time for all of us little ones. It seemed and felt like the most wonderful place on earth. The older girls and our home mother would decorate a tree. They would spend hours adding this and moving that. When they finished decorating our Christmas tree, they turned on the tree lights and it was the most beautiful thing I had ever seen. It was the first Christmas tree that I remembered, and if I had never been told about toys, it would have been all the Christmas I needed. I was so happy to be near that tree. Every chance we had to be in

that room I would just stare at that beautiful Christmas
tree. The older girls and our home mother would sing
Christmas carols, and we would listen to their beautiful
voices. I remember older children from other cottages
would come and sing carols outside of our cottage. I
wanted that feeling inside of me, wherever it was coming
from, to stay inside of me forever. As Miss Harbour and
the older girls told us Christmas stories, we learned more
about baby Jesus, Mary and Joseph, the three Wise Men
and Bethlehem.

Years later by tradition
Nancy reading to the children

Then of course there were the Santa Claus stories. I
just couldn't get enough of what was taking place. Oh Boy!
Is the rest of my life going to be this wonderful? The
reindeer pulling a jolly old man around in a sleigh seemed
so magical and real. In years when there was no blackout
ordered by the government during the war, lights were
hung on another gigantic Christmas tree in front of our
cottage.

Older girls singing carols
at our giant Christmas tree

Gray pulling strings of lights

The older boys and girls would help string lights on this tree, and the tree reached all the way up into the sky. It reached up forever and had a million lights on it. I guess that's one reason I really came to like this home where I was fortunate enough to live. Each instance of joy would eventually erase most of my sadness and uncertainty. Each event of joy and kindness would draw me closer to loving my Children's Home. The Children's Home spirit was beginning to develop inside me, even at this very early age. Being with this wonderful home mother and older girls on Christmas Eve was just one more gift of joy for us little ones. I hoped that my mother in heaven was freed from her fears of her children being unhappy. We were at the big home that she wanted for us! I always felt there was something missing in my life but at least some of the time, these wonderful girls and home mother made me happy. As the home mother and girls were making our Christmas Eve so special, we all struggled to stay awake. Eventually, all of the excitement just wore us out. There were a few children that could walk to their bed, from being so tired, but the remaining children had to be carried and gently tucked into their beds.

Christmas morning came and the excitement was overwhelming. Santa Claus did come, just as Miss Harbour and the almost grown up girls had said he would. Each child had a stocking hanging from the fireplace mantle, filled with all kinds of goodies. There were oranges, apples, raisins, hard candy and nuts of different kinds. There was still more to come as each of us had a present under that beautiful Christmas tree. The Christmas tree looked even more beautiful with all of the gifts lying under it. I was really the happiest child in the whole world. The excitement was overwhelming and I couldn't wait to see what was coming next. There was lots of joy getting to open a real Christmas present from Santa Claus, especially the first that I remembered. All of the children had smiles on their faces, a fitting reflection of all their joy. Our home mother and the almost grown up girls had pleasant smiles on their faces from seeing the joy their efforts had in making the children happy.

When I was older I found out just where all of those Christmas gifts came from. It was very humbling to know that children, just like us, gave their pennies and nickels and their parents gave what they could spare so that we children at the orphanage could have a Christmas. The many Sunday school classes, churches and just friends of the Children's Home made a miracle happen each year at this time. I am so grateful for the many blessings we received.

Getting back to Christmas morning, it really didn't matter who received a certain gift because we usually all played with each other's toys soon after Christmas morning. When all of the toys were out in the playroom, you can imagine the sight and noise of the thirty or so kids playing with all of those toys. The girls had all kinds of dolls, but sock dolls were common in those years. The boys had a lot of wooden and metal toys, balls and all sorts of boy things. While the girls received stuffed dolls, the boys received stuffed sock monkeys for Christmas! We would play until nearly exhausted from all of the excitement. After each time we played with our toys we would pick up every toy and put them into our junk boxes before we went to dinner or supper. We were taught in those years that the noon meal was called dinner and the evening meal was called supper. It was hard to give up playing with our toys just to go eat and take our daily nap. Those toys just had to be played with and I knew that they were lonesome in the junk boxes. We would eat dinner and then we had to go to bed for a while. When we were allowed to get up, we all hurried back down to the basement playroom. We got our toys out of our junk boxes and really played hard until suppertime. This routine would continue throughout the year with fewer and fewer toys surviving the rigorous daily play time. As the toys would wear out the older girls would put them in the trash. Well to me I didn't mind playing with a toy truck with a wheel broken off. As far as I was concerned I was happy with a toy truck with no wheels. I would put my broken toys in the back and under some other toys in my junk box so the older girls would not see them and throw them out.

Children just have to get plenty of rest. Our beds were lined up around the room and the boys were in one room and the girls were in another. When I was very young I remember the bed that I slept in seemed to be big enough for three or four kids, even though it was a small bed. Several times I would get lost in my bed under the cover. I remember one night in particular I was lost all night until the next morning. I searched for a way out from under my cover and it seemed that I crawled for hours. The covers were tucked in all nice and tight and it felt like the covers had a hold on me. I quietly cried all through that night. The next morning, one of the older girls came in to wake us up and helped me get out of my scary situation. That was one scary night. I never put my head under the covers again after that frightening experience.

I remember that the older boys were allowed to visit the older girls at a certain time during each week. The visit was always well chaperoned. Between the hours of seven to nine on Sunday evening, the older boys and girls could have a date or the boys were allowed to visit the girls' cottages and just socialize. They would talk and do things older kids did, I guess! There seemed to be a lot of teasing going on between certain ones. We never saw any kissing, as it was time for us to go to bed soon after the big boys arrived. I did see some of the older boys and girls holding hands. Stan Honeycutt, one of the older boys came by our cottage one evening. Stan started throwing a hatchet at an old stump. The stump was across the road from our cottage. The hatchet looked big and sharp to me and a little bit frightening. Stan could throw that hatchet and make it stick in that stump, so it seemed, almost every time. Each time the hatchet would hit that stump I would jump with fright. Well, I guess that I would have to learn that throwing a hatchet at a stump was normal big boy stuff. I believe the older girls were impressed with Stan's hatchet and the way he could throw it.

At times in the morning and afternoon, I could see the older boys and girls walking to R.J. Reynolds High School. Boy, were they big people! The older boys looked like giants. I often thought that it would take me a thousand years to grow as large as those big boys.

I remember that men would come to paint our cottage and one of them was named Charlie. Everyday when we would go out to play, all of the kids would walk by Mr. Charlie's ladder and say, "Hello Mr. Charlie." Once one kid said hello to Mr. Charlie every one of the kids had to say hello to Mr. Charlie. This went on for several days. Mr. Charlie was an older and very gentle man and would speak to us kids. He would speak in his soft toned voice, asking how we were doing and asking what our names were. He always had a smile and something cheerful to say. We thought he was very brave to be all the way up on that ladder. I was very happy to have another big person friend. I found out that smiling made you feel good and I sure liked to see big people smiling. It seemed that when big people were smiling, they were not mad at you for doing something wrong. That may be when I started smiling at everybody, and I've continued that habit all of my life. My troubles seem not to matter as much if I can smile. I believe that I've made hundreds more friends during my life because of my habit of smiling. Of course I will have to admit that the first Army Sergeant I met in boot camp was not at all amused! I had adults to tell me to wipe the smile off of my face before, but not quite as serious as my first Army Sergeant expressed himself. I believe that cost me twenty push-ups and being the first trooper whose name the sergeant remembered! Some years later in my military career, I was even able to get Admirals to smile, as I would salute them with a grin. Mind you, that was not all Admirals!

As time went on I found that I had a lot of big people friends that lived and worked at the Children's Home or sponsored a child at the home. Each child had a sponsor from a church somewhere in western North Carolina. At the time my sister and I went to the Children's Home we were sponsored by the Philathea class of Maple Springs Methodist Church in Winston-Salem. Mrs. Geneva Bailey and her daughter Linda would make visits to the orphanage to see my sister and me. I was so young at that time that I didn't remember their visits. Linda would later go to R.J. Reynolds High School with some of the older Children's Home children. Nearly sixty years after Linda and her family visited my sister and me at the Children's Home, Linda was able to get in touch with us. She sent my sister and me a photograph that was taken of my sister, Linda, and myself during one of their visits with us at the orphanage.

Fred, at three, Charlena and Linda
That sun is bright

After a few years the Susanna Wesley Class of High
Point Wesley Memorial Methodist Church began to sponsor
me. Mrs. R. J. Welch was the class correspondent. They
were so good to me! They were like real parents that lived
some other place. I was the luckiest child at the orphanage
to have such wonderful sponsors.

Easter was another exciting time for us. The trees and
flowers were beginning to bloom and the grass was turning
a pretty shade of green. It seemed that everything was
bright and cheerful. All of the older people seemed to be
happy and everyone dressed up real pretty when they were
going to church. The older girls would take us out to play
in the yard and let us find pretty colored eggs hidden all
over the yard. We had an Easter basket to collect our eggs
in, and when we would take a break in the shade from
hunting those eggs, the girls would break one open for us
to eat. I liked the taste of those kinds of eggs that the
Easter Bunny had left for us to find. Trying to find Easter
Bunny eggs was so much fun.

When summer arrived and it was warm enough for us
to go swimming, the almost grown up girls would take us
across the road to the Stockton cottage where there was a

32

large wading pool.

Baby pool

The pool wasn't deep but plenty large enough for all of us children to play in. In the middle was a sprinkler that helped keep us cool in the hot summer sun. Sometimes the water from the sprinkler seemed very cold, and I would get chill bumps. We would still run back and forth under the sprinkler. We could splash the water as long as we didn't splash the water into someone's face. We really enjoyed playing in that little pool every summer that I lived at the baby cottage. In later years I found out the baby pool was the favorite place for the older girls and boys to sit during their Sunday evening dates. After the water was let out the boys and girls would sit around the edge of the pool. Sometimes when the water was left in the pool, the older children would just take their shoes off and still sit around the edge of the pool dangling their feet in the cool water. The Stockton cottage was the home for the ninth and tenth grade girls.

Some of the kids would stay at the home for the rest of their youth until they graduated from high school. Many others would leave to go live with a family member or someone special in their lives. There were a couple of sets of twins at the Baby Cottage when I lived there. They were Roy and Ray Byrd and Linda and Brenda Brigman. Roy and Ray came to the orphanage just a few months prior to my coming. Roy and I would stay at the Home and graduate from high school together. Linda and Brenda had two older brothers named Arlis and Weldon. Arlis was much older but Weldon was near my age. Weldon and I would become good friends, and he would graduate a year ahead of me. Several of the boys that lived with me at the Baby Cottage would stay at the home for the remainder of their youth. There was Bob, Carl, Johnny, Jack, Roy and a few others. Over the years some of the   boys left the Home and others came to take their place.

Every year I looked forward to the different seasons to arrive, as the same exciting spirit would consume me. Christmas, Easter, Thanksgiving and Summer would be full of joy and more exciting each year as I grew older and one speck taller. Times between all of these exciting seasons were not always perfect, but where else on earth could one person be so fortunate to be cared for like I was being cared for. As we would grow older life would change from what we experienced at the Baby Cottage. I grew accustom to the caring and love by many of the older girls and my home mother. This created a hardship for me, as I would have to see each one for whom I had created an affection leave. When the girls graduated from high school they would have to leave the home and another younger girl would come to be my almost grown up mother. The feelings were real, just as in a regular family, "I guess." The day would come and the girls would just disappear; some never to be seen or heard from again! This was a part of my learning that I didn't care for. I longed for their return only to find that this sadness would be a common event annually after the school year ended.

Chapter Two

By age six we were big boys and girls. We would move from the Baby Cottage. The girls would go to one cottage and the boys would go to another. I would miss my home mother, Miss Harbour, and the almost grown up girls. However, the instinct to grow up and be a bigger boy was very strong and made the transition a little easier and more bearable. I went to the Anna Hanes Cottage, which would be my home for the next few years. This was like getting a new mother and a new home. I would even have some almost grown up girls at this cottage. Some of the boys that lived in this cottage grew up with me in the Baby Cottage. They were just a year older than me but some of the boys were new and had just come to live at the orphanage. I would have to learn about these "new boys" as they would be my new brothers, some for a long time! The girls went to the Smith Cottage. I sort of liked having a few sisters around but it was time for them to go in a different direction as dictated by age and gender.

There were all boys living at the Anna Hanes Cottage

and I began to learn how boys become men. Each of the new boys had their own personality. Competition and learning whom I could get along with began at this early age. Being a small boy, I began to develop a personality of protecting myself and being a little stubborn seemed to be a part of my personality. It no doubt developed while I was learning to survive amongst thirty other boys living in the same cottage. Conflicts rarely lasted out the day before they would be forgotten. That was a good thing because we had a long time to live together before we would be grown. The Anna Hanes Cottage was quite another experience. Miss Ruth Hunter was our new home mother, and I really liked her when I hadn't done something wrong!

Here we had a little more freedom and room to play with a little less supervision. We were allowed to go outside and play in the yard without any adult supervision, so we thought. The older girls and home mother looked out the windows often to be sure we were behaving like good little boys should. Oh! There had to be a few Rat-Tat-Tats on the buttocks at this cottage also. Being an adventurer I was willing to join in with a little mischief with some of the other orphan kids. Once in awhile, it brought unpleasant attention from our home mother. Learning from both ends seemed to be a part of my life but I enjoyed being all boy!

Also with more freedom came more responsibility. Each of us had a job assigned to us for a certain number of months and then we would switch jobs with someone else. Although we still had four of the older girls to help with our care, we were assigned chores that we were able to handle.

I helped Miss Holland in the kitchen for a while and learned the fine art of washing small dishes while standing on a milk crate, polishing silverware, sweeping and mopping floors, setting the tables and killing flies. I would help one of the almost grown up girls with washing the dishes in a big sink. Sometimes if the dishes were not too big she would let me help dry the dishes. She sometimes let me lean over into the sink and help wash some small dishes. While standing on a milk crate I could reach over into the dishwater. It seemed that we young boys would accidentally drop a dish every now and then while we were learning how to handle things. We learned to sweep the floors and every crumb had better be swept up when we had that chore. I found out very quickly just how serious Miss Holland's rules were for the operation of her kitchen and dining room. Miss Holland laid many Rat-Tat-Tats on the boys that had problems following her directions. She would use a fly swatter on our backsides if we didn't mind. I'll have to admit that I picked up a few licks myself from Miss Holland. She was a good woman though and really prepared good food for us. There seemed to always be plenty of food on the table at mealtime.

One of the older girls sat with a table of boys to help us mind our manners and to help serve our food. Food, placed on each table in large dishes, was passed around the table to each boy, always to the left starting with the head of the table. It took a while for us to remember all of the table manners that we were supposed to know. We would make mistakes once in a while and the almost grown up girl would correct us. Most of the time the girls were very nice to us. I always smiled at them so they would not be mad at me. I learned that while I lived at the Baby Cottage. I became very sad when a big person would get mad at me. I couldn't help but shed some tears no matter how big I tried to be. While the big girls were not in school, they would be just like young mothers to us. I remember one meal; Miss Holland had cooked squash for our supper. The bowl was passed all the way around the table and hardly anyone took any so I helped myself to an extra large portion. Well, I ate that portion and was ready for another serving. Miss Holland didn't like it much if all of the food she had prepared was not consumed. I asked the older girl at the table if I could have another serving of that good squash and she said that I could have all the squash I wanted. I was determined to eat all of that squash and, in the mean time, be a hero to all of the boys at my table that didn't like the squash. I was showing off just a little bit to gain friendship with some of the other boys. Having friends made life a little easier living with thirty boys every day of our lives. As I ate the squash I could see that the other boys were happy with me helping get rid of something they

37

did not want to eat. I ate and ate and ate and nearly finished the whole bowl of squash when suddenly, I felt I had really done something wrong. I became very sick which caused an early departure from our dinner table. After that foolish incident, I would not eat boiled squash for years. I loved fried squash but forget the other kind!

We boys often tried to show acts of courage so we would be accepted by those that were not really our friends. Sometimes bravery would help prevent your being picked on as much and having to get a black eye from one of the other boys. Sometimes we would have to take a licking on the buttocks, from our home mother, for our smart-alecky behavior though. Then again the licking on the buttocks seemed worth it if you could make a friend. If you didn't cry, that would show more bravery to the other boys. Although if you would cry, it seemed the home mother sensed we had had enough and she wouldn't spank you quite as long. Sometimes I would start yelling "oh, oh, oh," before the paddle ever hit my hinny in hopes that the home mother would have pity on me. The home mothers had a sense for some of us fakers and made sure we got enough licks to get our attention.

Miss Holland often made homemade ice cream for us on Sundays. She would make the ice cream in the ice trays, and on our birthday, she would also make us a birthday cake. One thing that I liked about working in the kitchen was the left over toast and eggs that Miss Holland would put on the top of the wood-burning stove. We were too small to reach up and get the toast and eggs so we just looked up at the eggs and hoped there was enough left over for each of us boys to get some. After we finished our chores, we would hang around next to that big stove and look up at those eggs until Miss Holland would see us. We looked like puppy dogs looking for something to eat but we really were not hungry. We just liked the taste of the warm eggs on toast. Usually there was enough as Miss Holland always looked after the boys that worked in the kitchen. When we finished our chores, Miss Holland would reach up and get the eggs and toast for us. Boy, did I love those left over fried eggs and toast, especially in the winter months.

Setting on top of that wood burning stove for a while made the toast and eggs a tastier treat than when we had them for breakfast. Once in a while she would let us have a couple of soda crackers. That was just like candy to us. When Miss Holland wasn't looking, we would lick our finger so the sugar would stick to it when we would put our finger into the sugar dish. Sometimes we could find the brown sugar, molasses or syrup in the pantry and sample those treats as well. We boys learned all of the tricks passed down from one generation of orphans to another. During the summer months, when we were finished with our chores and got our treat, we would swat flies until Miss Holland could see no more flies flying around before we were allowed to leave.

When we started first grade, we would come home from school at morning break and she would have a fresh slice of cabbage and some soda crackers and milk waiting for us. The old school house was just at the top of the hill so that made it easy for us little ones to come home for break or lunch. We were always out of school early in the first grade. I guess because we needed our rest. Miss Holland was a very hard worker, and I always did like her. I think she felt the same towards me. She always wore a hair net and her rolled down stockings were well worn and snagged from all of the hard work that went into preparing our meals. I liked being around that old big wood burning stove and smelling all the different kinds of food that she was cooking. Fresh biscuits sure smelled good to me, and I sure loved to eat the ones she made. She made good gravy to go on the biscuits. We had powdered eggs during the war and for a time after. I sure got used to eating them. Greens were a different story. I just had a lot of difficulty getting my greens down. The greens seemed to be a whole lot stronger in taste in those days. Sometimes we would have cooked turnips with the greens, and I couldn't eat cooked turnips. However I loved to eat them raw right out of the ground. We always had Cream of Wheat for breakfast with our egg if we didn't have grits. I would fix the wheat in many different ways to see if I would like it. I would put butter in it sometimes and sometimes I would put sugar and milk in it. Anyhow, I would find a way to eat it.

After working for Miss Holland in the kitchen, my home mother, Miss Hunter, assigned me another job of sweeping, dusting and mopping the rest of the cottage. On Saturday mornings we would hand-paste wax the wooden floors in the cottage. After we finished with the waxing we would rub the floors to a shine, teaming up and pulling each other from one end of the cottage to the other using old wool blankets or any other kind of rags that we could find. Those floors had to look just so. We seemed never to run out of energy. After lunch we were allowed to go outside and play and "PLAY WE DID." We played cowboys and Indians; we played soldiers and war and lots of other all boy games like marbles, jack rocks, trucks and tractors. We had lots of room in the back yard to run and a very large porch to play on when it was raining. We played hard all afternoon until called in for supper.

I can't remember how long Miss Hunter was our home mother before she left the orphanage. I just know that she left a void in my heart when she was gone. Even though she was stern in her rules, she always gave me a little extra hug now and then. A lot of times she would say to me, "You have the cutest little nose." She would then grab my nose and twitch it from side to side. That little bit of kindness made me feel good inside, as if she were my real mother. That little bit of attention would help fill the emptiness during all of the hours and days of wishing there could be more. I loved Miss Hunter.

Somehow I felt close to a lot of people at the orphanage, and kin to many of the home mothers and children. Maybe I was just wishing that I could have a real mother. I sensed that I could trust the home mothers, and I felt a longing to be accepted by them as if they were my own mothers. Oh, I received my share of paddlings just like all of the other rambunctious boys. I guess these were our years of learning what was supposed to be right and what was wrong. Everyday, I always wanted approval in whatever I did. When I would shine the floors or wipe something clean, I would look to see if my home mother or one of the older girls were looking. (Maybe Just For A Little Sign Of Approval Or Even A Split Second Of Love)! If I saw them looking I would attempt to make it look as if I were doing a special job at what I had been assigned. When they were looking, I would smile back at every chance in hopes of winning some approval from them.

Even with a real mother, I just couldn't see not having thirty brothers in my cottage and all of my new almost grown sisters. Bob, Carl, Weldon, Johnny, Jack, Roy and Ray moved with me from the Baby Cottage. "New" boys would begin to move in with us as some of the others would leave to go live with another relative. As the "new" boys came to live with us, we had to check them out to make friends with them. Some boys would naturally be sad from losing their parents, and the trauma was apparent for some time in many of the boys. Many of the boys would cry for a while. Some would not want to play but just wanted to be by themselves. After watching us boys that had been at the Home for a few years, the boys would eventually join in with all of the orphan fun. Soon there would be smiles on their faces, and then laughter, and it seemed their pain would be gone for a short time while we were playing. Before long you couldn't tell that they were "new" boys at all. At the time I didn't quite understand their feelings, as I could never remember this not being my real home. I heard of daddies and mothers but didn't know why I would have to have one. I believe that I sensed something different but everything was so confusing. I felt that I was doing all right so I'd just go about my business of being an orphan.

A lot of time during the day I was happy, playing with all of my friends; but something was missing in my life, and I couldn't figure it out. Receiving kindness from a big person overwhelmed me. I felt very special when an older person showed kindness towards me so much so that at times I found myself in tears but not as many tears as when I would get a spanking. Most of the time while I was engaged in playing with my brother orphans, I didn't have time to wonder what was coming next.

41

Miss Janet Carter was our next home mother at the Anna Hanes cottage when Miss Hunter left. She was a big woman and made us mind the way we should. Miss Carter let us play hard every day just as Miss Hunter had done. Everyone had better be on time though, when we were called in for supper. We would go inside and everyone would wash their face and hands and tuck their shirttail in their pants or bib overalls before each meal. We were sure to wet our hair before we went to the dining room. Somehow, Miss Carter could tell if we didn't wash our faces good. I think it may have been that you could see the streaks where the water had ran down our cheeks through the dirt on our faces! Miss Carter and Miss Holland sat at the head table and led us in our blessing. Each meal, all of us would say the same blessing together. It went like this:

"God is great, God is good,
Let us thank him for our food,
By his hands we all are fed,
We thank you Lord for our daily bread!"
Amen!

After the blessing we would all be required to eat in a proper manner. One of the older girls would remind us of how to be polite and how to eat our meal. She would show us how to hold our fork and knife and teach us how to ask for something on the table, always starting with, "May I please?" After supper the older girls would supervise all of the boys in getting a shower. The older girls would turn on the showers since we couldn't reach them. After the water was tested for temperature then we would take turns getting under the water. We would soap up and the older girls would see that we didn't miss any spots. We would turn around in a circle in front of one of the girls and then we were allowed to rinse off. If we would miss any spots the girls would scrub those spots and we surely didn't want to have a big girl scrub us hard in our ears and especially not in our boy parts. We were six years old and we were big boys now! That kind of treatment was for those little boys at the Baby Cottage! Miss Carter would always check to see if we had cleaned our ears. She would lightly tug at the ears while she looked inside and felt behind our ears.

It wasn't long after supper that we were off to bed. There were no televisions in the cottages in those years so the almost grown up girls or Miss Carter would read us a story. In the Anna Hanes cottage there was a long sleeping porch on the back of the building. All of the boy's beds were lined up from one end of the porch to the other. There were windows all the way along the porch.   In the winter time there seemed to never be any heat on that porch. When it was time to go to bed in the wintertime, we would run real fast to our beds and jump in and cover up. The older girls would check to see that we were covered up good. Then we would all say our prayers. It was the same prayer every night so we all could say it. It went like this:

> "Now I lay me, down to sleep,
> I pray the Lord, my soul to keep,
> If I should die, before I wake,
> I pray the Lord, my soul to take."
> Amen!

After our prayers, the older girls would leave and go upstairs to their big girls room. When we would go to bed the older girls would not have to worry about us getting out of bed because once we were tucked in for the night we would not dare move from under that warm cover until morning. During the summer months we could have the windows open to get fresh air. I really liked hearing the sounds of the rain on rainy nights.

The fall months also meant coal shoveling. A railroad coal car would be dropped off on a sidetrack at one end of the of the orphanage grounds. All of the older boys would shovel the coal from the coal car until it was emptied. It would take a week to empty a coal car. The older boys and farm men would bring us coal from the coal car that had been dropped off down at the railroad tracks. They would dump the coal down the chute into our coal bin. The coal would pile up high next to the chute and would eventually block up the chute opening. On some Saturdays Miss

Carter would have three or four of us boys get naked and shovel that coal to the other side of the coal bin. We were getting to be big boys now and could help with big boy things like shoveling coal. We were seven years old and that meant we were grown up enough to do heavy chores like shoveling coal. The shovels seemed to be about all we could lift at that age, especially after about a half hour of shoveling that coal. We started off with shoveling a half a shovel full of coal. By the time we were finished, we would only slide our shovels across the cement floor and pretend we had a shovel full. Miss Carter would be sitting in a chair watching us to be sure we were doing a good job. Along with each attempt of lifting that shovel, we would let out a little grunt; the coal shovels were bigger than we were and we wanted Miss Carter to know that we were working real hard. By the time we had finished moving all of the coal, we were black as tar. Miss Carter often lined us up and took pictures of us naked as newborn jaybirds. "At least we didn't get our clothes dirty," she would say! Then she would run us to the shower room and see that we got good and clean. Miss Carter was strict but a good lady, and I'm sure that the photos were taken in good faith just as if we were her own children. Today, some in America, including Congressmen and Religious leaders, would be stimulated by such things and misuse the photos.

Anna Hanes Cottage

At the Anna Hanes cottage, we had two long driveways that came down the hill and met at our front porch, like a big V. These long driveways were perfect for riding wheeled toys like wagons, scooters, tricycles and homemade soapboxes that we called crash derby buggies. During those years there was a riding toy called a Flexi Racer. It was the fastest ride in the world. The Flexi was designed to lay low to the ground just like a snow sled. Instead of runners the Flexi had hard rubber ball bearing wheels. The older boys were allowed to have Flexes and would ride them down our driveway. You would usually ride it with one knee on the Flexi and push on the ground with the other foot. The Flexi was so fast that you could ride down the driveway on one side and have enough speed to coast all the way to the top of the other side of the driveway. At times some of the boys didn't quite make the turn at the bottom of the driveway, and they would tear a little bark off the huge poplar tree standing next to the drive. Sometimes the bark (skin) would come off of them!

Leave it to one of the older orphans to come up with the idea to build crash boxcars similar to the soapbox derby cars. The boys would collect old wheels from broken toys, old metal wheels from broken wooden wheelbarrows or any other wheels they could find. They would nail together pieces of wood that resembled a soapbox car. There were some built with potato crates and some built with apple or vegetable crates nailed to a plank. Some had large all metal wheelbarrow wheels mounted on the back and small wagon wheels mounted on the front. The idea behind the soapbox challenge was to have the last car able to roll after running down the drive and striking the huge poplar tree. There were no trophies, just bragging rights. However, there were a lot of memories. There were upset stomachs, lots of bruises and, once in awhile, a broken bone. On a dare, sometimes a boy would drive his crash boxcar over the brick wall, just beyond the big Poplar tree. There was a drop of three or four feet from the top of the wall. A couple of years after moving from Anna Hanes I was old enough to build my own crash boxcar. One of the older boys helped me build it, and finally I was brave enough to make my daring run down that steep driveway.

I built the crash boxcar out of old junk from other cars. I put big metal wheelbarrow wheels on the rear of my car and old red wagon wheels on the front. I used bailing twine for a steering rope and my car had no brake. A wooden potato crate nailed to the platform board served as an engine cover. I even had headlights on my machine. I used old jar lids and nailed them to the front. Every nail we used was pulled from another board and bent straight so that the nail could be used again. Those nails were used over and over again. There was no such thing as a new nail. Oh, I did find "new nails," every time I mashed my fingers. Mashing my fingernails with a rock, trying to beat those old nails straight, was very painful. I found out that a while after the pain went away, I would get "new finger nails!" Most of the time we didn't even have a hammer to drive our nails into the board; we would just use a big rock. After I finished my magnificent machine, I went all the way to the top of the Anna Hanes cottage driveway and let her roll. One of the boys pushed as fast as he could to give me a running start. The noise from the large metal wheelbarrow wheels was very loud as I sped down the cement driveway. I knew that once my magnificent machine began to roll that there was no stopping it until it hit something! One of my runs met with disaster as a nail holding one of my rear wheelbarrow wheels wore in two. The wheel came off of my crash box after a short distance. The car flipped over and the axle came down on my leg, making a nice slice several inches long. My crash box derby career came to a "screeching halt." The home mothers and other staff members banned crash box derbies shortly after the many injuries occurred. I guess they decided to stop that crazy event before they lost one of their boys for good.

Bicycles were not allowed for the children at the Children's Home but we had our flexes to ride and there were plenty of challenges and dares to come with those fast rides. As we grew older we would race our flexes against each other. It seemed that we had to try everything the older boys did. As we grew up, there would be constant struggles between us to see who was top dog. Tempers would flair but would dissipate as fast as they had developed. We would find our own entertainment as we were playing. Anything someone could dream up was a game for us all.

I remember one rainy day when we had to play indoors. We built a puppet show stage out of a big cardboard box, and we all made puppets. We asked the girls at school to find us some old doll heads that we could use on our puppets. Now trying to come up with a script that made any sense or trying to find a story to match all of those unusual puppet characters was impossible. Our puppeteering efforts were short lived. Each boy had his own character that he wanted to play. Some wanted their puppet to be a cowboy; others wanted their puppet to be Tarzan or some other famous figure. Besides, that was kind of a short-lived and "sissy thing" to play, we thought!

When the time came for us to start school, we didn't have far to walk. There were not enough classrooms in the old school building to handle the first through the eight grades. The first grade classroom would be in the old school building but the second and third grade classrooms would be in other buildings around the campus. Coach Wilburn Clary was our grammar school principal and Mrs. Erma Pals was my first grade teacher. I remember her voice and personality even today. She was a short woman of medium build, just plum full of energy. She really put a lot of pressure on all of us children to pay attention and learn everything that we possibly could. All we had ever done in our short lives was play, eat, play, sleep, do a little chore, play, eat and play some more. Now why can't life be like that all of the time! I would have to dream of a way to make playing the most important part of life, just as it has been up until now!

My teacher had another plan for us children. This was where it all began with our chance at a good education. The discipline was already instilled in us from the way we lived and the way we were being brought up in our individual cottages. Now that's not to say we were perfect little angels because we each had our own personalities. Mrs. Pals had her little Rap-Rap paddle in her desk drawer if she needed to use it, but she also had a dunce hat and a stool in the corner. A Rap-Rap paddle was the most popular instrument for the teacher to use in those years. After proper contact with a child's buttocks, the Rap-Rap paddle seamed to do wonders for us misbehaved children. Many times I had my turn wearing that dunce hat and sitting on that stool. Believe me, that was much more intimidating than that Rap-Rap paddle. Mrs. Pals didn't want to hurt the children with that paddle anyway. I remember beginning to learn to read as Mrs. Pals would spend a lot of time in class reading to us, and we would try to read back to her. Most sentences had two or three words in them. It was hard learning how to say a word from a book, especially when there was a bird singing outside in a tree or clouds floating across the blue sky. I could dream of what the clouds looked like. Why couldn't that be part of school learning? Anyhow, I learned to make out some words.

One of the first things that I remember about reading occurred outside of classroom and at my cottage. We never were allowed to see the newspaper until we were much older, but one day I saw a newspaper lying on a table. I understood some things in the newspaper, and I could read some words. Just not big ones! I read the headlines of the *Winston-Salem Journal and Sentinel*. The headlines read, "Truman Fires Macarthur!" Somehow I could tell what the president's name looked like, and I was able to make out the rest of the headlines because I had started school, and I could read real words! I just knew that President Truman had shot General Macarthur and killed him. I didn't have any knowledge at the time just how much trouble President Truman had gotten himself into. I just knew that I didn't like the president anymore for a long time. Back in those days at the orphanage you didn't ask an adult anything. In fact, you didn't speak to an adult unless you were spoken to. That was the golden rule of respect to your elders there at the Home. Of course we would say, "Hey Mr. So and So" or "Hey Coach" or "Hey Pop" or "Hey" to a big boy or big girl! In school we learned that we could raise our hand, and after being called upon, we could ask a question. Most times when we raised our hands it was to let the teacher know we needed to visit the bathroom. We usually didn't have to say anything; we just held one finger out or two fingers out and she could tell that we needed to go! It was several years later before I found out that the president had not shot the general. An older person told me that the president had taken him out of his job. Boy, I sure was glad that the nice General Macarthur was not shot dead, but it still took a long time for me to not dislike President Truman.

Mrs. Pals was a firm teacher in discipline and taught us to do many different things such as: making valentines, drawing and coloring with crayons and my favorite class of all, "recess." We started learning how to wipe the black board as far up as we could reach. I remember our teacher driving to school in an old black business coupe and parking it just outside of our classroom window. We couldn't see out of our classroom windows because they were high off of the floor; I guess for big people to look through. We had a way of getting tall enough by standing up in our chairs when Mrs. Pals was not in the room. We could see the yard outside and where she parked her car. Once in a while, we would get caught standing in our chairs. Mrs. Pals would give us a little whack on the buttocks or make us wear the dunce hat to mend our ways.

Well, I couldn't wait for school to let out and we would get to go home because there was a lot of playing that had to be done, and I was ready. Of course, first we had to take our nap! We had four Seesaw rides that kept us occupied for hours. We had a line of swings that were a lot of fun. There was a horizontal ladder that we called a handle bar or hand walker just off of the play porch. Our sandy yard was perfect for playing with our toy soldiers or our toy trucks and tractors. There was never a passing moment that we didn't take full advantage of the time we were allowed to play outdoors. With thirty boys in our cottage, we could always find a friend to play with. Different boys had different personalities and each liked to play a certain way or play with certain toys. Once in a while we would get caught climbing on the chain link wire that enclosed our play porch. Now that was a reason for another "hinny popping."

I remember when the soldiers, sailors, and airmen came back from World War II. One day some of them came to the home in trucks and jeeps and paraded all over the Children's Home campus. Real army trucks and army jeeps with real GI's riding in them left a lasting impression on me. In later years I found out that many of the Children's Home boys left the home early to go and fight in the war, and after the war was over, many returned to finish high school, but not to the Children's Home. Junior Sprinkle was the only boy to serve in WWII and return to the Children's Home to finish high school. He did so because he had no other place to live. He played sports with the other boys but didn't have the same work routine. Junior left the Home and served in the Korean War. Wounded in his leg, he was the lone survivor from his squad after a fierce battle. Patriotism and pride were instilled in us from the very beginning at the Home. Many of the Home children came back after college or after the war to be teachers or to help run the Home in some other capacity. Most would give their entire adult lives to the care of other children at the Children's Home.

We held our Sunday school in the auditorium. Coach Bill Edwards, a very good Bible story teller, and "Pop" Woosley would tell us about things in the Bible. "Pop" always had to have his time with the children. He would bring a different family to the front of the auditorium each week, and tell everyone where they came from. He would then tell a story about some happening when he went to pick them up and bring them to the orphanage. He told about children that would hide from him, and all sorts of funny things that happened. At the time my sister and I had come from the furthest distance and "Pop" loved to tell about it. It seemed that he wanted me up in front of the group more than anyone else. He was always very kind to me and would always hold his hand on my cheek or rub my head very gently while he was talking to the other kids. All of us loved "Pop!"

When we were at the Anna Hanes cottage we all wore short pants, but in the wintertime we had a corduroy or plaid wool jacket. I can remember being so cold at times with those short pants on. I guess they figured that we were young and should be running around all the time to stay warm. We finally were allowed to wear long pants when the weather really turned cold. I remembered it snowing a lot in the winter months there at the Home and it seemed that when it snowed it was quite deep to us little tots. The big boys shoveled snow from our outside doors and porches. The boys would always be playing as well as working. Some of them would ride their coal shovels down the steep hills beside our cottage. It looked like so much fun, and I couldn't wait until I was old enough to ride a shovel like that. Some of the older girls would be outside, and the boys and girls would throw snowballs at each other. Then they would always make a big snowman in the front yard of the cottage. I remember the girls putting pieces of coal from the coal bin in the snowman for his eyes, nose and mouth. They would use broken tree twigs for his arms. The snowman almost looked real to me; almost like he would move at any minute. I would look at that snowman for long periods of time just waiting for it to start moving. The snow would bring another good fortune to us. The older girls would gather up some snow and Miss Holland would make all of us snow cream. Boy, that was good! She would always make sure that the snow was the second snowfall of the year. She said that the first snowfall cleaned the air of all the impurities.

Well, I got through my first year of school; then second grade came along. I really thought that I was growing up fast. I was smarter and could do many things. I could draw, knew lots of ABC letters, color pictures and could read from books with three words in a sentence. I was also smart in daydreaming. My teacher would be reading a book and it seemed that I would become part of the story. A lot of times I would drift off thinking I was one of the characters. I really liked a teacher that could send me off into my own dream world. I would be the brave knight that saved the princess or a frontiersman blazing a path across America. A lot of times after the teacher had finished reading the story, I would still be engaged in my own world of thought of how I would be in the story. My eyes would be wide open, and I would be focused on one spot in the room. I guess my teacher sensed that I wasn't there with her in the room, and she would call on me by asking a question about what she had read. Well, a lot of the time I would just say, "HUH!" I knew she was making noise about something, but I couldn't tell you what she was saying. I only knew where I went in my story! I often wondered where or how my story would have ended if I hadn't been pulled out of my dream world. I just thought that what the teacher was trying to do was send me into my own dream world. Anyhow, I really enjoyed going there and what she was doing for me. Some children went to sleep just as they had been trained to do. Nearly every night at bedtime, our home mother would read to us until we would fall asleep. This was confusing! In the classroom, while our teacher was reading to us, one had better not fall asleep or they may get to wear the Dunce Hat! Oh well, I guess we would figure it out sometime!

Second grade was held in another building called the Brown building. We were in the basement but there were windows on one side so we could see outside. Mrs. Donnie Huband, née Matheson, was my second grade teacher. She was a very pretty lady and was a very good teacher. She was also raised as a child at the Children's Home so there wasn't much room for us kids to get into too much mischief because she knew all of the tricks. Of course I didn't know that she had been raised at the orphanage until I was much older.

There was a long rock wall beside the driveway at our cottage. Everyday we would walk up the driveway on the way to our second grade classroom. There just happened to be a lot of yellow jackets that nested in that rock wall. Some of the boys, being mischievous as they were, would stir up the bees by throwing rocks at the places where the bees would come out of their holes. The next boys that came along after them were surely in for a real surprise. There seemed to be hundreds of those yellow jackets. It was a sure thing that who ever came by next was going to

be stung. The boys would wait just over the hill, out of sight, and break out laughing when one of the boys got stung. That dirty trick stopped after the trick was played on them, and they got their buttocks spanked by the home mother. Of course, being a typical orphan boy, you must know that I was not involved in that kind of prank!
(Orphan Humor)

I had a lot of fun in the second grade but there were a few disastrous events that would occur with me. One morning my Anna Hanes classmates and I were walking to school just after a very deep snow had fallen. There was a big drainage ditch that we all had to cross if we took the short cut to school. The night before, the winds had blown the snow into drifts covering the ditch. As we were crossing the ditch, I slipped and fell into the deepest hole. I immediately knew that I was in serious trouble. I kicked and struggled to get out of that ditch that was full of wet leaves and covered with a snowdrift. I finally got out of the ditch with only my feelings a little tattered, but when you live in a cottage with thirty boys, there has got to be a lot of teasing. Being laughed at by the other boys was bad enough, but what got the biggest laugh was, I came out of that ditch missing one shoe. Well, there I was, being laughed at and having to walk the rest of the way to school in the snow without one shoe. I didn't have to walk too far though. When I got to school Mrs. Huband dried me off and sent a couple of boys back to find my shoe. When the girls learned of my adventure they were also amused at my misfortune, but soon schoolwork was back on schedule. I got through that trauma but wouldn't you know it, another surprise was about to surface!

It was getting close to the Christmas season, and all of the girls and boys were going to draw and paint Christmas decorations so we could decorate our classroom for the Christmas Holidays. Each student was assigned a different art project to accomplish. Some would make snowmen; some would make paper cutout chains with all of the different Christmas colors, and some would make snowflakes from white paper. Other children were chosen to cut out and paint reindeer on brown paper. The

53

reindeer were to be painted from the water paint colors that were mixed by Mrs. Huband. She had instructed us on exactly how to paint the reindeer so all would look alike when they would be hung on the wall pulling Santa's sleigh. There were eight of us and it seemed to be several days of painting before we were finished with our reindeer. I took my time so my reindeer would be the prettiest. Well, when everyone finished their individual projects, Mrs. Huband began hanging all of the beautiful decorations on the wall. She put up paper snowflakes and colorful paper chains. Everything was beginning to look like Christmas. I was really proud that I had painted the prettiest reindeer of all, so I thought! I just couldn't wait for everyone to see my reindeer hung on the wall! I knew that I would become the most popular boy in my class and especially with Bonnie and some of the other pretty girls.

Mrs. Huband finally got around to hanging Santa's sleigh. Then the first child handed her reindeer to Mrs. Huband to go in front of the sleigh. Oh! It was really looking pretty! Then came the second and third reindeer. Now, finally, the sixth and seventh and mine would be next. The pressure was building because I just knew that all of the kids would gasp with joy at the beautiful reindeer that I had painted all by myself. Mrs. Huband said, "Freddy, let me have yours," and with a big smile and a pounding heart I rushed up and handed Mrs. Huband my reindeer. She lifted it up to fasten my reindeer to the wall in line with all of the other reindeer. All of a sudden the room became quiet. Then a few, "ahhhs," and then laughter such as I had never heard before! I mean everybody was laughing, even the pretty girls that I thought I would be impressing! Everyone was laughing until Mrs. Huband quieted the class. Then it hit me like a ton of bricks as I looked back up the wall. I had painted the prettiest reindeer but I had painted it going in the opposite direction! It WAS funny, but I was very disappointed in myself. There were no more smiles on my face. I thought that I had ruined one of Santa Claus's reindeer. I received a pretty stern one-way discussion from Mrs. Huband about following directions. I hastily painted the backside of my reindeer with Mrs. Huband's help. Then Mrs. Huband hung my reindeer on the wall, this time going in the same direction as the others. At least we saved the reindeer! I believe that teachers know when a child tries hard but sometimes makes a mistake.

Mrs. Huband had a lot to teach us that year, and I really enjoyed second grade. I remember our first trip walking all the way to R. J. Reynolds High School to watch the play "Peter Pan." Now that was something to see. Every child in grammar school was lined up in a row and walking all of the way over to R.J. Reynolds High School. That was a long way to walk for little folks with short legs. We walked all the way to the end of the orphanage, across Reynolda Road and up a steep winding hill. The play was magical as the big people were like real characters and the scenery looked real. I can still remember the impression that the performance left on me. Who would ever think that kids living where we lived would ever see anything so real? Mrs. Huband was always friendly to me for the remainder of the time that I knew her. In later years after I had left the Home and when I would be able to get away from my military duty, I would come back to our annual Homecoming at the orphanage. In those years the Homecoming was held on Easter Monday. I always looked forward to Mrs. Huband being there so that I could give her a great big hug. Teachers could be a mother figure to us just as some of our home mothers were. In those years, discipline by the teachers was used to correct a problem child very quickly. It seems to have worked, as there was very little trouble from the children as they grew up in the Children's Home school system.

During this period, I was growing all the time but it seemed that most of the girls were taller than I. In fact most of the boys were bigger also. I didn't let that slow me down from competing or accepting all of the challenges that orphan life had to offer. Bruises, broken bones, black eyes and bee stings were common occurrences in our quest for manhood!

At this age, I heard about rabies for the first time in my life. There was a stray dog wandering around between the boys' cottages one day and a dog was one of those animals that we just didn't see often. Dogs were just not allowed at the Home with all of those children. Naturally, a dog drew a lot of attention from all of the children. Several of the boys touched that stray dog. The dog was later shot for having rabies. I believe that three of the boys there at the Home had to go through the whole series of rabies shots. I remember someone saying the boys cried because they said that it hurt them to get the shots in their stomach. They said the needles were twelve inches long, and that was enough to scare me to death! I really became aware of stray dogs after that incident. I would never get around stray dogs if I could help it, NOT UNLESS they looked like they needed petting or needed something to eat or needed a warm place to sleep or something like that!

Somewhere about this age I got a real taste of hospital life. I had to get my tonsils removed at a hospital somewhere in town. I was very frightened being at the hospital because I don't ever remember being away from all of my other orphan brothers. I could see outside, through the glass window, into the yard, but there were no orphans out there playing. It hurt to have my tonsils removed, but I loved that ice cream they gave me to help make my throat feel better. I remember the nurses being so kind to me like I was someone special. Even with all of that nice treatment, I couldn't wait to get back to my cottage with all of my brothers, and I never wanted to go anywhere again. Oh, I dreamed of going places, but I would have to take all of my orphan family with me or it would be awful lonesome by myself. Now where could I go and carry all of my four hundred brothers and sisters with me?

Well, life would continue at The Anna Hanes cottage as the snow fell on Christmas Eve. It seemed that snow gave Christmas that extra touch of something special. It made things much quieter than usual. I remember listening for the reindeer on the roof and just knew that I heard them at one instance during the night. The Christmas season always touched me in a special way at the orphanage. Every year we had a Christmas tree and it seemed always to get prettier each year as the home mother and girls

would decorate the tree. Seeing the other children happy
and full of joy was almost as good an experience as getting
my gifts. Getting to see the Christmas play that the older
children preformed every year at the orphanage school was
so magical. I was learning many new Christmas carols and
beginning to understand the Christmas story. I got some
nice toys for Christmas. I got a scooter, a horse head on a
broomstick that we called a hobbyhorse and some cowboy
things. We all loved playing cowboys all over our big play
porch and back yard. I would ride my horse all day and
my horse would never get tired. My horse was faster than
any of the other cowboy's horses. My horse could rare
back and say, "Neigh! Neigh!" I kept my horse for a long
time and had a special corner for him in my junk box.
Santa brought horses for a lot of the orphan boys at our
cottage. My horse got to run with all different colors of
horses. You should have seen our play yard with all of
those horses running and chasing each other. We could
ride our scooters on our big driveway. We would make
motor sounds as we raced each other pushing our scooters
along.

Chapter Three

Soon it was spring and then summer, and I found
myself being moved from the Anna Hanes cottage to the
Norfleet cottage where the eight and nine year old boys
lived. I felt just as I did when leaving the previous cottage.
I would miss being at my old cottage; but at least this
cottage was right next-door, and I could come over and ride
my tricycle and other toys down the steep driveway. I was
still a little nervous about meeting my new home mother
and wondering if I would like her and if she would be good
to me. Then there would be bigger boys that I would have
to get to know. I would also be entering the third grade in
the fall. I found out that Mrs. Sifford, the home mother at
Norfleet, was a very nice lady who loved all of her boys.
She would have to have a lot of patience to experience the
spirited group of boys that we were. We were a very active
bunch and we ran wide open all day.

Mrs. Lou Belle Sifford With Robert
(One Of Lou Belle's Boys)

There were a lot of learning experiences that we all
would go through at this age. First, Mrs. Sifford would be
the one to tell me that my father had gone to heaven. That
hurt for a while, but she had at gentle way about her of
making that kind of pain go away. She held me and
hugged me while she was telling me that my dad was no
longer here. She held me until I stopped crying. She didn't
tell me how my dad had died, probably to spare me any
unnecessary grief! I only slightly remembered seeing my
father once in my life, but being told that my father had
gone to heaven was still a shock to me. "What would I tell
the rest of the boys in my cottage?" I couldn't brag
anymore of just how good a daddy I had. I wondered,
"Would they think any different of me?" I was told that he

came for a visit when I was very young. My memory was so faint that I couldn't remember what he looked like or who he was. I was told that when he did come for a visit that he left a pistol for me to keep, so that I could take care of myself when I grew older. I really remembered none of that visit, but I did wish that I could have remembered hearing my parents voices and being near them. I didn't let the other boys know how I felt inside. I had always bragged to the other boys about my daddy. I had told the boys how big and strong my daddy was. I had told the boys in my cottage that my daddy had a whole dump truck full of money. Shucks, we were so poor that my mom and dad couldn't even afford to give my sister Charlena and me middle names. With my daddy gone to heaven that also meant that I was a full-fledged, certified orphan boy. "Orphan" was a name that we boys all were proud to call each other at the Children's Home. It just made you feel like you belonged to a family with a whole bunch of children. If you could laugh at being called an orphan, then living like one didn't matter as long as there was someone to love and care for you.

Before taking the Norfleet job Mrs. Sifford worked as the sewing room supervisor. She had several of the older girls working with her. They were responsible for sewing up torn clothing, patching what they could and sewing on a lot of buttons. The clothing was then cleaned and hung up to be handed down to the next child that could wear the item. I'm sure she was good at that job, but I am thrilled that she decided to take the home mother's job when "Pop" Woosley asked her.

Mrs. Sifford was the perfect person to have as the home mother of the Norfleet cottage. She was always like a mother to all of us boys, but somehow I felt an extra bit of love from her. I hope that all of the boys felt the love from her that she made me feel. Mrs. Sifford would always try to see that we were happy, and she joined in on a lot of our boyhood games. She would play horseshoes with us and played a pretty good game of it. I can still remember her now pitching those horseshoes. One of her arms was broken when she was a young girl and it didn't heal back completely straight. That didn't slow her down one bit and she always kept up with her boys. She would pitch the ball for us boys to hit and taught us to play fair. Boy, she would even get down on the ground in her dress and shoot marbles with us. That was my kind of mother! I would even like to have this woman for my own mother! She would teach us how to throw horseshoes and how to make a ringer. She loved to rock in her favorite rocking chair on the front porch during the warmer days. There was no air conditioning in those days where we lived. The front porch always seemed to be cool as it was high off of the ground and there was a nice view from the porch.

I didn't have to worry anymore about how good my new home mother was going to be to us. She was like an angel to us but did make us mind. I knew though that she loved us all, and I liked being in her cottage. She didn't mind helping us. She showed us how to comb our hair, and at times she would let us sit in her chair with her as she read to us from a storybook. Mrs. Sifford would step right into a fight between us and stop the bullies from beating up on the little fellows. She would sit us down and talk to us about how bad we were when we would get into trouble. Spankings were given only if you really needed one. They were few and far between at Mrs. Sifford's cottage. She had a way about her that showed each of us love but she demanded respect.

All of the boys our age wore short pants most of the time for school, Sundays and special occasions. We wore bib overalls to work. Bib overalls and work boots were the everyday work uniform except during the warm weather months. Then we went barefooted to save on the wear of the boots. The overalls were more suited for doing more grown up chores and for playing real hard. Some of the older boys were lucky enough to have regular work pants like blue jeans.

We all had jobs to do at this cottage that carried more responsibility. There were no almost grown girls living at this cottage so we had to do more of the work ourselves. However, some of the almost grown up girls would come by

61

on certain days and do some of the harder chores that we could not do. I remember one of the girls that weren't too much older than we were. She was there to help us wash windows, as we couldn't climb on ladders. She was a beautiful girl. All of the older boys liked her and so did I. She was very nice to us. I loved being her helper boy, holding her ladder when she washed the windows or whatever else I was asked to do.

Sometimes one of us would get sick and have to stay in the infirmary with Miss Smith. I never really liked being indoors, let alone being stuck in the infirmary. The older girls who worked there made things a little more interesting for us boys.

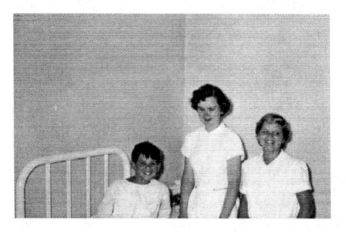

Fred, Muriel and Sara Ann
Do I get to go home today?

During the summer months we were sent to work on the vegetable farm, usually called the "truck farm." I never did understand why! If you were raising vegetables and not raising trucks, why would anyone in their right mind call the farm a "truck farm?"

At the truck farm we not only raised vegetables but we had a hog processing room, a potato storage shed, a smoke house for curing hams, a tool room that carried enough tools for all of the boys to use, a tractor shed and a large cannery where we would can all of our fruits and vegetables to last through the winter. The cans were then stored in part of the cannery and issued out to the different cottage kitchens during the year.

As little children we didn't have to work all day on the farm. That all day work would come in due time as we grew a little older. We would pick some vegetables or learn how to hoe the grass out of the middle of the rows of vegetables. Sometimes we would take turns pulling the rope that was tied to a small plow with a wheel on it. We would plow the small patches of fields where we grew small vegetables like beets, radishes and carrots. There was an old persimmon tree in the pasture just behind the truck farm sheds. Once in a while, in the fall of the year, we would climb over the fence and try to knock some persimmons out of that tree. Occasionally we would see a opossum up in the tree trying to get some persimmons to eat. I remember one day I ate some persimmons before they had a chance to get really ripe and got the worst bellyache. It seems that we would learn a lesson from all of our stupid antics, but there at the orphanage we seemed to try everything. There was always something or someone to laugh about. If there weren't a lot of humor, there would have been a lot of sadness in our lives.

After we went home and had our lunch, we would go back to the truck farm for a few hours in the afternoon. Sometimes we would get there before it was time to go back to work and just lay around on the grass under two big popular shade trees playing mumble peg. If no big people were looking, some of us would grab a carrot out of the carrot patch, which were only a few feet away from where we were sitting on the grass. We would go back to work for a couple of hours, but we would get off work in time for our cottage's turn at the swimming pool.

The old pool

After an hour in the pool, there were still lots of time to play and always a lot of new land to explore. There were always balls and bats, footballs, yo-yos, cap pistols, cork guns, jack rocks and of course jack knives that we had to play with. The boys that were lucky enough to have jack knives would teach us how to play mumble peg. Mrs. Sifford would always warn us about playing mumble peg and would always tell us not to stick the knife into our foot. We would play mumble peg barefooted. That was much braver than when wearing shoes. Mumble peg was a game that was won or lost on how good you could control the jack knife while flipping the knife in the air and making it stick into the ground. It was a very popular game in our days at the home. I guess these were the toys that lasted long after the other toys were well worn out.

We get to go fishing.

Eddie Newsome, one of the staff workers, and Coach Gibson took us fishing one day and taught us how to rig our hooks and put the worm on the hook. Most of us had a bamboo pole and some had a sapling limb on which to tie their string. Somehow I wound up with three poles, maybe thinking I could catch more fish!

Fred with three poles

Charlie/Fred/Arthur/Bill/Weldon/James/Melvin
Eagerly awaiting ride to go on another fishing trip

I remember one day we found a big chunk of molded cheese. There seemed to be a couple of blue jays that were really excited about diving down and picking at that big chunk of cheese. Well, we came up with an idea to try to catch those birds. We found an old wooden box and placed the box over the cheese. Then we found a piece of string and tied it to a small stick. We then placed the stick in a position to prop up the box. This would allow the birds to get to the cheese. We then hid behind a tree and waited for the birds to come. When the birds would walk under the wooden box, we would pull the string and hopefully catch a blue jay. We tried many, many times and different ways to catch those blue jays. We finally did catch one. We just knew that we were great hunters and boy was I proud. We didn't know how we were going to get that big bird out of our trap, so I lifted the wooden box very slowly and slid my hand under the box grabbed the bird. That bird was really upset when we pulled up on that wooden box. I just had to let the big bird go free. That blue jay started pecking at anything that was within its reach. One peck on the hand and that was all it took for me to let go of that bird. I didn't try to catch another one of those blue jays. That bird was going to eat my hand along with the moldy cheese!

A lot of times on rainy days, we would be stuck inside

and had to play in the playroom. I remember one day I got my first lesson in electricity. Some of the boys would trick us and tell us how to put a bobbie pin in an electrical outlet. We were young and didn't realize the danger at that age. Most of us fell for the trick and stuck the bobbie pin into the socket. One experience with this trick was all that I could stand, and I never got near an electrical outlet again while I was young. When I stuck that pin in the two holes, I felt the power of electricity hit my fingers with the worst kind of tingling. I snatched my hand back and it really hurt. My fingers and hand were swelling up and turning blue. It just seemed that nearly every boy had to try it one time. That was just one more of the dares that we would all be challenged with while we were growing up at the orphanage. It would be one more chance to experience orphan humor. There were always those that had been tricked before, and they were just waiting for a good laugh at the expense of the next victim. Needless to say, anyone of us could have been killed by this diabolical trick. I learned by experiencing this misfortune, and I knew early on in my life that electricity was nothing to play with. Electricity demanded respect anytime you were near it.

In the late spring as the weather became warmer, everybody could put their shoes away and go barefooted until the cold weather came back in the fall. First, every boy at the Home had to walk the entire Home property looking for anything that could hurt someone's foot. We picked up every piece of glass, nails, barbed wire and anything else that could cut someone's foot. There were wheelbarrows and buckets filled with all matter of sharp objects. To make it look more impressive to "Pop" Woosley, some of the older boys would crush up bottles and collect junk from the trash pile. Well, I think "Pop" Woosley knew some of this was going on, but he thought the home grounds were safer for the kids to take off their shoes for the summer. He gave the word that it was all clear for every one of the children to take off their shoes. There was one more important surprise with this privilege. Everyone had to have an up-to-date tetanus shot. This had to be done before barefoot day was declared because we worked barefooted around the barns and pastures. I just wished they had developed a honeybee shot because the home grounds were covered with clover and it seemed that I would get stung about every week!

"Pop" finally declared barefoot day and it wasn't long after that the swimming pool was opened. The pool was old and the concrete was rough but it was a hole full of water and that was where we would have a lot of fun. Each cottage had a certain time during the day in which the children could use the pool. I was always cautious around the pool because it took a while for me to learn to swim. The bigger boys would hold our heads under the water and that really scared me for quite some time. I would stay near the edge of the shallow end so I could get away from the older boys. I would swallow a lot of water before I learned to swim. I was so skinny that I would sink to the bottom every time I tried.

Ah! But I couldn't let that stop me from swimming, especially if the girls our age were looking around the hedges that surrounded the swimming pool. I would dog paddle for a few feet at a time but never got too far from the edge of the pool. At least at the edge of the pool I could grab hold and it would look like I could swim. Well I couldn't get by with that for long because everyone of the children had to pass a swimming test before they were allowed to swim in the deep end of the pool. After a year or so of choking on the chlorine water I braved the deep end of the pool, especially when I saw that the girls were able to swim in the deep end. I finally passed my swimming test. I did a lot of belly flops from the diving board and swallowed a lot of water trying to impress some of the pretty girls that may have been looking my way. It took some time for me to master swimming techniques in the old pool. I always looked forward to swimming time each day because once in a while, we would see our favorite girls getting out of the pool after their swim time. During those years we all had a lot of favorite girlfriends.

During the summer, all of the children who had some family or friends from churches would be allowed to leave the Home and go on vacation for two weeks. All of the other children who didn't have a place to go would pack up their clothes in a cardboard box and move to another cottage for the two weeks. There was one cottage open for the boys during this period, usually the John Neal building. There was also one cottage open for the girls. I believe it was the Stockton or James A Gray cottage. Anyhow, the children who stayed behind would carry on the necessary work chores while the others were on vacation. The cows had to be milked and the pigs had to be fed. There was also some canning of food to be done.

Over the years, some of the children never returned from vacation but settled back in with their families. Often it felt like losing a good friend or brother or sister. Even today I still feel close to all of the children that I knew, and I often think of them. When it came time for everyone to go on vacation, I had no place to go or anyone to go with. I would stay at the Home and do the necessary chores until all of the other children returned from vacation.

Another one of Mrs. Sifford's boys was in a similar situation. His name was Tom Reece or "Tinker" as we called him. Mrs. Sifford said that all of her boys would have a vacation that year and she was not going to leave anyone at the Home to work. She told "Pop" Woosley, the superintendent, that she would take "Tinker" and me with her, on her vacation, to her niece's farm in Danville, Virginia. Those of us who didn't have parents were sure lucky to have a home mother like Mrs. Sifford. I was so happy to get to go somewhere on a real vacation. Mrs. Sifford packed our clothes, toothbrush and comb in a cardboard box and off to the bus station we went. "Pop" Woosley drove us to the bus station, put our cardboard boxes on the bus, and off to Virginia we went. Boy, did we have fun fishing for catfish, running all over the farm, and riding on the tobacco sleds with the big folks. We would go fishing on the Dan River and catch big ole catfish and sometimes we would catch a big ole slimy eel. Mrs. Sifford and Margaret, her niece, would show us how to kill the eel. We would draw an X on the sandy bank and lay the eel across the X. Then we would lay Mrs. Sifford's handkerchief on top of the eel. After a while we could peek under the handkerchief and see if the eel was still wiggling. So, now I am an expert on cat fishing and the art of handling freshwater eels. We explored the barnyard to see all of the farm animals and looked over that strange looking barn called a tobacco barn. We walked in the pasture and down by the creek, doing boy things. I hope we weren't much of a problem for her as we tried to mind our manners like we had been taught. We were excited about everything that went on at their farm. It was a great vacation and this is just one example of how Mrs. Sifford loved all of her orphan boys in her cottage.

The next summer I went to Statesville with some of the other children that didn't have anywhere to go on vacation. A church group invited ten of us boys and girls for our two-week vacation. "Pop" Woosley drove us there in the Children's Home bus. The church was out in the country, and the Rev. D.T. Huss was the pastor of this wonderful group of Olin people. Each family would take a child to their farm for the two weeks. I stayed with a real nice family, the Mondays, and had a great time. They had a nice big farmhouse with a real big yard and lots of huge shade trees. Everything seemed so peaceful there on their farm. The Mondays had a son named Jimmy and after we sized each other up for a bit, we got to be real good friends. Jimmy would take me fishing, show me all over the farm and let me help milk the cows. Jimmy's dad would let him drive an old vehicle called a "doodle-bug." It looked as though it was made from and old truck that was chopped down to the frame. They would use the "doodle-bug" to pull trailers and equipment around the farm. Well, Jimmy would let me ride with him all over that farm and we really had a good time.

All of the neighbor farmers would visit each other's farms during harvest season or to raise a barn. One day Jimmy and I traveled with his family to another family's farm to help them get in their hay. I remember the man at the other farm asking me if I would like to ride on the tractor to another field. I was a little frightened because I would be standing next to those big wheels turning around

70

on the tractor, so I said that I would rather ride on the hay wagon. I climbed up onto the wagon and we took off. We traveled down a gravel road that looked like a washboard. The hay wagon had hard rubber wheels, and I was in for the ride of my life. I just knew that wagon was going to shake me to death. My teeth vibrated and chattered and my whole body felt like it was coming apart. Once the farmer started driving down that road, he never turned around to see how I was doing. I couldn't find a spot on the trailer that was the least bit comfortable. I said to myself, "Please let me off of this hay wagon!" When we got to the other field, I was dizzy and half sick, but at least I was finally off that wagon.

Every family brought a picnic dinner and there was enough food to feed twice the number of people there. After lunch one of the young boys who lived at the farm we were visiting asked me to play with him, and I found myself in a game I had never played before. I was not going to back out and show the young boy that I was just plumb full of fear. The boy said that he was going to drop a board on his pet dog's head and run to an old truck and jump inside before his dog could catch him. I felt that I could run as fast as the young boy, but I didn't want to hurt the dog. I just knew I could make it to that truck and get inside before that nice doggy could catch me. The boy went first. He dropped the board on that nice dog's head and took off for the truck. He ran as fast as he could with the dog growling and nipping at his heels. He jumped into the truck just in time and closed the door. It looked pretty scary to me, but I couldn't show any fear in a real man's challenge. I just had to prove that I could do the same trick. Well, it was my turn so I rolled up my britches legs and rocked back and forth several times to make me go faster. Finally I had enough practice to make me faster, and I got my bravery all together. I dropped the same board on that nice doggie's head and took off running as fast as I have ever run in my life. I know that I was running faster than the other boy, but I didn't make it to the truck before I felt something sting my buttocks. Down I went and that big nice doggy was not so nice anymore. That big doggy was getting even for the both of us dropping

71

that board on his head. The doggy got real mad and jumped on top of me growling and fussing. I felt the dog's teeth all tangled with my teeth and then the doggy tried to shake me apart like a rag doll. The boy started screaming and his mother ran out of the house and pulled the doggy off of me. The boy's mother took me to the local country doctor who used metal clips to hold the bite tears in my face together. I was so frightened by the attack that I felt very little pain. Mr. and Mrs. Lee Boggs were the owners of the dog, and I felt bad that I upset them so much. They were very nice people. It just seemed that when there was a lesson to be learned, I always picked the most exciting and hardest impacted ones. Back at the orphanage, this would have been one of the most humorous things that ever happened, but here on the farm, they took it very seriously.

Afterwards, I went back with Jimmy and his family to their farm and back to being a kid again. Jimmy and I ran all over the farm just as if nothing had happened. Mrs. Monday always had dried apples or peaches in a flour sack at the back door of the kitchen. Jimmy and I would grab a hand full every time we went out the door to do boy things. We would go to the fishpond on the neighbor's farm, and fish every chance we could.

Chickens ran all over the farm and the mother hens nested in just about every spot in the barn. There was a hen house for the laying hens to lay their eggs, and we would collect the eggs every day. Some of the mother hens had baby chicks, which I thought were the prettiest little creatures as they ran all around the farmyard. Once in a while I would catch one of the chicks and pet it for a while before I would give it back to its mother.

One day an old stubborn mule got loose from a neighbor's barnyard and ran up and down the dirt road in front of Jimmy's house. Jimmy and I decided that we were going to lasso that mule and carry the mule back to the neighboring farm. We ran to the barn and got a nice length of rope that would hold the mule if we caught it. We just knew that we could catch that big, stubborn mule. We

72

went out by the road and hid behind a big oak tree. Every time that mule would pass by, one of us would take turns and jump out at the mule and try to lasso the huge steed. We came close to catching the big steed a couple of times, but it probably was just as well that we didn't lasso it. Mr. Monday came running out and said if we had gotten a rope around that mule's neck, that the mule would drag us to death before it would stop. Oh, it was a thrill while we were trying to catch that mule though! My heart was beating a mile a minute. I could just see me being the one to catch that big steed and my friend Jimmy thinking I was as brave as Randolph Scott, Tom Mix or Roy Rogers.

Jimmy and I would ride his "doodle bug" tractor all over the place as we helped with the chores on the farm. We would milk the cows and feed all of the animals. We would help Mrs. Monday as she put different kinds of fruit out to dry, on a piece of metal, in the yard. She would slice the fruit into certain sizes and lay the fruit out on pieces of tin to dry in the hot sun. The dried fruit was as good as any candy and had to be a lot better for us to eat.

One day Jimmy and I went to the barn to milk the cows. One of the cows was in another pen with her newborn calf. I wanted to pet that pretty little calf so I climbed over the fence and jumped into the pen. I mean this was the prettiest little animal that I had ever seen. The calf had a very light brown color to it all mixed with white. The calf was just lying there in the straw as I began to pet it. Suddenly Jimmy shouted, "Look out Fred!" I jumped to my feet and turned around and all that I could see was cow horns on the front of a cow's head coming directly at me. At that time Jimmy said, "Jump through the fence, jump through the fence!" I was scared to death as I turned and ran towards the fence where I saw a gap between the boards. I didn't even try to climb through that fence, as there was no time for that. I dove through the fence headfirst. Before I hit the ground on the other side, I heard the mother cow crash into the fence behind me. I lay there for a while as Jimmy came running over to see if I had been hurt. Jimmy asked me, "Are you all right?" I lay there with my heart pounding out of my chest and couldn't half get my answer out. "Yep, I'm all right." I said to Jimmy, "That mama cow sure got mad at me for petting her baby calf." Jimmy said, "You got to look out when you get around mama cows and especially the young cows." Well that was enough excitement for that day. I was learning a lot of lessons at this family's farm.

I remember getting my first bowl haircut in the front yard of their home. One Saturday morning all of the men folk took turns in a chair as Mrs. Monday and her beautiful daughter would place a bowl on the men's head and cut off everything that hung below the bowl. It didn't bother me to get a bowl haircut because I fit in with everyone else. Even though, I still wanted my hair to grow out a little bit before I went back to the orphanage. My haircut looked like the kind of haircut that one of the Three Stooges always wore in their comedy movies. Then the ladies would put a little taper on the sides that made it look a little better. Mrs. Monday's daughter was a very pretty, almost grown lady, with pretty auburn hair. She would ride with an almost grown up man, in his own car, to the movies in town on Saturday evenings and to church on Sunday mornings.

Well it finally came time for the other orphans and myself to meet "Pop" Woosley back at the church for our trip back to the Children's Home in Winston-Salem. When the Monday family packed my cardboard box with my clothes, there was a special gift that Jimmy and Mr. Monday had for me. They gave me my very own yellow handle jack knife. Boy, would I be something when I got back to the orphanage! I really enjoyed being with my new friends on their farm, but in the back of my mind, I missed being with all of my brothers and sisters back at the orphanage. At that time Mr. Monday gave me a box with holes punched in it. I knew right away what it was because I could hear a baby chicken inside. This was really something to have my own baby chicken. I guess Mr. Monday knew how attached I had become with the baby chicks. I gave lots of hugs that day to all the Monday family for all the kindness they had shown me. I can still picture the farm and that wonderful family, and I think of them from time to time.

We all met "Pop" Woosley at the church and rode home in our bus. I couldn't wait to get back to the orphanage and show off my new pet chick and my jack knife. When "Pop" heard that little chick, he wasn't so sure that my having a baby chick was a good idea as there were no dogs, cats or any other pets allowed at the cottages. Mrs. Sifford, our home mother, met us when we arrived back at our cottage. Pretty soon I saw "Pop" and Mrs. Sifford in a discussion, and it didn't take long for them to make up their minds about my baby chicken. Mrs. Sifford had talked "Pop" into letting me keep my pet chicken.

Then "Pop" carried me over to the infirmary and turned me over to Miss Anne Smith, our nurse. Miss Smith took me to the Baptist Hospital to let the doctors look at my face and remove the metal clips that were put in my face after the dog bites. The doctors at the hospital said that the country doctor really knew what he was doing because my lips and jaw looked very good. The doctors and nurses at the Baptist Hospital were always good to us orphan kids. I knew my way around that hospital early on in my life because of my many visits resulting from my very mischievous and active lifestyle.

After I got home from seeing the doctors, I went back to my cottage to see my pet chicken and show off my jack knife to all of the other boys. My pet chicken had to be looked after, and I had to make it a home. Mrs. Sifford gave me the rules for keeping my pet. The chicken could not stay next to the cottage, so I built my pet chick a home behind the cottage. Before long that little chicken was old enough to lay eggs. All of the boys would carry food scraps and crushed eggshells and feed my chick everyday. Mrs. Sifford told me the old eggshells would make the new egg shells harder and keep them from breaking so easily. The eggshells would also provide my chicken with enough grit for its craw.

When that chicken started laying, she laid an average of one and a half eggs every day. Mrs. Sifford came up with an idea. She said, "Why don't you carry the eggs across

the highway on Reynolda Road to a grocery store and sell
them?" Wow! I had become a businessman! That grocery
man would pay me twenty-five cents for every dozen of
those eggs that I would bring to him. I was the richest
nine-year-old orphan in the whole wide world. Business
always has its risks, and I was about to discover a serious
flaw in my business. That business was going great until
my pet chicken picked a new spot to roost. The chicken
wanted to roost right next to the front porch where Mrs.
Sifford rocked in her rocking chair. I tried and tried to get
my pet chicken to go back to the backyard to roost, but the
chicken had its mind made up. I guess my pet chicken
thought that it was good enough to roost anywhere it
wanted. I surmised that the chicken wanted to be near
Mrs. Sifford, in her rocking chair, when the sun was
setting. My pet chicken was just not going to learn where
the right place was to roost.

Norfleet Cottage front porch
with Mrs. Sifford's rocking chair

It was bye-bye chicken because the area around the
front porch looked just like a barnyard with the entire
flavor! Mr. Simpson, the Home's business manager raised
chickens in his back yard so Mrs. Sifford asked him if he
wanted to buy my pet chicken. Mr. Simpson bought that
chicken for four dollars and seventy-five cents. I sure
hated to see my chicken go but at least it had a good home
living with the other chickens that Mr. Simpson raised.

76

When I was a little older, once in a while I would walk by Mr. Simpson's house to see if I could see my pet chicken amongst the others. I couldn't pick it out of the bunch of chickens he had in his pen. I often wondered if a dog had gotten to my pet or if possibly it made a nice Sunday dinner!

I was just about the right age to start playing football. At the orphanage we started playing tackle football with real helmets, shoulder pads, a smaller football and a real coach at the time we reached sixty pounds. We had an eighty-pound team, a hundred pound team, a junior varsity team and a varsity team. The first order of business was competing for my own uniform. Our uniforms were in big boxes in the girls' dressing room at the gymnasium. Sometimes the uniforms were just dumped into piles on the floor so we could pick through them easily. We used the girls' dressing room to get our uniforms during football season. Uniforms were handed down over the many years from varsity down to junior varsity down to the eighty to hundred pound team and then to the sixty to eighty pound team.

It was very difficult trying to walk after I had donned the uniform. I put on a pair of shoulder pads that would slide off of one shoulder or the other because the neck hole was larger than my shoulders. I put on a jersey that the sleeves came past my knees. I put on a pair of pants and the kneepads were past my toes. The pants had hip pads built inside them with pockets inside the legs to hold the thigh pads. It was best not to put any thigh pads in the pants because the pads would be below my knees. I had only seen other boys wearing a football uniform, but I had no idea how everything was supposed to fit. I really had a difficult time getting a uniform, but I made up my mind that it wasn't going to stop me from playing football. I continued looking through that big pile of equipment scattered all over the floor. I started looking for a pair of shoes. Finding two of the same kind was hard enough. Some of them still had the old leather cleats. The shoes must have been thirty years old. Some of the shoes had the round screw on cleats and some of shoes had leather cleats that were rectangular shaped that came to a point and were nailed onto the shoe. It didn't make any difference to me because I was going out on that football field and play football. I picked up two of the smallest shoes that I could find that looked like they were a left and a right. I slid them on and wow! Did I need to stretch my feet? I thought if I could put some of those old dirty socks in the toes of the shoes then I could possible wear them. I scavenged through the pile of shoes for three or four pieces of shoestring and began tying the shoes to my feet. I tied a piece of string a couple of holes up from the bottom on each shoe and then tied a piece near the top holes. When I finally got those shoes to stay on, I was ready to go and impress my very first football coach. I stood up to run out the dressing room door and found out I had a slight problem. The shoes were old and limber, let alone too long. When I stood up to take a step, the shoes folded in half, and I fell right to my knees. I got up and said to myself, "I'm going on anyway." I knew that practice had already started, and I was in a panic to get out to the field. I wanted to make a big impression my first day. I adjusted my step to walk more on my heels. I grabbed a helmet out of a box full of old ones and headed out to the football field. In those days we had old leather hand-me-down helmets with no facemask. My first football coach must have been really impressed. I could tell by his smile. I had my sleeves rolled up a half dozen roles so that I could get my hands outside of the sleeves. I had my pants tied with shoestrings as high as I could get them but the thigh pads were as wide as my chest and were still below my knees and the kneepads were on top of my shoes. I could tell that that coach liked me by the grin on his face when he turned and looked towards me.

Our future uniforms, handed down,
(From 20 years ago)

I knew my football coach, Bill Edwards, from school because he taught the older grammar school kids. He was a giant of a man and always seemed friendly to us young kids at school. I just knew it would be easy for me to learn how to play football from such a nice big man. I just knew that I was going to have an easy time learning this game. Coach Edwards had a little different attitude when it came to his great eighty-pound football team. Teaching us how to get down, how to know when to go and who we were to block or tackle must have been a nightmare for him, but somehow he managed to pull us together. He had one good instrument of persuasion. I would get down ready to go and sometimes my shoes would bend in the middle. I would fall forward and be off sides. Then I would hear this giant of a voice shout out, "Way to go Tanner, way to go!" Then the dreaded words, "Come here, bend over and touch your toes." I had seen that giant of a man kick some of the other boys in the buttocks, and I was not enjoying thinking that I would be next in line. I knew that I was going to be kicked plumb out of sight. I bent over and touched my toes and began to flinch at every sound or motion. The anticipation was overwhelming as I glared back at this giant. About that time, Coach Edwards reared back with his number nine foot. He swiftly brought it forward as I closed my eyes, clinched my jaws and puckered up for the boot of my football career. I felt the mighty giant's SIZE NINE make contact with my buttocks and over on my face I went. Coach Edwards just barely made contact with my bony buttocks, and I flinched and fell forward. I got up in anticipation that there may be another kick in store for me but Coach Edwards said, "Now get back over there and go when it's time to go!" After that I sure was going to try to do better the next time when it was time to go (if only I could understand when that time was supposed to be)! Coach Edwards was a gentle giant after all. He loved us and would never want to see any of his boys get hurt. I found out later that he was raised at the Home as an orphan just like me. He came back to the Home during WW II, after completing college, to help children and give them a better chance at life. Coach Edwards and I seemed very close from that day on. He found some donated equipment that fit us better, and we had a great time learning the game of football. One other incident that I remembered well happened while we still had those old uniforms. I was running out for a pass from Coach Edwards, and I turned my head around to catch the football but I couldn't see it. Everything became dark! My helmet was so large that my head turned around inside of the helmet. I believe that was part of the reason Coach Edward found us some other uniforms that were closer to our size.

I just knew that I was going to be a big star football player some day. Coach Edwards would let us all play, and I was getting better every day. Better at what, I didn't know, but I thought that I was getting better! I sure didn't like being on the bottom of that pile every time! I couldn't wait to get my breath after everybody got up off of me and the dust cleared.

One year when the professional football teams came to town to play in a pre-season game at Bowman Gray Stadium, we were invited to play during the halftime. Coach Edwards divided us into two teams and we scrimmaged each other. The crowd was overwhelmed as they enjoyed seeing us play as much as they were enjoying watching the pros. We were so small and it must have been humorous to watch us play tackle football. Everyone wanted us back to play at halftime whenever there was a pro game in town.

Coach Edwards did his best to make us all football heroes. He really gained my trust in him. There was a lot of humor in his personality. The way he was with us young orphans created a lot of respect and admiration from us towards him. He never swayed from that human decency and kindness the whole time that I grew up at the orphanage. The words he spoke were always words of encouragement, decency and honor. I would develop a thought of him over the years as not just an ordinary man but also a great man.

Each day we walked down to the administration building for school as our third grade class was taught in the basement. A new addition to the old school was being built so that all of the grammar school classes could be taught under one roof. I really enjoyed all of my classmates and especially some of the pretty girls. Bonnie was my favorite and Dorothy and several others were good friends, I thought! But they liked other boys, and I don't think they even knew I was around. Mrs. Folger, my third grade teacher, was a very stern. She really meant business when it came to our paying attention and doing our work. Boy, was this a shock. Not a week went by that for some reason I didn't get a hand spanking from Mrs. Folger. She would call me to the front of the class, grab my hand by the fingers, bend the palm out and spank my palm with a wooden ruler. It hurt and at times a few tears leaked out of my eyes. Showing bravery in front of the boys and especially the girls just didn't work. I tried to do what I thought I should but for some reason, I'm sure it was I, Mrs. Folger just seemed to pay special attention to everything that I did.

Soon the third grade came to a close, and I was thrilled. There was Field Day that was a great event for me each year and "No More Mrs. Folger!" The report cards were handed out and boy was I glad to see mine. I loved summertime at the orphanage and looked forward to dogpaddling in the pool, eating watermelons and playing after we got off work on the farm. I opened my report card and read down the list of grades. There was an A; there was a B-; there was another A and then a shock hit me. There was a big fat red F on arithmetic. That was really bad but it got much worse. There was a space reserved for the teacher's remarks and Mrs. Folger had recommended that I remain in her class for another year. That had to be the end of my life. I thought, "Oh no," I just couldn't handle another spanking on my hand. I thought that just because my arithmetic summations were a little bit different from the rest of the class, they were not that much different. I just couldn't stay another year in her class.

The worst part was parting with the classmates that I had grown accustom to being with, especially the girls. I would no longer be with my special friends. Oh, well, they may not really have known that they were special to me. All of my orphan brothers would be a grade ahead of me and they would move to the next cottage, and I would be left behind.

The next school year I would have Mrs. Folger again but we would be in the new school addition. The new school addition had very nice classrooms. I don't know whether the new school addition or being in a building with other classrooms seemed to mellow Mrs. Folger a bit. It didn't mellow her to a point where she entirely gave up spanking my hand with a ruler though! Well, I lived through another year with Mrs. Folger and had fewer hand spankings. In the long run it didn't hurt me to stay another year in Mrs. Folger's class. I had started school the youngest in my class. I also would get to stay another year with Mrs. Sifford at the Norfleet cottage. That was all worth the trouble to get to stay with such a nice lady that treated me as if I were her own son! The summer season would come and go as we worked some in the fields and played a lot.

As Christmas season arrived, each of the cottages would receive a Christmas tree. We just knew Santa would be coming very soon. Mrs. Sifford would let us help decorate the tree. We couldn't handle the pretty glass balls but we helped hand other stuff to Mrs. Sifford because she could reach a lot higher than we could.

There was a Christmas program at our school auditorium each year and at the end of the program Santa Claus would come and give us a present. This Santa Claus really was Santa. I knew it was he because he was very jolly and had a big tummy. That was what I was told, and I believed it. It had to be Santa! What a great time for all of us young children! Some of the boys didn't believe that it was Santa but I did, even though he did seem like I had seen him in July! In September! And maybe November! I know, I'll ask Coach Edwards if it was really Santa, if I can only find him! He should know because he looked like he could be kin to Santa himself!

I can remember, so well, every Christmas season when Mrs. Sifford would let us walk to Winston-Salem with her. She would have every one of her thirty or so boys walking along with her to town before Christmas would arrive. That was a long way for us to walk but even more of an effort for Mrs. Sifford to walk. She would take us to several stores and let us look at toys on the shelves. We would go to F. W. Woolworth and Walgreen's Drug Store. That was really a treat for us boys, as we had never seen such a sight as the shopping district in Winston-Salem at Christmas time. All of the stores were decorated with lights and the street lamp poles were decorated with bows and lights. There was a chill in the air that made it feel like Christmas time. Every Christmas shopping trip, Mrs. Sifford would buy us an ice cream or drink at Walgreen's Drug Store. The store shelves were full of toys and other things for adults. It was a very exciting trip to get to look at all of the things on display.

I found out later just how much Mrs. Sifford was paid to care for us boys during those years. She was paid about forty dollars a month but often treated her orphan kids with part of her salary. She would take some of her own money, that she had saved during the year, and would spend her money on some of her boys who would not get much for Christmas, if not for her. She wanted to see that all of her boys were treated equally in any way that she could. After giving her entire adult life to the care of orphan children, Mrs. Sifford only received a minimum allowance from her Social Security when she ran out of energy and reluctantly decided to retire. During her service as home mother at the Norfleet cottage she had cared for four hundred and six boys, an average of two years for each boy. The boys would always be known, to anyone that she could tell, as Lou Belle's boys. She would give her entire adult life to the love of her boys just as if they were her own sons. Often she would give not only of herself but what she had so faithfully earned in salary.

When we would get home, Mrs. Sifford would let us look at a toy book while we were writing our letters to Santa Claus. It was really a hard decision to ask for something in our letters to Santa. After everyone had written their letter to Santa, Mrs. Sifford would collect them and send the letters to Santa. At the time, we children didn't know that Mrs. Sifford would be the one to go back to town and buy our Christmas gift. The Orphanage would give Mrs. Sifford money to buy us gifts for Christmas. She spent many days shopping for our Christmas gifts. As she would gather the gifts, she would store the gifts in the basement of the Superintendent's home. "Pop" Woosley would help Mrs. Sifford and the other home mothers gather their children's gifts. They would spend days in the Superintendent's basement wrapping each of their children's presents while the children were in school. There was a lot of secrecy to this operation because I never saw Mrs. Sifford go to the Superintendent's basement. On Christmas Eve, all of the older children would meet at the basement of "Pop" Woosley's home and would help carry the gifts to each of the little children's cottages. This would be late at night after all of the children were tucked into their beds and dreaming of the Christmas day soon to arrive. Mrs. Sifford would always make sure that Christmas was special for each child in her cottage. She would read us Christmas stories and tell us about the manger scene that she had put out for display. She made our Christmases a special season by her own individual caring for all thirty of us boys. Why would any boy want to live anywhere else but here and be one of Lou Belle's orphan boys?

The gymnasium and dressing rooms were right next door to where we lived in the Norfleet cottage. The gymnasium was built underneath the Duke cottage, a cottage for older boys. Living in the cottage next to the gymnasium had its advantage. On Friday nights, when we didn't have to be at school the next day, Mrs. Sifford would let us watch the varsity girls and varsity boys play basketball at night when we had a visiting team come play our team. That was a really big deal to us young boys. The gymnasium was small with the backboards bolted directly to the brick wall. There was a padded mat hung on the wall under each basket so the players would be less likely to get hurt when they would charge towards the basket for a lay-up. Seating was limited to one side and you had better bring something to sit on because the seats were hard concrete steps. We orphan kids seemed to make out all right sitting on cement as I think our buttocks were conditioned for such things.

Coach Edwards was also the girls' basketball and softball coach and he always took care of his girls just as he cared for all of us. Coach Clary was the varsity boys' baseball, basketball and football coach. Coach Clary had been quite an athlete himself in college. He wasn't raised at the home but he had the same spirit as the home developed into us. Coach Clary was the grammar school principal and later became the Children's Home's assistant superintendent.

Coaches Edwards, Clary and Gibson

At the Norfleet cottage we ventured further and further away from the cottage and all over the orphanage grounds. We went all the way to the big farm where the big boys worked for Mr. Angell and Mr. Gray Todd. We saw the mules and would pet them when none of the big people could see us. I remember one mule was named Mary.

The Mule Barn

We saw the older boys hoeing the corn, getting in the hay with pitchforks and, once in a while, we saw the mules all hooked up to the farm equipment. I couldn't wait to be an older boy so that I could do all of those big boy things. I couldn't wait to be an older boy just to get out of my bib overalls and get to wear work pants with a belt! All of the older boys wore blue jeans. Some of them called the jeans "Roebucks." This was a brand sold by Sears Roebuck and Co. Some were called "Bells" that were made right there in Winston-Salem.

The orphanage had just dug out a new baseball field below our cottage. This is where we practiced our little boy's football. This big ball field made us a playground that seemed to extend forever. It was huge. The old baseball field was in front of our cottage and in front of the old school building. Sometimes, at the old ball field, the older boys would hit baseballs out of the field and hit cars parked on the road below. Sometimes the balls would hit the infirmary just across the road. On occasion a windowpane would be broken from a well-hit ball. Later varsity boys played baseball games on a corner of the football field. The new baseball field would be a welcome sight for Coach Clary as he was as sincere in his job as any major league coach or manager.

This old ball field would become the girls' softball field and the young boy's soft baseball field. The young boys played with a ball that looked like a baseball but was a little softer. During those years of school we began to see more of the older orphan children and we were involved with more activities like school plays, Christmas programs and all kinds of sporting events. There was football, baseball, basketball, softball and recess.

Back at the Norfleet cottage we were still enjoying our freedom. We could go right behind our cottage to the new ball field and watch the varsity boys practice baseball under the coaching of Coach Clary.

He was a tough coach and serious about that ball team. There were big boys that could really play ball. I heard that "Red Smith" knocked a baseball over the fence and the fence had to be a mile away. I had found baseballs in the soybean field below the fence. I often wondered if one of them was hit that far by "Red." "Red" was always one of my favorite big boys. I remember the Boyette brothers (Bill, Tom and Junior), Charles Schrader, Bill Proctor, Julian King, O.T. Williams, George Holland, Buck Hall, Dan Stutts, Dick Hayworth, David Poole, the Shuping boys and many more of the older boys that were my heroes. We would hear about them from time to time and would see them when they would come back to the Children's Home's homecoming that was held every Easter Monday. When the older boys would make a mistake or were late for practice, Coach Clary would make them run laps around that big field. The amount of laps depended on the severity of the offense. I have seen some of those boys running long after practice, and they looked like they couldn't take another step. These boys were in good shape and could do anything and win over anybody in the world.

I was in the infirmary one time with a broken bone or sick when Julian King was brought in with a broken leg after a football game. I just knew he was a superman. After I got out of the infirmary, I had bragging rights at my cottage because I was in the infirmary with Julian. I told every boy in my cottage that I was in the infirmary with a big boy that broke his leg playing football.

One year our varsity football team lost every game except the very last one. They were supposed to lose that one because the team they were playing was the number one team in the conference. This orphan team just wasn't going to let that other team beat them. I remembered hearing those older boys as their helmets clashed against each other in a fierce battle. The pounding of their shoes on the ground sounded like horse's hoofs, and when they came close to the sidelines, I could feel the vibration where I was sitting on the ground. Our team fought with all its might and at the end of the game had won over the best team in the conference that year. That team was Monroe and the year was 1950. I was lucky enough to get to see that game as Mrs. Sifford marched us single file to the ball field when we had home games. We sat on the grass, out of the way of all of the big people, and watched the game. That was some game!

This was the first year that Bill Adkins played varsity football. Fifty years later I ran into a man that found out that I had grown up with Bill in the orphanage. He introduced himself as John Caldwell. He asked me if I knew Bill, and I told him that I was his water boy when Bill played sports. He mentioned to me that the hardest he had ever been hit on the football field was by Bill Adkins. This man had played for Mt. Airy and went on to college at NC State.

The big boys never ceased to amaze me while they were playing sports at the Home. Some of my heroes would leave one year and there were many more the next year playing in the most spirited game of football. They didn't have to be the favorite player as they were all my big brothers and that made them all my heroes. "Red" Church was the head manager and my hero as well!

Life experiences were coming at a fast pace for me. There were a few more black eyes that I received at this cottage. We would get into little fights with each other but they seemed to be over as fast as they began. Then everyone would go right back to playing with each other. Most of the time we were all very close friends. The older I became, the more challenges I had to deal with. There was always a bully somewhere in the group that had to show they were tougher than any one of the other boys. There were a few boys that were just down right mean, and those few would make life miserable for some of the smaller, weaker boys. Some of the boys were a little shy and that also seemed to attract these bullies. With thirty boys in a cottage you had to deal with a lot of challenges. There was a lot of name-calling and from what I remember the name-calling touched just about every kid unless you were real big and strong. We would just call the big bullies names behind their backs so they wouldn't hear us!

I guess the hardest thing for boys my age was to be picked when we were choosing up sides to play a game. Some of the boys were just not as big as others and a few never got picked unless there weren't enough players for the game. Being a smaller child at that age, I knew very well the feeling of not being picked to play. When the older boys would move up to the next cottage, then we would become the older boys to the younger ones that were moving into our cottage. There was always something else to do at the orphanage though. The only problem was to find the time to do all the playing that had to be done. I never remembered a day growing up that I was not busy trying to get all of my playing done in the time that I had. Sometimes we considered getting into mischief, playing! I found myself always thinking of how to do something or make something.

One year I received an electric train for Christmas from the Sunday school class in High Point that sponsored me while I lived at the orphanage. Each child had a sponsor from one of the many different church Sunday school classes in western North Carolina. At Christmas and sometimes on our birthday our sponsors would send us a gift. The sponsors that I was lucky enough to have sure were nice to me all of the time that I was living at the orphanage. I played with my electric train for years. Mrs. Sifford would let me put my track together in the living room and she and the other boys would watch that train for hours. Mrs. Sifford always loved to see her boys happy and encouraged them to do things that made them happy. She didn't want her boys to get into fights, and when they did, she would break them up and talk to them for a long time after a little gentle paddling. She always treated each boy as if he were her own child.

Mrs. Sifford watched each boy as he did his studies and always helped those that were a little behind in their work. She looked at each report card and talked with each boy about how they were doing in school. If a boy were not doing well in conduct, then she would also have a long conversation with that boy.

The living room was a special room that we were only allowed to go into if we were in our Sunday best or in our pajamas. A lot of times, Mrs. Sifford would read us a story from a book. We really loved times like that since listening to a story from her was like being a part of the story. We would all lie around on the floor around her chair and some of us would fall asleep before she would finish reading for the night. Mrs. Sifford was proud of that living room and we helped her with the cleaning and dusting. The furniture was beautiful and there were plenty of windows from which any activity outside could be viewed.

Sometimes Mrs. Sifford would take us on day trips to Winston-Salem, and sometimes she would take us for walks to the farm and pastures. Once she took us to the radio station to watch a disk jockey, and the man talked to us while we were on the radio. She also took us to the tallest building in Winston-Salem, the Reynolds Building, and let us go all the way to the top and look out over the city. When we went to the pastures, she would show us where we could get a safe drink of water from the spring in the creek. The spring had very cool water and was located under several shade trees. We could sit in the shade on a bed of thick grass and fall right to sleep. Sometimes we would carry sandwiches with us and have a picnic under the cool shade trees. There was a small church that sat on top of a hill in the pasture. Mrs. Sifford would take us to this church, and she told us that one of the former orphan children was buried beside the church. The child's name was Polly Wray. We were told that if we would walk in a circle around Polly's grave and if we would say;

"Polly Wray, Polly Wray what are you doing down there?" Then listen carefully, she would say, "Nothing."

All of us boys took turns going around and around that grave. We tried talking to Polly over and over and over but we couldn't hear her say nothing! Each time we would visit her grave for a couple of years we tried, but she would not say anything! She would say nothing! Oops! I got it.

There was an old cemetery behind the church that kind of gave me the creeps. I had just never been around dead people before and didn't feel comfortable being there. I would always keep my distance from the graves. I wouldn't let any of the other boys know that I was afraid. The orphans before us named the church "The Little White

91

Church". It was a very pretty Moravian Church nestled in amongst the large Oak trees. We could hear the church bell ring on Sundays from our cottage about a mile away.

Mrs. Sifford would show us where the blackberry patches were located and she would show us how to pick the berries. We would pick enough blackberries to carry home and Mrs. Blankenship, our cottage dietician, would make enough pies to feed the whole cottage. This beautiful pasture and creek would provide us with a much larger playground for the rest of the time that we would live at the orphanage. I would grow to love this awesome playground and found myself over the years spending many hours roaming every inch of this wonderful place. In fact I liked being there so much that I spent a lot of my school study time there instead of doing my studies. When I think back of the days we played in the woods and pastures, I often think of Mrs. Sifford when she introduced us to this playground. I will always keep her close to my heart and am thankful that I was lucky enough to be one of "Lou Belle's Boys!"

Fred
One of Lou Belle's boys

After I retired from the military I was able to visit Mrs. Sifford from time to time. She lived in a retirement home in Huntersville near Charlotte. Anytime that I was traveling near the area I would stop in to visit with her. Many of the other Children's Home children would also visit her. I guess Phillip Hutchins was the most frequent visitor of all her boys. She always kept in contact with many of girls and boys that she knew at the orphanage. I received cards regularly, and I would respond in hopes that it may give her an enjoyable moment. She loved to hear from her boys and always wished them happiness. She had known where each boy had come from and the sadness that many had faced as a small child. In her mind they were still her boys and she would always be there for them for as long as she had a breath left in her body.

One day Wyndell, Mrs. Sifford's son, phoned me informing me that his mother had peacefully passed away. She had lived well into her nineties. She had recently broken her hip and began to fade. She lost weight rapidly and even this was not her main concern. She slipped into a coma. As she was taking her last breaths she awoke long enough to speak her last sentence to her family. Her voice spoke softly the words "My Boys, My Boys" and Lou Belle left us so peacefully.

I was fortunate to get to be one of Lou Belle's pallbearers. I know there would have been a hundred boys there if only we could have gotten in touch with all of her boys. I believe Lou Belle will see some of her boys on the other side, and I know she will also be taking care of them there. I can see her now walking in the meadows in heaven with her boys in hand. She will be looking down at her boys to see if their faces are clean and on each face shine a bright smile.

Lou Belle wrote a poem, which pretty much expresses how she lived.

I want your will in everything

I open my eyes; I see the light.
GOD has kept me through the night.

I lift my voice to Him and say:
"Please keep me through this day.

Let Your loving grace to me abound,
Keep me safe and keep me sound.

Keep me faithful from day to day
And never let me go astray.

Be with my loved ones everywhere.
Keep them in your watchful care.

Be with the sick, Dear Lord, I pray
And make them better day by day.

Help those in trouble; they need You too,
Stay close beside and bring them through.

May words I speak, heart meditation too,
My Lord and Savior, be acceptable to You.

This is my prayer to You I bring.
I want Your Will in everything.

Lou Belle Robinson Sifford

Chapter Four

It was finally time for me to move up to my next cottage. I wanted to move up with my friends but I sure hated to leave Mrs. Sifford. Mrs. Sifford packed my cardboard box with all of my belongings, and I moved up to the Tise Two cottage and met with my new home mother, Mrs. Jamesina Reynolds, a very slender and proper lady. Tise Two and the next older age group, Tise One, were in the same building but separated by a brick wall. One of Pop Woosley's great innovations was hiring the mothers of admitted children to be housemothers or to perform other functions at the Home. Mrs. Sifford's son, Wyndell, was a Home resident as was Mrs. Reynolds' daughter, Ina Clare. Others that I recall include Mrs. Speight, Mrs. Shores, Mrs. Gibson, Mrs. Gary, Mrs. Lettie Sue Smith, "Nanny" Hartman, and Mrs. Hatcher. Mrs. Sifford said that she had originally applied to Barium Springs Orphanage to admit Wyndell but the superintendent told her that it would be a conflict of interest and a violation of the principles of whatever organization was constituted of the child caring institutions of that day to hire her as an employee.

However, he told her, Oscar Woosley was known to bend those principals from time to time. So she and Wyndell ended up at the Home. I guess Pop discovered that these women had a greater dedication and more interest in the children's welfare than those available from other sources.

Mrs. Reynolds always tried to encourage us to think of something to make or something to do. She spent a lot of time looking over our shoulders while we were doing our homework and trying to see that we did our very best. Miss Tula Harrelson, who worked at the campus laundry, shared living quarters with Mrs. Reynolds and helped her keep us boys in line. Miss Harrelson was a mighty strong lady and certainly none of us young boys would be foolish enough to cross her. I believe this is the time that we learned to signal each other when some adult was near and we were not exactly behaving! We would shout the word "CHIGGERS" and everyone would be on the lookout for an adult coming. Chiggers would stick with us for the remainder of our time at the orphanage. I must have heard the word "chiggers" a thousand times as we surely engaged in a lot of mischief and boy's play as we grew up.

Miss Harrelson let it be known that if there was any trouble with any of us boys that she would straighten us out. I surely believed every word she said and didn't get into "too much" trouble while I stayed in Tise Two. In a pretentious display of authority, she let it be known that when there was trouble from one of us, she would put us in a mattress bag and scrub the cement floor with us. I never saw any one of the boys get that treatment probably because she left such a strong message for us to remember

Tise Two cottage had a cement floor in the basement with our lockers and showers located there. The wooden stairs between the floors were open to the outside air. We would really hurry when we moved between floors in the wintertime because it was very cold. Sometimes snow would blow in on the steps, through the large openings in the brick walls. The second floor was our study/playroom combination. On this floor each boy had a junk box for his toys and a chair at one of the tables for study time. We did our homework there, and on rainy days we could play in this room. We would walk outside and up the steps to the top floor where we slept. Before we had television, Mrs. Reynolds would let us listen to the Amos and Andy or a mystery show on the radio on Sunday nights. We would all go upstairs to bed and no one would make a sound while the Amos and Andy show was playing on the radio. By the time the show was over, every one of the boys had fallen fast asleep.

One year we were allowed to go all the way to the other end of the pasture and into the orchard. We were told that the president of the United States would be coming by in his car. He would be coming right by the orphanage on Arbor Road. This was a big deal to all of the orphans, and we all scurried to get a place on the orchard fence. Pretty soon we saw a line of big black cars coming down Arbor Road. I was in my bib overalls and work shirt, but I didn't know that anyone was supposed to dress in their Sundays to see an important man come by in a car. Sure enough as the cars passed one by one, there was the President that I thought had shot General Macarthur several years earlier when I was learning to read and understand words. I guess I could wave to the President of the United States. I waved from where I was sitting on top of a fence post and he looked straight at me, smiling and waved back to me. I really saw a famous man and he waved to me.

The president was going to the site where the new Wake Forest University was going to be built. A bunch of famous people was going to meet him there and dedicate the land for the university. A lot of the land, around where the college was being built, would become part of our extended playground. We used to walk to the Reynolda property and catch fish in their pond when the adults were not there. One of the boys would catch Muskrats in the creek and sell their hides. I caught a few but not as many as Ward would catch. There were real nice woods all around the college site. Some of our farm fields were near the area so we knew how to get to the property to have fun.

My Sunday school sponsors from High Point always

kept in touch with me. Once in a while, "Pop" Woosley, our superintendent, would let my sponsors take me to High Point for a visit with them. I would visit their church, the Wesley Memorial Methodist. The Sunday school class that sponsored me was the Susanna Wesley class. They were so good and loving to me. I remember on one visit Ms. Norma Dutton came from High Point to pick me up. She drove me all the way to Holden Beach to stay with her family and friends. It was the first time that I had seen that much water in one big hole. There was so much water that you could not see to the other side! On the drive to the beach, there were bridges to cross that fishing boats passed under. There was lots of sand and a lot of heat bearing down on that sand. There were a group of boys playing cowboys and army and stuff so Ms. Dutton let me go play with them. I took off through the underbrush and up the sand hill and made friends with the other cowboys. My shoes soon filled with sand while I was climbing the sand hills. We would choose up sides and have a battle. I had a good time playing in the sand. I had never seen big sand piles before, "only red dirt piles." It seemed that everybody was running all the time that we were playing, and I began to feel a little sickly. I went back to the house and really got sick from being in the heat. Ms. Dutton put me to bed for the rest of the day, and I felt a little better by the next morning. There was no cowboy playing the next day, but something I loved even more and that was fishing. She took me fishing and we had a ball. We walked the beach and picked up large shells. Ms. Dutton told me that some of the shells had the sound of the ocean inside of them when you put the shell next to your ear. That was really exciting to carry the ocean around with you in a seashell. The beach and the fishing boats were amazing to me. I really liked what I experienced at the beach, but if I ever came back for another visit, I would have to watch out for that heat. I surely didn't like that overheated feeling.

On another trip to High Point, the husband of one of the ladies in the class took me on the train with him. I went all over that rail yard, engine house and switch track. I climbed on every train engine and car in the yard, even the caboose. That train was gigantic and must have weighed a thousand million pounds. The nice man let me take a train trip with him on his daily run for the High Point, Thomasville and Denton Railroad. I helped him drive that train all the way to High Rock Lake and back to the train station. I blew the horn and rang the bell at each rail crossing, and I even got to ride in the caboose. The excitement was overwhelming. Boy, was I somebody! I wish I could have taken all of my orphan brothers on a train ride and let them pull the whistle chord. There is no way they would believe me when I told them that I helped a man drive a real big train. When Saturday came, the same nice man took us to the movie theatre to see a cowboy movie. He bought us a bag of popcorn, and I ate the whole bag by myself! He bought us candy and a drink; and I tried to consume the candy and drink, but it was just something I wasn't use to with all of the other excitement going on. I didn't feel well on the way back to their house, and when I got home, I had a big surprise for them. I got sick and threw up on their pretty carpeted floor. I really felt bad about it. They put me to bed for the rest of the day and by the next day I was ready to go again. I had learned my lesson, and this time I didn't plan on eating any of those delicious treats.

There were other sponsors in Ms. Dutton's Sunday school class that I stayed with on some visits to High Point. Mr. and Mrs. J.R. Adams had a son and daughter, and I stayed with them sometimes. Their son Jimmy really showed me a good time. I believe Jimmy liked one of the girls in their neighborhood. I have always remembered that Jimmy gave me the yo-yo that had been his personal toy. It was a real pretty yellow yo-yo and boy, did it work well! I learned a lot of yo-yo tricks from Jimmy. We would also pitch a ball back and forth and do all sorts of boy things. Mrs. Adams would take us to the High Point Country Club and we played in the pool with Jimmy's friend R.J. Welch and a bunch of other kids. They were all just a very nice bunch of folks.

I really had a great time, but I missed being around all of those homeboys and girls back at the orphanage. I did meet one other man who grew up at the orphanage. His name was Jake Harris and he ran a barbershop in High Point. I met a Fire Chief at a fire station who showed me a real fire engine. I will never forget that giant of a man as he tapped me on the arm, and I looked up at him. He opened up his hand and nodded to me to look. I looked in his hand and there was the shiniest real silver half dollar. He handed me that pretty half dollar piece and as I looked back up at him, he was smiling and winked. I said "Thank you," to the nice Fire Chief as he rubbed my head. It really doesn't take much to make an orphan child happy, just a little sign of love and a shiny coin as often as you can afford it! Everywhere I went with my different sponsor families, I was treated with the most kindness that could be possibly shown to a young boy. I learned to smile early in my childhood and while I was with them I was smiling all of the time. I loved being with my sponsors, but I was always happy to get back to my real home at the orphanage. That was the real home where I loved to be. At the orphanage I felt more at ease with all of my brothers and sisters near me. Things just seemed natural there. I could always tell my story to the other boys, a story of where I had been and what I had experienced.

Back at the orphanage things were really happening for me. I was back in school in the fourth grade, and I really liked my teacher, Mrs. Butler, most of the time. She was a pretty lady and also pretty strict on us children. She had very black hair and wore dark rimmed glasses. I was having a very difficult time with cursive writing. At that time, we were graded on how well we could write. Everyday Mrs. Butler would have me stay in at recess period and write some sentence a hundred or so times while everyone else was out playing. I thought my hand was going to wear out, and every time I thought I was getting good enough, she would make me stay in again. We had a writing grade on our report card. Every time the report card came out, I would get an "F" on writing.

Well, leave it to me to complicate matters. I was at the ripe age of beginning to flirt with girls. One day when the weather turned colder, I just happened to be walking by the Cornelius cottage on the girls' end of the campus and saw some pretty girls, about my age, playing in the yard. I just couldn't pass up the opportunity to show the girls how nimble and strong I was. I stopped and grinned at the girls for a while and they smiled back. I said, "Hey," and they said, "Hey," right back! I made a few other jibberish comments and thought I had better think of something else to say or do before I embarrassed myself by just standing there. I thought to myself. There is a stone wall and a cherry tree just a short distance away from the wall. If I could run and jump off of that wall, grab hold and swing on that limb, I would really be somebody! My brain never thought that I couldn't make that jump, not with all those pretty girls standing there. I went ahead full speed, ran and jumped off the wall for that cherry tree limb. I said to myself, "Oh boy, I'm going to make it, I'm going to make it, I'm going to be a real hero to all of those pretty little girls!" I'm going tooooh maaa!#*?#*UFF." I grabbed that limb and knew that I was going to be a hero. Well, my hands grabbed the limb like I had hoped, but my hands spun around on that slick bark and down I went. I hit the ground with a crunch and a thud. I saw a lot of stars and felt a terrible pain in my arm. When I fell, I had put my arm behind me to catch my fall. There was a large root from the cherry tree right on the spot where I had fallen, and my arm snapped as I hit the ground. The girls were asking me, "Are you alright? Are you alright?" I tried to answer but I was dizzy; I was seeing stars; my arm really hurt badly, and I couldn't talk. I was out of breath from the fall. So, I sat there for a few minutes until I got my breath back and the stars cleared a little bit from my head. I got up rather slowly and began walking away as if nothing had happened. I just had to cry but not in front of those girls. All I could get out of my mouth was, "Bye" as I turned my head and headed home to my cottage. I felt of my arm. It wasn't the same shape as it was before, and it hurt so badly that I had to let loose with the tears. Well, here I go again, back to Miss Smith at the infirmary. You guessed it, my arm was broken! She carried me over to the Baptist Hospital and let the doctors set my bones and put a cast on my arm. When the next school week came around, I just knew Mrs. Butler was going to let me go out to recess with the other children but that was just not going to happen. I believed that Mrs. Butler would feel sorry for me and show me a little pity. After all, I was in a little pain and had a big cast on my arm. Mrs. Butler thought that since I had foolishly gone out and broken my arm, that I should learn to write with my left hand. So my recesses were still far away. I did learn to write with my left hand and eventually was good enough with my right hand to go out and play at recess with the other children. All of that writing somehow helped me with my spelling as the next year I became the top speller in the fifth grade. That put me into the school championship spelling bee. I enjoyed the rest of that year in the fourth grade, especially recess and all of my pretty girl friends. At least I thought they were my girl friends! I would let them be if they wanted to be. It was all confusing to me but it felt good while I was confused. I would never jump off of that wall again while trying to make friends with some pretty girls. On the other hand, maybe!

As spring came around, Coach Edwards asked me to be the big girl's bat boy and water boy for the softball team. There was no question that I would like to be the bat boy and water boy for the prettiest girls in the whole wide world. They were Evelyn Daniels, Sue Gary, Sissy and Jo Walters, Faye and Raye Horton, Ina Reynolds, Nancy and Betsy Carpenter, Sylvia Staley, Frankie Wilson, Sara Ann Hauser, Mary Elizabeth Johnson, Norma Jean Lawing, Joan Willis, Becky Moore and so many more beautiful girls. There was not a more beautiful group of girls in the world than the girls that lived at the Children's Home. Maxine Dowell was one the pitchers and boy was she good at not only pitching but hitting as well. I had the job of chasing those foul balls in practice, and I found out just how far those girls hit the ball. On the girl's softball field, the outfield sloped down hill and the foul balls would roll forever. I got more of a workout than the girls during their practice, just from chasing foul balls. Some of the girls had their favorite bat. I remember Sylvia liking a long black bat, Faye liked the big fat bat we all called the potato masher.

Blanche, Maxine and Coach Edwards

During the season the girls' team would play other teams out of town and occasionally on a Saturday they would go all the way to Chapel Hill to play. I always remember, when I think of those days, when all of the girls would shout together, "Hey Coach, Stop The Bus, Maxine Has To Go!" Maxine would still be so wound up from trying to win the ballgame that when she got on the bus she always had forgotten to visit the ladies room or outhouse, depending on where we had played. Maxine played ball like I like to see it played. She gave all of her efforts to win right down to the last second or last out. That seemed to be the spirit of each of the girls on the teams at the orphanage. Maxine's talents on the basketball court were equally impressive as her softball game. She scored 57 points in one game. She was an all round sportswoman and was later inducted into the Forsyth County Sports Hall of Fame. Our friendship is still strong, as it is with many other brothers and sisters.

Coach Edwards would always stop somewhere on the way home and buy the ball team and the batboy a cone of ice cream. Of course we have to remember that Coach Edwards liked ice cream as well as anyone I have ever known. Coach Edwards was a great man and loved every orphan child. The girls always looked after me while I was their batboy. They seemed to take special care of me to be sure that I didn't get hurt. They always said nice things to me and would offer me a piece of gum or candy if they had it. I even got to see my big sister play and that was a real treat. I was always proud to have a pretty sister like Charlena for my very own. She loved me and was always good to me.

Growing up also meant even more responsibility. We all worked at the truck farm at this age, learning how to hoe the grass out of the middle of the vegetable rows. We also learned how to pick the vegetables when they became ripe. As we were walking with our hoes on our shoulders, headed out to a distant field, I would always grab a carrot or radish or a tomato as we passed by the different fields on the way to work in another field. It sure tasted good when break time came.

One boy was always chosen to be the water boy, maybe a boy with a broken arm or some other injury. He would provide us with water since the fields were very hot in the summer time. Sometimes if the boys had a nickel, the water boy would cross the fence in a black neighborhood and go to a colored man's store and buy him a soda pop. Soda pops cost four cents plus a penny deposit on the bottle, and back then, there were a lot of different drinks that they don't have today. There was *Nu Grape, Strawberry, Tru Ade, Cherry Wine, R. C. Cola* and *Orange and Grape Nehi Sodas*. The *Coca-Cola* was in a small bottle with a foreign town's name on the bottom. Most of the time, we would drink spring water from the creek or bring a bucket or jar of water from the farm shed. We had to have something to drink because it really got hot working in those fields.

Many times while we were working in the fields during the hot summer we would take a break in the cover of the trees where one of our springs was located. There would be several tall pine trees there in the woods. Instead of resting in the shade, some of the boys would challenge each other by racing up a pine tree. After a few times climbing those tall trees, I learned that it was much more enjoyable to

have a cool drink of water and rest before we had to go
back to work in the fields. Yes, it was a lot more fun to
watch other boys race up the trees while I was lying back
in the shade. I was learning boy things all of the time,
however, sometimes very slowly!

It seemed like hoeing corn was a never-ending job.

There was a cornfield behind the infirmary that we
boys had to hoe. Mr. Johnny Horton was our supervisor
on those hot summer days. He always called me "Tammy"
instead of Tanner. I can still remember his voice when he
would say, "All right Tammy and you other boys, lets get
back to work a hoeing this corn!" I think all of the young
boys liked old man Johnny Horton. He talked a little slow
but wasn't too hard on us while we were working in the
fields. One day several of us decided to race to the other
end of our row. We thought that if we got to the other end
faster, that we would get a longer rest break. We could see
ourselves lying in the grass under the big cherry tree
sipping on cool water. We put our hoes to work digging at
the hard, dry red clay. We dug the grass and pulled the
suckers out of the cornrows at the same time. We were
bent over with our backs to the sun and never stood up
until we reached the other end of the row. We all stayed
pretty close to one another until we finally came to the end
of our row. When we got there I stood up and became dizzy
and had to immediately sit down. Everything was

spinning, and I was getting a terrible headache. I told one of the other boys that I didn't feel right and he called Mr. Johnny over to look at me. They put a little water on my head, as I was hot as a firecracker. Mr. Johnny told the boys to carry me to the infirmary. I had overheated myself in our race to our resting spot. Here I was again going to the infirmary and having to stay in bed. I wasn't confined too long, about a day or so, before I was able and raring to get back outside. I didn't like being inside of a building, especially in the summertime. However, sometimes when the pretty older girls came in to bring our dinner or something to drink, we considered it well worth a day or two of having to stay in bed in order to get all of their attention.

We had started getting a little pay, called an "honorarium," for the work we were doing on the farm. Each child would get graded on the basis of how well he or she did his or her work. If you goofed off, then you would get less money at the end of each month. We started off getting twenty-five cents a month. We would get twenty-five cents and the orphanage would put twenty-five cents in savings so we would have a little money when we graduated from high school. By the time we were seniors we would get four dollars and twenty-five cents a month. The money was ok because we realized that the home was feeding us and putting us through school. You really had to watch your spending if you wanted your money to last until the end of the month. If we wanted a piece of clothing that was not issued from the fitting room, we had to save our allowance from one month to the next or either try to find a Saturday afternoon job at someone's house. The fitting room was the room where you would trade in your clothes when you outgrew them and get a "hand-me-down" piece of clothing or a new piece of clothing if there were any available.

One job that I really didn't like was picking okra. I loved fried okra but didn't like it boiled. The plants were taller than I and when the leaves rubbed against my body the itch became unbearable in the hot sun. Most all of the time that we worked at the truck farm, we just wore a pair of bib overalls and no shoes. Our feet became so tough that walking on gravel or pavement in the hot summer sun never bothered us. When there was okra to be picked, one thing was certain, we wore our shirts.

There was a field where we grew potatoes. We called this field the "rose bowl." It was shaped like a half rose. Mr. Boose, the truck farm manager, or Mr. Hege, his assistant, would dig the Irish potatoes with a turn plow on the back of a tractor. We would pick up the potatoes out of the dirt and put them into potato crates or bushel baskets.

Picking up potatoes

Mr. Johnny Horton would watch us to be sure we got all of the potatoes out of the dirt. We used a potato digger that was shaped like a hoe but had prongs instead of a blade. A lot of times we would just rake the potatoes from the dirt with our hands while we were on our knees in the soft dirt. When we filled the crates we would load two crates onto our wooden wheelbarrow and push the wheelbarrow, about the distance of four football fields, down the gravel road to the potato shed. The wheelbarrows had steel wheels on them so every time you would hit a bump, it felt like your teeth would jar loose.

The roads were made of broken up sandstone from a sandstone pit nearby. Earlier orphans named it the "gravel pit." The older boys would dig the gravel with picks and shovel the gravel onto a wagon or truck to be spread wherever there was a low spot in the road. This kept the roads drivable all year long. I lucked out when I became old enough to do this kind of work and only had to work in the sandstone pits a few times. As the orphanage began paving more of its roads, the less gravel had to be dug. When we rolled the wheelbarrows down the gravel road, we would always try to stay where the truck tires had packed the gravel down smoothly. When we reached the packing shed, we would unload the two full baskets, pick up two empties and push the wheelbarrow back up the road to the field. In later years we loaded the potato crates onto the farm truck to carry back to the shed.

One tradition at the orphanage, handed down from the older boys to the younger boys, was the art of making slingshots. Year after year the older boys would make a new slingshot. We would watch the older boys, as they would craft their own special slingshot. There was very little difference between one boy's and another boy's slingshot. When hunting season came, never later than Thanksgiving Day, all of the boys were ready. Boys like "Buck" Hall, "Tuffy" Brown, "Red" Church, Robert Stewart, Larry McCarn, Robert and Ronnie Tuttle, Sam Murdock, Clarence "Kissel" Russell, Kenneth Sykes, Dale Speight, Wallace Stafford and many others were always crafting and using their slingshots to hunt squirrels. They would take the fork from a dogwood tree that was the right size to fit their hand. They would then tie the two outside limbs to the center limb with a piece of wire forming a perfect (U) shape. Then they would bake the wood over a fire to dry the wood into the shape they wanted. After untying the wire from the fork, the fork would remain in the "U" shape. Next they would carve the middle limb out and the forks would be shaved of its bark. Red rubber was popular back then because some inner tubes from car tires were made of synthetic red rubber. The real rubber was needed during WW II so the rubber companies developed the red synthetic rubber. The natural black rubber did not stretch nearly as good as the red synthetic rubber. In later years we could buy gum rubber at the Bocock Stroud Co. sports store in town. With two strips of red rubber and a piece of shoe tongue our slingshots were ready for action.

A lot of the boys got into trouble with slingshots but you know that I would NEVER do anything mischievous like that. It was "those other boys" that did it. One day a group of us boys were walking to the fields with our hoes on our shoulders. There was this gigantic hornet's nest up in a tree along the path leading to where we were going to work. A lot of times I would carry my slingshot to work with me in my bib overalls. As we were walking along, a few of us decided to hang back and let the others get ahead of us. As we started to cross the creek, I jumped in and picked up a handful of pebbles. We were going to take a few shots at a hornet nest located up in a tree along the path to the field where all of the boys were headed. So I took the first shot since it was my slingshot. I was very accurate with a slingshot. As I pulled back the pocket with the pebble and released it, I could see that creek pebble sailing through the air straight to its intended target. I heard the sound of the pebble smashing into the hornet nest. Thud! Then immediately I heard screaming from all of the boys as the hornets came out for revenge. It seemed as soon as that pebble hit the nest, those hornets were down my back. This was one of the unusual days because I was wearing a shirt. Would you believe that those hornets were able to go down the back of my shirt? I was running faster and yelling as much as the other boys. The hornets not only went down the back of my shirt and stung me, but two more stung the side of my head. Many of the other boys were stung as well. Mr. Johnny Horton had a time getting all of those boys back to that field to start working. He kicked my hind parts good fashion, and I got roughed up by a lot of the other boys for quite a while after that stupid trick. I got the black eye that I was asking for. I paid a terrible price for what I had done. Mr. Johnny Horton took my slingshot and broke it into pieces, but that wasn't the first one that I had owned nor would it be the last one for me or for most of the boys. I was an expert at making a slingshot, and I would own many more before I left the orphanage. We were very lucky that someone was not severely injured from the projectiles of our slingshots. These weapons were plenty strong enough to kill a man, or at least to put an eye out.

One day I was chasing a big squirrel and the squirrel ran to a dogwood tree and crawled into a hole. I wanted to get that squirrel, and I thought of the many possible ways of catching it. I didn't have a glove with me so I couldn't trick the squirrel and make it bite my glove and then snatch it out of the hole. First I tried a twig to see if the squirrel would bite it. The squirrel was just becoming angrier, and I could hear it fussing each time that I tried to get it out of the hole. I finally became impatient and looked down into the hole. Ah! I could see the squirrel's tail, and I came up with a real stupid plan. I figured I could grab that squirrel by the tail and jerk it out of the hole before it could bite me. I reached my hand into the hole real fast and grabbed that squirrel's tail and before I could turn loose, the squirrel's teeth went right through my fingernails. I snatched my hand from the hole and out came the squirrel. The squirrel came out so fast that it jumped right out onto my chest, knocking me to the ground. The squirrel and I hit the ground at the same time, and I thought that squirrel was going to eat me up. All that the squirrel wanted was to be free from some orphan boy trying to make its life miserable. The squirrel took off running to another larger tree, and I began to worry about my bitten fingers. They hurt pretty badly. Sometime later I would be diagnosed with Cat Scratch Fever although in my view it should have been called "Squirrel Bite Fever" because the squirrel's bite is where the fever came from. I learned my lesson about getting a squirrel out of a hole. Always use a glove and extend the glove fingers several inches from the end of your fingers so you can trick the squirrel into biting the glove, all the while thinking it had a good bite on your fingers. Most of the time that trick will work, but if you are not an orphan boy with a lot of trial and error experiences, then I would recommend you find an orphan boy to teach you how it's done before you suffer from much unnecessary pain. Wild animals have a nasty disposition when they are cornered. I guess the good Lord looked after us orphan boys as we went through a lot of pain, but with all of the pain, we survived despite our very aggressive life learning experiences!

I remember one year that I had to have some surgery done on my arm at the Baptist Hospital. While I was on the table with the doctors standing over me, I started crying a little and the doctors thought that I needed more numbing medicine. So they told the nurse to add a little more medicine. She added the medicine, and I continued to tear a little. The doctors thought that they were cutting too deep and they showed great concern about what was going on. Finally the doctor asked me if it hurt; and I said, "No." Then he asks me, "What's the matter? Are you afraid of the operation?" I said, "No." Then he asked what he could do for me. So I told him, "Make me well before tomorrow because tomorrow is hunting day, and I won't be able to go hunting if my arm is not well." That's what I was crying about. All of the doctors nearly fell to the floor chuckling! The doctor said that he would wrap my arm up real tight and maybe I would feel like going hunting tomorrow. I felt much better after he had told me that he would wrap my arm real tight so that I could go hunting. The next day was Thanksgiving, our big hunting day, and out with the other boys I went with my sling shot in my hand. I had great difficulty using my arm as the doctor had stitched the wound and wrapped it very tight, and I had to wear a sling to support it. My arm ached all day; and I had headaches, but that did not stop me from going hunting. I followed the other boys all day, as I wasn't going to miss out on the big Thanksgiving hunt, our main day of the year for hunting. My hunting skills were greatly diminished, and I wasn't much use to my hunting party, but the excitement of getting to go hunting on Thanksgiving Day was enough for me to endure the pain from the surgery. I would have to go back to have the stitches pulled out in about a week. I knew that I had strained my arm in my attempt to hunt with all of my friends but it was well worth it, so I thought! When I went back for a check up, my stitches had been pulled loose but my arm was already healing. I wouldn't tell the doctor that I was a little reckless with the care of my arm. I did tell

111

him that I went hunting on Thanksgiving Day, the day after my surgery, but I think he knew that was my intention in the first place.

Eddie with boys chasing rabbits

One time, I saw Red Church, Robert Tuttle and Wallace Stafford make a slingshot out of a whole tree. They took two big long strips of red rubber from an inner tube and fastened them to the forks of a small tree behind the wood-chopping shed. Then they tied a section of leather from a football to the pieces of rubber. It took two of them to pull that slingshot back to fire but they could shoot half bricks at least seventy-five yards. Boy, what a weapon! If one of us were ever hit with that slingshot projectile, we would be dead for sure. They did hit a squirrel once with a big rock. That squirrel was still stuck in that oak tree's bark several years after that with the tail still blowing in the wind gusts.

As we grew older, our territory for playing became

greater. We had two large pastures, one on one side of the home property and one on the other side of the property, to play in with lots of woodlands. One day we got into a friendly battle with some of the colored boys who lived in a colored community near our pasture. We had our slingshots to do battle with. We also would pull up some tall dried weeds that made good spears. We had bow and arrows that we made from tree limbs and shoestrings. On this particular day, the colored boys brought BB guns to play war with us. We got to know some of the local colored boys who lived next to the orphanage. There seemed to be one that was the main leader. His name was Alvin and he was a little older than we were. Alvin and his friends would come over to our woods from time to time and play "cowboys and colored boys." We got to know some of the colored boys well as we played often in the woods.

On this particular occasion at the start of our battle, we found out real quickly who had the firepower superiority. We engaged in a fierce battle for a few minutes, but soon their BB guns won out and we had to take cover where we could find it. We hid behind trees or logs on the ground and we still would try to get off a shot once in a while. Every time that we tried to look over our log or tried to look out from behind a tree, we would get peppered in the face with those BBs from the BB guns. We soon came up with a plan. If we could draw fire from them and force them have to reload, we could charge their positions at that time, the moment they were out of ammo. We peeked out from behind our positions and every time we would get shot in the head with a BB. Our faces looked as though we had run into a bees hive, but our plan finally worked. We charged with our slingshots and spears. You could hear the creek pebbles and marbles from our slingshots bouncing off their heads as they ran for all they were worth. We were throwing the spears at them and overwhelmed them. The battle didn't last long after that charge as their hands were in the air in surrender. We always played fair and when it was their turn to surrender, we honored the surrender and stop firing at them. It was a good thing that our home mothers didn't know of our battles or we would surely be in for a whopping on our buttocks. I guess our home mothers thought it was a normal thing to see her boys with scratched up faces and black eyes from all of the rough playing we did in the woods and pastures.

On another day, we were in the other pasture behind the gravel pit where the creeks come to a fork. We had borrowed a big rope from the dairy barn and tied the rope high up in a tall oak tree. The tree was on a high bank and one of the limbs that hung over the creeks below was the place we tied the long rope. We were having the time of our lives swinging over the gully with the creeks below. We would take turns swinging on that rope. It had to be thirty or forty feet down to the ground when we were out over the creeks, or so it seemed to us. Suddenly old Alvin sneaked up behind us and took a shot at one of the boys while he was way out in the air, hanging from that rope. The BB hit the boy and stung him pretty good, but he managed to hang on to the rope. A big argument ensued and Alvin swore that he was not shooting at the boy on the rope. After the argument cooled off, old Alvin wanted to join in on the fun. It was hard to keep a grin off of our faces, and we all said Alvin could join in on our fun. It must have been orphan intuition as everyone thought of the same thing at the same time. Alvin laid his BB gun against a tree and we let him have the rope. As he began his run to swing out over the creeks below, everyone rushed for his BB gun. The first one there grabbed the gun, cocked it and aimed it at Alvin swinging out over that creek. As the boy fired the BB gun at Alvin, you could hear him scream. Only this time Alvin let go of the rope and was headed down into the creek below. He was yelling all the way down until he hit the bank on the other side of the creek. Every one of the boys could not stand up from laughing so hard. When old Alvin moaned, they laughed even harder. Some of them were saying, "That will teach you to shoot one of us orphans!" Old Alvin wasn't hurt bad and was able to get up, but I think he learned a lesson that day. You can only get by with so much when you mess with an orphan. We all got back to our normal arrangement of getting along. We knew Alvin came from a poor family, and at times we picked him some vegetables out of our farm fields for him to take home. We were not allowed to do that but at the time it just seemed the right thing to do. His mom always spoke kindly to us when we walked by Alvin's house on the way to the colored man's store to get a drink. She had that real friendly southern charm about her with a great big smile. We never had any real fights with the colored boys, and we never really meant to hurt anyone seriously, I think!

Before long, we knew every inch of the orphanage, and we had a lot of fun playing in all the woodlands and fields. We made bow and arrows to hunt with and play target shooting. We made camps in the woods from old limbs and burlap fertilizer sacks. I guess you could say that the camps were our clubhouses. We would climb a tree seventy five to a hundred feet in the air just to back up a dare. One tradition was to climb trees and get baby squirrels to raise as pets, and then turn them loose when they were big enough to start biting us. We would climb up the tree to where a nest would be located. Then we would put on a glove and let the fingers stick out as far as we could without the glove falling off. We would stick our hand into the nest and if the big squirrels were in there then they were sure to bite down on the fingers of that glove. As soon as they would bite down on the glove, we would pull them out real fast and they would fall to a lower limb and not be there to jump in your face. We did the same trick if the squirrels had a hole in the tree for a nest.

Baby squirrels were our companions.

Many times boys would get into a fight over some disagreement. Sometimes the fight would get pretty intense with several black eyes and blooded noses the norm. The other boys would just gather around in a circle and see who would fare the best during the fight. They would just cheer on the one that they wanted to win. Usually an adult would hear the commotion and break up the fight. Once in a while there would be a twin or a brother that would jump into the fight to help the other. That's usually when someone else would jump in to make the fight fair. Fair fighting was always considered as one on one, even though sometimes the size of a big boy seemed awfully unfair. After the fight was broken up, usually the boys were back to playing with each other by the next day. Fighting was not a fun thing to deal with. There was always a feeling of no one winning. If I did feel like I had won then I always felt bad about any harm I had done to the other boy. Mostly I was always on the losing end with a black eye and tattered feelings!

Those were the days when we would see all of the pretty girls a little more often. We would see them at school, at ballgames and at Sunday school. The orphanage had more pretty girls than anywhere else in the whole wide world. I started getting the feeling that I might sort of like some of them. But to begin with I didn't know HOW to like a girl. I had tried that "liking thing" before and ended up with a broken arm. I just had to find out how to do this "liking thing" without getting myself killed. I liked a lot of them and didn't want to just pick one. I soon found out that a lot of the liking might not be all my choice. Things got real confusing for a year or two. I liked a lot of the girls but one day one of them almost beat me up. That really made things more confusing. Later in life I saw her and she explained to me that she really liked me, and that is why she tried to beat me up. I guess she wanted to get my attention! She was a pretty girl but I think we never were boyfriend/girlfriend. Maybe for a day or so! I decided to be nice to her so she might not try that "liking thing" again. A lot of the girls were bigger than the boys at that age. I can remember getting a lot of hard looks from the older boys when I would be nice to one of their girlfriends. One day one of the boys gave me a black eye when the boy thought that I was being too nice to the girl he had claimed for his girl friend. Now that was really embarrassing for a girl to see you get beat up by another boy.

Irene
We all liked her.

117

Anyhow, things started making a little more sense as time went on. I had my special tree in the woods that I would climb and carve my sweetheart's initials and my initials with a plus sign between them. I had to climb that tree more than once because it seemed that when I picked a sweetheart there was always a problem. After a while she always found another boy that was taller, more handsome, flirted better, had more candy or something, so there I would go again, back up that tree, to carve my next sweetheart's initials.

My Friend Tree

First, I had to say, "Hey" all over again and see if she would say, "Hey" back to me and smile. After a few of those "Heys" then I could tell that she was my special friend. It really all depended on how she would say her "Hey!"

Along about this time Coach Clary ask me to help "Red" Church as assistant water boy for the varsity boys' football team. I think "Red" had something to do with getting me the job. At that time there was one other water boy who was about five years older than I. I was much younger than any water boy who ever had that job. Being water boy meant that I would be working in the gym. My job would be to help clean up the old gymnasium. I would clean out the ashes in the old potbelly stove and replenish the stove with wood and coal. That was the only heat that the older boys had in their dressing room. I also would clean up their dirty laundry and clean and put polish their shoes. I would also put oil on a real wide dust mop and then push the big dust mop across the gym floor to get up all of the dust. I remember that Loy Witherspoon and David Poole, older graduates from the orphanage, once lived in the girls' dressing room during the summer while they were attending college. It didn't take much for orphans to be satisfied in those years as long as they had a place out of the weather. While they were trying to finish their college careers, they were grateful to have the dressing room in which to live.

I didn't do a lot of carrying water to the boys on the football field after being run over a few times when I would get in their way. I was a small boy and too slow getting the water bucket and dipper onto and off of the field so "Red" had to do that job. One game I ran onto the field with "Red" to give the boys some water. Several of the big boys ran right over me when they turned around real fast. That was embarrassing since I spilled the bucket of water and had to find a spigot to refill my bucket. When I came back with a fresh bucket of water, Coach Clary put me on the bench so that I wouldn't get hurt. Now that was something! I was the only water boy in history who was benched by the football coach. In addition, I didn't get to see much of the game because the big boys would stand up in front of me so they could cheer on their teammates. At least I got to be with my heroes. At that age I was not allowed to go to the out of town games with the older boys because they would come home well after my bedtime. It didn't hurt to be the big boy's water boy because they sort of looked after me when a bigger boy would pick on me.

"Red" taught me how to run the gym, but it wasn't long before we had a brand new gym. Only this gym had a skating rink around the outside of the basketball court. The old gym had the basketball goals mounted directly to the wall on each end of the building. Thick pads were hung on the wall under the baskets to help prevent the players from being hurt as they ran to the basket. The new gym had basket goals hanging out far enough from the wall so no one would be hurt. It had nice dressing rooms for girls and boys and also a scoring box built high above the gym floor. I was taught how to repair skates, and I played the music when the kids skated. I would check out the skates to the different cottage kids as their time came to skate. I loved to skate and bought my own shoe skates with my savings. I still helped "Red" and Coach Clary with the upkeep of the sports equipment and with the lining of the ball fields. I had to pick up all of the stinky jocks and jerseys and scrub the showers and locker rooms. But that was all right with me because it sure beat forking cow manure and living with that manure smell on my clothes every day. It was quite a while before I became the number one water boy and got to carry the keys to the gymnasium. All of those shiny keys made you important. "Red" always carried his keys clipped to his belt loop and he looked mighty important. When you were in charge of the keys you had a lot of big boy friends. When they wanted something from the equipment room, they had to come to "the boy with the keys."

Coach Edwards worked part time as a football official and when he was assigned to officiate a college bowl game or a regular college game, he would bring his football shoes to me for my special cleanup and polishing. He would always give me some change for the special job. I felt proud just to get a chance to clean and polish Coach Edwards' shoes. He was one of my big time heroes.

Coach Gibson, our other coach and teacher, started a Boy Scout unit for us. He and one of the other workers, Eddie Newsome, were our scout leaders. They both were raised at the home. Coach Gibson also taught older kids in the eighth grade and coached junior varsity football, baseball and basketball. Mr. Eddie Newsome helped manage the dairy farm operations. Our dairy farm produced a lot of milk and we also raised some beef cows. Mr. Eddie had to be seven feet tall or very near that height. We used the old gymnasium and our old second grade

classroom in the basement of the Brown building for a
scout hut. Coach Gibson and Eddie Newsome taught us a
lot about scouting and how to build things. We had a real
table saw, a jig saw, drill press and every kind of tool we
needed.

All of these fancy tools were a bit dangerous so we
spent a lot of time learning how to use them correctly and
safely. Once in a while though someone would slip and
have an accident. One day, Jerry Graham and I and a few
other boys, were building birdhouses. We were cutting the
pieces of wood on the table saw when the wood slipped and
the end of Jerry's finger flew off. I turned off the saw and
wrapped a rag around his hand and walked him to the
infirmary to let Miss Smith take care of him. He turned
white as a sheet, then green and almost passed out. I was
pretty scared myself, but that feeling passed away after we
got him to the nurse. Miss Smith carried him to the
Baptist Hospital for treatment. We went right back to
doing things in the scout hut. We built birdhouses, bird
feeders and a lot of the equipment that we needed for
camping. We made fishing reels from old used thread
spools and tinker toys and fishing poles from bamboo. The
Hanes family lived across Reynolda Road and they had a
bamboo thicket on their property. We figured they
wouldn't mind if we borrowed a few stalks of bamboo for a
good cause. We would follow the creek, through the large
culverts that passed under Robinhood and Buena Vista
roads to get to the bamboo thicket. We would use small
screw eyelets and run the fishing string through them to
make a good fishing pole. Sometimes we didn't have real
hooks so we would bend straight pens. Sometimes it
worked but most of the time the fish would jump off the
pins. We made our own backpack frames from wood and
our backpacks and breechcloths from canvas. The only
thing we could afford in the way of a scout uniform, at first,
was a neckerchief with our scout troop colors.

Fred/Winfred/Ward/Gilmer/Bill/Graham
David/Bob/Talmadge
Boy Scouts fishing
(Old Mack Bus in rear)

This would identify our troop when we had outings with troops from all over the area. We really didn't need the neckerchiefs, as none of us could afford a scout uniform. We certainly stood out with the type of clothes we wore when we got together with other scout troops in town and around our part of the state. It didn't matter about the uniforms; we were proud of who we were and proud just to be real Boy Scouts. We couldn't see that we were any different from all of the other scouts unless we were looking in a mirror. It wasn't long though that Coach Gibson managed to get us scout uniforms.

Coach Gibson with his scout troop

Boys playing snatch the bacon

New Uniforms
(Great cooks)

Boy, were we proud! I think it really made a big impact on a lot of the kids in maturing and learning a little more about life besides school and work. Each one of the boys carved their own neckerchief holder. A lot of them were Indian heads and some were braided leather. I remember our troop number was Eighty-Three.

Coach Gibson would take us for weekend camping trips and some of the time Mrs. Gibson and their two small children, Linda and Stevie, would go with us when they could. We went fishing, hiking and did all kinds of fun things. I remember one outing when we were climbing a mountain with a sheer drop-off of many hundreds of feet. Coach Gibson told me that if I wanted to look down from that cliff that he would hold my feet. I was too afraid to look down or to even get near the edge of that drop off. It was a long way down, and I just wasn't going to look. He finally convinced me after some of the other boys looked down as he held their feet. I got down on my belly and slid out to the edge of that drop off as he held my feet. Wow! That was something to see. The tops of the trees seemed to be a mile down. I thought right then that he had in his mind that he wanted me to trust people and to overcome fear.

I wonder sometimes if Coach Gibson ever spent any time at home with HIS family. He taught school, coached sports after school and ran the Boy Scout troop on scout nights and on weekend outings. He was doing for us kids all of the time that I knew him at the orphanage. He was doing an awful lot of jobs, probably the work of two good men.

Coach Gibson with Stevie and Linda

He left after graduating in 1938 to go to college. Later he became a fighter pilot in the Navy during World War II. After the war, in the late forties, he returned to the Children's Home, to a place that he loved, and helped children as he had been helped as a child. Twenty-five years after Coach Gibson and his brave squadron of navy fighters helped save our country from certain death, I found myself in the same skies doing my military duty.

Fred, Proud to serve

I saw first hand, the evidence left from the deadly battles that he and his fellow servicemen and women had fought to preserve our freedom during WW II. The only thing missing from the battle sites was the blood and bodies of our brave service men. I saw the many airplanes that were shot from the sky, ships that had been blown to bits, landing craft and tanks that were blown up by the Japanese and never made it to shore.

Iwo Jima; Invasion vehicles cover the bay.

War machinery was still visible and strewn all around many islands in the Pacific. I swam out to the planes and landing craft and put my fingers and hands through the mortar and bullet holes and tried to imagine what the servicemen felt before they died in such fierce fighting. On Midway, Marcus, Iwo Jima, Guam, Saipan, and Yap Island and all the way to Southeast Asia I saw just how those brave men died. I experienced the miserable weather in which the men fought and died. From Attu Island in the Alaskan chain, through Dutch Harbor, Adak and the many islands in between, it was literally a survival situation just being there. I lost friends in several air disasters while they were trying to carry out their missions in this very dangerous environment. I know that Coach Gibson lost friends in many of these places, and I realized why he wanted us to be brave and patriotic to carry on our country's necessary duties with pride, patriotism and bravery. I thought of this great man often during my military career, and I still think of him today. He dedicated his entire adult life so that many of us young boys would have a better chance at life and at survival if we had to face the same fate that he and his crews faced.

Many Children's Home boys and girls have served our great nation during its many wars. I have often wondered if the good Lord looked after orphans whenever they were in harms way. I often think of my orphan friend, James Hope, who was nearly burned to death in combat in Viet Nam. James overcame his burns and survived the war. There are hundreds of Children's Home boys and girls that have served with honor and they all seem to be survivors. Many have been injured in combat and a few have died. They have served in every branch of service as marines, airman, sailors, nurses, USO volunteers and soldiers. My orphan brother Bobby served in the Marine Corps during the Viet Nam war and died in a V. A. Hospital, never overcoming the impact the war left on him. Recently I heard from a friend that one of the older boys that I knew at the orphanage had passed away. He was a real hero of mine while he lived at the Home. His name was Roger Dale Holder. He had served in the marines during the Korean

War and was honored with the Purple Heart for the wounds he had received during that campaign. Another was Junior Sprinkle, after being wounded, the only soldier to survive from his platoon when the enemy overran their position in Korea. If there was a need to serve our country, you can bet orphans were there serving proudly to defend our freedoms.

At times during my military career, I found myself a little frightened or uncertain by what I had to face. Always on those occasions there seemed to be an ever present memory of my life at The Children's Home, and still in my mind, I would hear, "Make Me Proud Of You!" "I'm Here With You!" I often thought and asked myself, "If today is my day to die, will my Children's Home family know and care?" I can't ever remember not volunteering for any mission during my entire military career. When it came to pride, the Children's Home, where I grew up and called my Home, put a lot of it into me. When times got tough or a little frightening for me, I always felt someone standing beside me helping me to stand tall. I remember being called out on rescue missions over the ocean in the middle of the night. Many times we would be in the middle of a severe storm. At times the salt spray from the high waves would cover our windshield as we looked for any signal from a troubled mariner or downed pilot caught up in the storm. One miscalculation from any one of our flight crew and we would become the victims of the storm as well. Unfortunately many of our crews never made it home, giving their lives trying to save others. Sometimes one of our engines would fail on our plane, and the storm would make flying with an engine out a little more difficult and tense. On occasion the lighting would strike our plane and knock out the radar and part of the flight instruments. Without the radar we could not see the bad storms we were flying into. Oftentimes we would fly into storm cells that would tax the structural strength of the plane itself. As flight engineer I could hardly monitor the instrument panels; and the pilot and copilot were doing their best to keep the plane level. The plane would be bouncing around so hard that we thought the wings were going to break off at any second, and our crew in the back were all strapped in their seats to avoid the evident danger of injury. Once we were descending through bad weather in the North Atlantic without radar. We broke out of the weather at a few hundred feet above the water and everything turned white. Just as we broke out of the clouds we were heading directly into an iceberg that reached into the clouds. We took immediate action back up into the clouds as everyone shouted "Iceberg." It was the largest iceberg that I had ever seen and to this day I don't know how we missed it! Each time that I found myself in those kinds of severe hazards, one man in particular seemed to always be present with me-"Coach Gibson". Sometimes I sensed his chuckle as he would say, "Atta boy Fred, it ain't nothing, you can do it." I had this feeling that many more people were around me and that they were there looking after me. At any rate I sure felt braver and prouder that I could be doing my job with a whole team of good orphan people there looking after me.

Over the years at the orphanage I had a lot of heroes. Many of the older boys were good to me and would take the time to speak a kind word to me from time to time. The older boys would kid us and play tricks on us, but it felt to us that they cared and really wanted to be a friend to us. I mean, after all, they were the only older brothers that I had ever known. The very way that they conducted their lives was a big influence on the way I wanted to be. I found it difficult to be like some of the real good older boys at times. I just had to try every thing that I thought boys should try to do. Maybe they were mischievous as well. I just didn't know it. Their bravery on the football field and the determination to succeed helped make me a braver person. Even the boys my age and younger, that I played sports with, gave me inspiration to succeed in every mission. As a team or with a group of boys, we could handle any hard work task or win any challenge. My home mothers and teachers had a lot of influence on me, but the older girls were also an important part of my life. I say this because many older girls helped raise me for a good portion of my life at the orphanage. These almost grown up girls bathed me, cleaned up after me, dressed me and taught me to dress myself, taught me to tie my shoes, fed me and taught me manners while learning to feed myself. They took care of me when I was sick, tucked me in at night and taught me my first prayers. Now I would say that is pretty impressive in my thoughts that these almost grown up girls are also my heroes.

Many times while I lived at the Home, I wondered why the girls never had a chance to have a Girl Scout group. The girls seemed to really be guarded at the Children's Home. They were not allowed as many freedoms as the boys had. At the time I didn't understand that some girls might get into trouble if not supervised somewhat, but maybe if they would have had the chance to experience a scout program like we did, there might have been a different mindset with the girls. There were good girls there at the Home, but it just seemed that they were so confined. I believe that living like that everyday made some of the girls take risks at any available opportunity just so that someone would love them or show them affection. Don't get me wrong, there was a strong moral and religious message presented to all of us at the Children's Home. There also may have been a strong desire for the girls to have personal attention from someone they considered special maybe because of the lack of their own family and/or the lack of love from some home mothers. Many of the home mothers were strong disciplinarians, but I believe some lacked the understanding of just how much love was missing in these girls' lives. I guess it was hard for some of the home mothers to show the necessary love to that many children living in one cottage. I'm sure that the girl's home mothers were good women but they didn't want to show one girl love and not another. A lot of the girls would go through their entire teenage life without as much as being asked for a date or even a dance at one of our few social events. That had to be difficult for some of the girls, especially if there were no one to confide in. That seemed to be the norm at some cottages. That's why I say that the Children's Home girls should have had the opportunity for special programs such as we had as boys. A special program like the scouts would have given the girls a little release from the feeling of lack of love and confinement. Thank God in most cases the girls were able to pull through those trying years. They were some of the prettiest and sweetest girls I've ever known.

What do you know? The girls finally did get to be part of a Girl Scout group. Miss Willa Whitson started a group for the girls and the girls loved it. She was the head dietician at the Central Dining Hall where most of the girls ate their meals. In her spare time, Miss Whitson would teach the girls about scouting and would take them on outings. Miss Whitson would later marry Mr. Eddie Newsome, leave the Home and move to Davie County.

At the end of our school year, it was time for another field day. On this particular field day I was sick and in bed at the infirmary. I could hear the loud cheering coming from the Alspaugh Field, our football field where we held our field days. It was named after Mr. John Alspaugh, a staunch supporter and contributor to the Home. On this special day, lanes were marked off for running different distances.

Mike/Tony/James provide muscle here.
Field Day Tug-O-War

There were sack races and relay races and the winners were awarded ribbons. We had a jumping pit for high jump and broad jump. All of this excitement was just too much for me lying in that bed in the infirmary. The most

131

excitement we ever got lying back in the back rooms, where
the boys usually stayed, was when one of the pretty older
girls would bring us juice or a pill to take. Even a small
airplane, from Reynold's airport, puttering across the sky
or a rooster crowing from Dad Shaver's chicken house next
door was some excitement. I made up my mind that I was
going to field day. I was very scared but I was determined
to go anyhow. I grabbed my clothes from the cabinet by
my bed and put them on. I slipped quietly down the hall
and down the stairs to the basement and out the back door
by the old dental office. I felt a little weak from being in
bed for several days, but that wasn't going to stop me on
this special day. Being caught by Miss Smith was ever
present on my mind as I walked slowly down the road to
the football field. I was trying to think of something to tell
my teacher as I walked along. By the time I got there I was
feeling pretty bad but I wanted to see all of the fun. I found
a spot in the shade and sat down and then I knew I had
really messed up because my teacher looked over and saw
me. She knew right away that I was not supposed to be
out there on that field. With some assistance from the
older kids, my teacher sent me back to the infirmary.
There I had to face the Home nurse, Miss Smith. Miss
Smith gave me a couple of pops on the buttocks and put
me back to bed. She was definitely not pleased with what I
had done, and she was going to make sure that I would
never do that stupid trick again. I got over that day but
when I looked in my cabinet the next day, there were no
clothes. All I had was a gown with the back end opened. I
surely wasn't going anywhere. She had locked them up in
some secure place so that I would not be tempted to take
another stroll. I spent several more days at the infirmary
and was very happy when Miss Smith said that it was time
for me to go back to my cottage. Being under special watch
from her was no fun. It seemed that when it came time for
her to give me a shot in the buttocks, the shot seemed to
sting a little more than usual, and I believe it was because
the needle may have gone quite a bit deeper into my
buttocks than was necessary. I definitely believe that she
had the upper hand in controlling my behavior. Miss
Smith was a very strict nurse, but I guess that is the way a

nurse would have to be who was responsible for four hundred or so children.

As I grew older, I realized just how many children were at the Children's Home. There were more than four hundred and that's a "bunch" of children. Miss Smith and a few of the older girls looked after nearly a hundred of us children at one time during a bad flu season one year. All of the rooms were full and not a space left in the hallways on both floors of the infirmary. Children with measles created another bad time for Miss Smith and the girls that worked for her. They had to care for so many at one time. Sometimes at morning sick hour, children lined up outside of the building all the way to the street some forty feet away. We would come with a wide variety of injuries or sicknesses and stood in line waiting to be called inside to see the nurse. Some of the children were very sick and standing outside in the cold. That seemed unbearable. The girls were in one line and the boys were in another and there was no talking while you were there. Discipline was mandatory anywhere around the infirmary. I remember one of the girls telling me that she had developed pneumonia while standing outside in the cold weather waiting for her turn to be called inside for care.

Over the years I would spend many more days under the care and watchful eye of our nurse, Miss Annie Smith. It seemed that I tried everything possible as a young boy and there were a lot more broken bones and stitches in store for me in my near future at the Home. In those years I really didn't know just how much care I did need from Miss Smith.

Chapter Five

Well, a few years had passed at the Tise II cottage, and I moved over to the other side of the building known as Tise I cottage. I would stay there for a couple of years. This cottage was getting old and actually had some serious electrical problems. One night the fire truck had to be called because of an overheated and smoke filled electrical panel. Our home mother, Miss Little, tried to make sure we thought it was no big deal so that we would not be afraid. I always had a plan that if we ever did get trapped up on the top floor, I would grab my mattress and throw it out the window onto some tall bushes, then jump out the window. It really would have been another orphan game to us boys as we were just plum full of daring and trickery.

Every year, during the summer, The Men's Bible Class from Centenary Methodist Church would provide enough watermelons for the entire family of orphans at the Children's Home. There were more watermelons than all of us children could possibly eat. I mean they were real good watermelons too!

"Pop" with children eating watermelon

"Pop" Woosley loved watermelon as much as any of the children. During several of the years, I ate and ate and ate watermelon until I couldn't possibly eat another bite. I didn't learn my lesson the first year, and I paid the price for over indulging more than one time. Those watermelons were so good, and the other boys would challenge me to see who could eat the most pieces. I really enjoyed the contest and would pay the ultimate price for my stupidity. About an hour after I finished my last piece of watermelon, I would get the worst bellyache you could possibly imagine. I would be sick for a while, but I would do the same stupid trick the next year. After we finished our watermelon feast, we would carry all of the watermelon rinds to the hog pen and let the pigs have a feast. The pigs really loved the watermelons as much as we children did.

Miss Sara Little was my home mother at the Tise I cottage. She was a very sweet and nice lady and did her best to keep us boys under her control and look after our welfare. She was a small lady with a soft-spoken voice and hair as white as snow. She let me play with my electric train under her supervision. She would let us listen to her records on the victrola. We kept that victrola wound up and we would listen to songs in the evenings and on rainy days. One song that I remember playing all of the time was "Alexander's Ragtime Band." I guess it was something about the music that kind of caught my interest. I liked that music along with the Big Band rhythms from the World War II years that were still popular in those days.

On Sundays after lunch, Miss Little would have Mr. Thompson, a Baptist Minister from town, come to visit with us boys. Mr. Thompson was a real good man. He would bring us all kinds of Christian crafts to work with. He would bring us bibles and teach us bible stories. He would challenge us on different parts of the bible and we would compete with each other in various games dealing with the bible. I never saw Mr. Thompson after I left that cottage, but I always wanted to tell his children or grand children, "Thank you for letting him have the time to spend with us boys." Mr. Thompson would stay until three o'clock, when visiting hours would start for the entire orphanage. The little kids had to nap until three o'clock and the big kids did homework or big kid things. I heard later in life that Mr. Thompson's son was working for McQwen Lumber Company in High Point. An orphan brother in Charlotte, Johnny Tuttle, ran into him. The son had to explain to Johnny who his father was. Small World! Anyhow, young Mr. Thompson, if you read this, "Thank you and your family for letting us have your dad for all of those Sunday afternoons." We will never forget him and the sacrifice of your family to let us share his precious time with us.

Anyone that wanted to visit a child at the Home would check in with Mrs. Bess Gary in the administration building. Mrs. Gary would call the home mother and let her know that the child had a visitor. Usually the visitor was a parent or some family member, but sometimes a church sponsor would come to visit. I had an aunt, Aunt Louella, who would come to visit me once in a while. She was my daddy's sister. She couldn't come very often because times were tough for her. She was trying to raise her family all by herself. She worked in a cotton mill at night to be able to provide the bare essentials for her family. I went for two weeks on summer vacations with her, in Gastonia, when I was a little older. She had three sons named Virlin, Steve and Lester.

Visiting was over by five and it was back to orphan life as we knew it. We would say our good-byes to our family or friends and usually it was time for us to have our Sunday evening supper. Every Sunday night we had nearly the same meal. We would usually eat sandwiches, usually peanut butter and jelly or banana, and this would give the lady in the kitchen a little breather before she would begin the next week in the kitchen all over again. It was nice to have real family come to see you, but I always looked forward to getting back with my orphan buddies when they would leave.

I never really knew any of my distant family until I was a little older, so my feelings of family was living with my brothers, sisters and adult care givers at The Children's Home. Some members of my family would write occasionally and send pictures of their family. Uncle Roy and Aunt Lizzy had five children. There was Edward, Charles and three beautiful girls named Blonde Dell, Thelma and Ora Mae. The girls were all pretty like my sister Charlena. Aunt Mae and Uncle Fred Bynum, Aunt Sally and Uncle Winslow King, Mrs. Ora Mae and Wiley McGlamery all would send pictures but since I never remembered seeing them, my only memory of them was through their letters and pictures. They were all very loving letters with support in the situation in which we were living. They all knew that my sister and I were in a good place to live and grow up. Uncle Garnett and Aunt Arizona Swanson were members of the Masonic Lodge. They helped support the Oxford Orphanage in the Eastern part of the state. I got to know Aunt Louella and her children Virlin, Steve and Lester, as they would come to visit me on Sunday afternoons.

I remember when our cottage got a television set. Boy, what a change in life! We could see Cowboys and Indians right inside that box in our own cottage. We saw the Howdy Doody show, the man with the bubble machine and people fancy dancing and singing. There were programs on TV that showed real bands playing music. I really liked that Big Band music and watched that program as often as I could. Miss Little also liked that kind of program. There was the Gillette Cavalcade of Sports that showed live boxing matches. We boys really liked that program. Everybody had his favorite cowboy hero. I was always amused at Gabby Hayes and all of his sidekicks. The Lone Ranger and Tonto, Gene Autry and Roy Rodgers were our favorites, unless we could go to a movie in town and see Lash Larue, Tex Ritter, Hopalong Cassidy, Randolph Scott, Davie Crockett, Daniel Boone, or Tarzan. We would watch the test pattern for quite some time before the regular programming began. Sometimes we waited an hour before the regular television programming started. We would wait to make sure we didn't miss anything that might be coming on. This was real television and even the test pattern was still magic to us. We stayed up until at least eight or eight-thirty at night. Then our home mother would rush us off to bed.

Tise 1 And 2
Sixty boys lived here.

We all had chores assigned to us at this cottage just as we had at the other cottages. Some of us would clean the outside stairs. Some would be assigned to clean outside or clean the basement or dormitory. Sometimes we would help Miss Little wash the windows on the top floor where we slept. She would have us sit in the windowsill while we washed the outside of the windows. She would hold us from falling out the window, by leaning against our legs. It seemed a little frightening as there was cement on the ground just below. We would wash the outside of the windows while she pointed to any spots that we had missed. She always kept a tight grip on us from inside so we would be safe. I guess that is one-way confidence is built in youngsters while they do chores like that. I did feel a little brave when the other boys were looking up at me from the ground. We all liked to show off our bravery.

We were getting to be big boys. Every time one boy grew an inch taller than another boy, there seemed to always be a challenge. With thirty boys to a cottage this seemed to be an ongoing event for years to come. There were a lot of black eyes in those days, but we all seemed to get over it. "Vick," one of my good friends, and I would play in the woods all of the time. He was tough as nails and would try anything. Often he would get hurt, but he would get right back up as if nothing had happened. We would play real hard together all of the time, but once in a while we would get into a fight. I remember one scuffle that we had that scared me a little more than the other times. He got the best of me and had me on the ground. "Vick" grabbed a hatchet and put it right on my forehead and acted as if he was going to rear back and crack my skull. I think he realized what he was doing and dropped the hatchet and walked off. He was a little tougher than I was, and it seemed that most of the time "Vick" got the best of me. We would get over any differences we might have had and go right back to playing again. I don't know what ever happened to "Vick." I believe he just didn't come back from summer vacation one year. "Tinker" was another friend that I lost. A lot of my friends would just disappear when summer vacation time came, then a "new boy or girl" would come to the orphanage in their place. I really didn't like losing my best friends like that because I never got to say good-bye. I guess I would have to train a "new boy" to make slingshots and bow and arrows and learn how to get around in the woods and pastures.

"New boys" would come and some things would change. Our girl friends, which we thought liked us, would

139

be very eager to check out the "new boys." The boys that had girl friends had to find another after their girlfriend became friends with a "new boy." Sometimes this would create a situation where a conflict would arise. On a number of occasions there would be a scuffle or a fight then things would go back to normal for a while until another "new boy" would arrive. Sometimes there would just be words spoken. Nevertheless, the transition seemed to be relatively harmless and forgotten in a short time. There was a certain loss when one of our friends would not come back from vacation. We would go on with our everyday activities but we wanted to know what happened to our friends. We would start over with the "new boys," teaching them all of the tricks that had been pulled on us over the years by the older boys. We would teach them how to catch the yellow nosed bumblebee to make their friendship, and they just had to know how to make a slingshot. We had to teach them everything that we had experienced, which they had missed out on, while we were growing up at the orphanage.

As we grew older, there were fewer and fewer confrontations. I was glad of that because I was always smaller, and being spirited as I was, I paid the price for being small many times. I really felt that all of the boys were and are my brother orphans. We played a lot of marbles while we lived at this cottage. The yard was sandy/clay just about all the way around the cottage. That made it good for playing marbles.

We had a handle bar or horizontal ladder set that we all would swing from. We would challenge each other to see how many bars we could skip, as we would swing from one end to the other. We were still the mischievous little orphan boys, just a little older.

Some days I would walk up to the wood shop where Mr. Binkley and one of the orphan boys worked. Mr. Binkley was in charge of all the building maintenance. He was a nice older man. He talked very low and slow and didn't have a whole lot to say. He was always making or repairing something. The orphan boy that helped him was named Ravanelle. Ravanelle could make just about anything. Mr. Binkley would teach him how to use the different wood tools. Ravanelle was always good to me and let me watch him make things. He would hand carve a mortise and tendon corner on a wooden box and make it go together real pretty. He would use very sharp chisels and chisel a real small piece of wood from the board each time that he would hit it with a leather mallet. It seemed to be real tedious work but he had good concentration as he mastered the job. Ravanelle was one of the older boys who was friendly to us younger boys and took the time to answer our bothersome questions. He would let me stay in the wood shop while he turned on the machinery. Most of the equipment was driven by one big motor turning a long shaft in the overhead. Large belts from pulleys on that shaft drove the equipment. That was something to see with everything moving at one time. He would be sure that we young boys didn't get near all of those drive belts. Ravanelle had an older brother named Bob who had the same kind of personality. Bob would graduate from the Home and go into medicine. Ravanelle would graduate and go into dentistry. Memories of both of those brother's and their sister's friendship has stayed with me all of these years. They just seemed like real family to me.

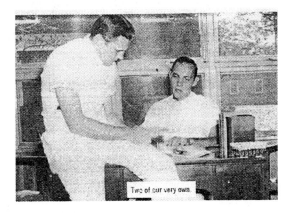

Two of our very own

Dr. Bob Stepp and Dr. George Holland
"My Heroes Turned Doctors"

When I was that age I would bring home just about

any kind of wildlife animal for a pet. We would catch bumblebees in our hand. Of course you had to know not to catch the ones with black noses, only the yellow nose bees wouldn't sting you. The black nose bees would sting. It was some time before we would trust the older boys to tell us the truth about the bees. We had been tricked so many times before. Eventually we would work up enough nerve to grab a yellow nose bumblebee. It was true; the yellow nose bee would not sting, but sometimes we would make a mistake and grab a black nose bee and would pay the price with a stung hand. We would tie a piece of thread to the bumblebee's leg and let it fly around. Sometimes we could only find June bugs and we would tie a string around their leg and watch them fly. We would catch jars full of lightning bugs and carry them to our dormitory for entertainment when we had to go to bed.

I always had a frog or a garden snake in my pocket. One day I brought home a nest of brown snakes and kept them in a bucket beside my bed. I would bring them bread and lots of bugs to eat. I had a piece of screen wire over the top of the bucket to keep the critters from crawling out. Black snakes would always try to bite you. I thought brown snakes were garden snakes and never had one of those bite me. I would always be careful and learned in time how to handle them. I had been bitten a few times by black snakes and some other kinds of snakes but the bites never really hurt much, and the snakes were not poisonous. Among this nest of brown snakes there was a mama snake and a whole lot of baby snakes. I didn't know what kind they were, only that they were brown with different colors on their backs. One day Miss Little was checking to see that all of our beds were made correctly and that the bedroom was clean. She found my bucket and took a look inside to see just what I had brought home. She was really frightened to find that I was keeping a family of snakes next to my bed. She immediately called for help and Coach Clary came to the rescue. Coach Clary carried the snakes in the bucket out of the cottage and disposed of them somewhere. I certainly wasn't going to ask Coach Clary where my pet snakes were. When I got home, I got my buttocks whipped good. I found out then that those snakes were copperheads. I didn't bring home any more brown snakes after learning just how lucky I was. Occasionally I would bring home black snakes and green snakes. However, I would still play with the wildlife in the woods and creeks. We would catch terrapins and keep them in a box. They were easy to feed but when the home mother found them she would turn them lose. Baby opossums were cute when they were very little, but they stunk and had a very bad disposition when they began to grow a little older. They would try to bite anything that came close to them and snarl out of their slobbering mouth as if they were trying to frighten you away. They really weren't our favorite pets of choice. We would only bring one home when we couldn't find another friend that day. The wildlife had a pretty tough life at times with some of us boys looking to have a friend to play with at any opportunity. Baby chipmunks, flying squirrels and fuzzy gray squirrels were our favorite pets. Baby rabbits were hard to keep. I will have to say that one particular older boy became my friend because he didn't know whether I had a snake in my pocket or not. Before I pulled one out of my pocket one day, he used to grab me by the head and give me a Chinese hair rub. After I scared him half to death, he kept his distance from me. He was afraid of snakes and blood. I knew he would never bother me again because I could make his life miserable. His name was "Tuffy" and he became a real good friend of mine.

We used to dam up the creeks with piles of rocks and swim in the water when it became deep enough. One day we were really having a ball running and jumping into the pond that we had built. We would run and dive in doing a belly flop to see how much of a splash we could make. Suddenly someone yelled, "SNAKE," and we thought that they were kidding with us. We turned around and there was a big fat water moccasin no more than a few feet away from us. I had never seen a big snake like that before in that creek. We jumped out of that water as fast as we could jump. The snake slithered up under the bank of the creek and disappeared. There was no way that we were going back in that water hole. We knocked the rocks out of the way to let the water out of our dam. There would be no more swimming in that creek for me. We would have to go upstream a ways and build another swimming hole. When we built this little dam we would let our baby ducklings swim in it. When we were allowed to go to town, we would buy a baby duck and bring it home. Taking care of our baby ducklings kept us busy playing for hours. The ducklings never seemed to last long because the opossums and stray dogs would get them.

There was a tree that we called a "Monkey Pod" tree next to the creek. It grew long pods that looked like long cigars. In the past, we had seen the older boys pull the pods from the tree after they had dried out. Then the boys would light them up and smoke them like a big cigar. You know that we just had to show off amongst ourselves and try everything the older boys did. So we gathered a couple of "Monkey Pod" cigars and found a box of matches and tried the same trick. I had never smoked before, but I tried everything the other boys were doing. They lit up one of the cigars, and I did the same. I puffed just as they did as I had seen older men puff cigars. I was really impressing all of my friends and coughing just like them. The smoke was getting in my eyes and making me cry. But they were doing the same thing so I thought that was what was supposed to happen. I puffed and puffed some more and began to get dizzy. I didn't want the other boys to think I was a sissy so I tried to keep up with them at every puff. It wasn't but a minute later that I found myself sitting on the ground with my head spinning. I thought to myself just how stupid I was for getting myself all dizzy like that. All of the other boys were laughing and having a good ole time. I was just dizzy and wanting my head to stop spinning. One of the other boys said that I needed to take my time when I would puff on that cigar. He didn't have to worry about that anymore because I was not going to smoke any more "Monkey Pod," EVER AGAIN. I hope!

I remember one day in the woods behind the infirmary, Ted Barnett, "Vick," another boy and myself were climbing trees. Ted decided to climb this real big poplar tree. He was about seventy-to-eighty feet up in the tree when he started out on a limb. We all knew that poplar limbs were very weak, but Ted was going out on that limb anyway to check out a squirrel's nest. We shouted, "Ted don't go out on that limb, it's going to break!" Ted said, "It's just a little bit further." It seemed that before he could get the words out of his mouth, he moved out a few feet more then we heard that limb crack. Poplar tree limbs make a sound like a loud pop when they break. Here came Ted falling towards the ground. I knew Ted would die or be hurt badly when he hit the ground. Someone was looking after Ted that day because he hit one limb that started him spinning and slowed him up a bit. Each time that Ted would hit a limb, the limb would flip him back in the other direction. Then as he got about ten feet from the ground another limb caught him across his nose, turned him upright, and he landed on his feet and fell over backwards. He was a little dizzy and bleeding pretty bad, but Ted's main concern, when he got his bearings, was how to explain what had happened to him when we got back to our cottage. He didn't want to get into trouble for climbing trees. One of the boys had died in the past from falling out of a tree. I believe Ted already had a broken nose before so one more broken nose wouldn't bother him much. We all went back to the cottage and helped Ted wash the blood from his shirt and his face. Both of his eyes turned black and his eyelids were swollen nearly shut. When Miss Little saw him he told her that he had tripped on the straw floor mat and fell against the door. I could sense that she was suspicious of what Ted was telling her, but I think she knew that Ted didn't want to get in trouble. We often had to change our stories a little bit as we were into mischief like growing boys should be, maybe! It just became natural for us to try things and to overcome the dangerous risks that came with it. Ted was tough as nails and would try anything.

At the Tise II and the Tise I cottages we ate our meals at the Central Dining Hall. We were the only boys that ate there with all of those beautiful girls. The Central Dining Hall was a building between the girl and boy's cottages and the place where all of the girls ate their meals. Mrs. Edith Fincannon, Mrs. Pauline Gibson and some of the older girls cooked the food and the older girls would help clean up. Mrs. Byrd ran the dining hall and boy was she strict. I got into trouble from talking more than one time in the dining hall. Every time we would not mind our manners or would do something she thought was not right, she would grab us by the cheek and twist our cheek between her fingers and thumb. If there was a more serious infraction she would send us to Coach Clary's house. We didn't want to go to Coach Clary's house but some of us still managed to get to visit with him anyway. It was always embarrassing because Coach Clary's daughters were about our age, and we didn't want them to hear what we had done to get into trouble. We definitely didn't want them to hear us cry if we were to get a spanking. I mean after all they were very pretty girls and we were supposed to be big strong almost big boys.

I remember one day when one of the young girls who worked at the dining hall was hurt while she was helping clean the stairs that went up to the second floor. She was a very pretty girl named Vivian Ann. She was reaching over the stair railing to dust the other side and slipped and went over the rail and landed on the floor below. I really was worried about her when I heard how badly she was hurt. It seemed that I always felt sadness when one of the orphan children would get injured or was sick.

On Sunday night from 7 to 9 the high school boys and girls were allowed to date. The boys could go to the girls' cottages and sit with them for two hours and socialize under close supervision of the home mother. Once in a while the older boys would give us a quarter if we would shoot out the street light in front of the big girls' cottage before their Sunday night date time. I guess they wanted to sneak in a long good night kiss without the home mother being able to see them quite so well. Most of us were very accurate with our slingshots and a quarter was a lot of money to an orphan boy.

I enjoyed getting to eat in the Central Dining Hall because on occasion I had a chance to see my sister. It felt good to see her because the girls and boys were kept separated except during sporting events, school, Sunday school or church. There was a large bell outside of the dining hall that one of the girls would ring to let everyone know when it was time to come for the prepared meal. I loved my sister very much and of course it didn't hurt that she was always eating with the rest of the pretty girls. She had a lot of friends that I got to know like Bobbie, Blanche, Ruby, Sara, Doris, Voncille, Maxine, Toni and many more. I couldn't wait for that bell to ring. I always tried to look nice when I went to eat there. I would wet my hair and comb my hair for ten minutes. Gosh, I've never seen so many pretty girls in one place. Most all of the girls' cotton dresses looked pretty much the same and nearly the same color. They all wore brown shoes most of the time. Occasionally they would wear brown and white shoes. Even with their plain dresses and brown shoes, they looked very pretty.

I could have sat on the steps and watched all those pretty girls all day long, but we always had to go back to our cottage when we finished our meal. Gosh God was sure good by having all those beautiful girls at the Home.

Bonnie

Bonnie was promoted to the fourth grade when I had to stay behind in the third. She was up there with the older group of children now. I guess that was the way it was supposed to be because she was much older and she didn't ever know I wanted her to be my special friend. She was six months older than I was so it worked out for the best.

All of us boys thought we had the girl of our dreams but many of us would be disappointed. You see a lot of the boys would pick a girl and claim that the girl liked them. Sometimes the girl really didn't like the boy that had chosen her to be his own. Oh boy, there was a lot for me to learn about this so-called girl friend thing. Every time that I thought I had it figured out, another girl told me that she was the one that liked me. The girl that I thought was my girl friend said that she liked someone else. We would sit at the dining room table and look across to the far end of the dining room and see if the girl that we thought would be our girl friend was looking back at us.

Central Dining Hall

We didn't want any of the other kids to see us looking, as we didn't want to be teased by the other boys. I must have had a dozen girl friends that I dreamed of speaking to me. If a pretty girl would say "Hey," I just knew that she was in love with me. Later, in school, I would write a plus sign in between our initials if none of the other boys were looking. Worse yet, I had to be careful or I would get a black eye for flirting with some other boy's girl friend. Saying "Hey" meant to me that I loved her or that she loved me or something like that, I suppose. This love thing was a strange world to me, but during those years, it was a period of time that I enjoyed and felt warm and gentle towards another person. I guess we had nothing else to give except love. I believe this was also a time when I began to stump my toe more often and stumble when my mind began to drift and not pay attention to where I was walking. It seemed a time when I began to do all sorts of stupid things. I guess the girls didn't know just how important I was in their lives or just how important they were in my life.

There was a large swing set beside the big dining hall and once in a while the girls would be swinging in the swings. We would stop by and try to be friends, or would you call it flirting with the girls? At this age we didn't know much about what we were doing. We would push the girls real high in their swings until they screamed for us to stop. It just seemed to feel good to get to push a pretty girl in her swing. I would push all day if my favorite girl would let me. Sometimes we boys would get into the swings and we would swing so high that it seemed that we would be ready to swing over the top. Swinging like that seemed to get the attention of some of the girls, but it also got the attention of the girl's home mother. When the home mother saw us being daring brave little boys, she would run us off and tell us to go home.

Sometimes we would pick cherries from the big cherry tree next to the large swing set. This was the same cherry tree that I was rushing through the cornfield to get a longer rest period after hoeing my row of corn and got overheated. In the summertime it was a lot of fun to climb that cherry tree. The tree provided us with a lot of shade while we were eating our freshly picked cherries. Ah! What an orphan life! Barefooted, bib overalls, a hand full of sweet cherries and a hundred beautiful girls just waiting to be called someone's sweetheart! I thought! I wished! Well, things would come in due time in my wonderful orphan world.

As we grew a little older we did more grown up things. When snow season came, we rode sleds on every steep hill at the orphanage. We would get into snowball fights with the girls and hope that there was some attraction with a certain one. In later years we ventured off of the orphanage grounds and rode the steep hills over at R. J Reynolds High School, which was across Reynolda Road from the Children's Home. R. J. Reynolds was the high school that all of the Children's Home children would attend after the eight grade. We would ride snow sleds at R.J.R. if we were lucky enough to borrow one. If we had no sled, that didn't stop us. We would ride coal shovels, old Coca-Cola signs, pieces of tin, old barrel boards from wooden barrels or anything that would slide in the snow. There was a fence that ran along the railroad track at the bottom of the hill. A lot of times we would be going so fast on our sleds that the fence was the only thing that would stop us before we would hit the railroad tracks. We were a daring bunch of boys with little fear of getting hurt.

Splitting firewood

On Saturday mornings we had to split firewood for the wood burning cooking stoves in all of the cottage kitchens.

In the warmer seasons, we would run up and down the roads rolling our barrel rings, guiding our barrel ring with a piece of baling wire, stick or a coat hanger.

Sometimes we would find an old tire and push it and roll it for hours up and down the road. All of our toys were worn out but we found anything that wasn't tied down and made a plaything out of it. Marbles and horseshoes were the games that the older boys liked to play. We began to learn the games, especially big boy marbles, as we hung around the older boys and watched them play the game. Some of us younger boys really thought we could challenge the older boys after we had watched them play the game for quite a while. The real serious marble and horseshoe games were played up by the old school house and in front of the Duke and John Neal cottages. These cottages were where the high school boys lived. Across the street, next to the old school, was a real sandy area that was perfect for playing the game of marbles. I watched Arlis Brigman, Bill and Donald Buchanan, Ravanelle Stepp, Eugene Wallace, "Red" Church, Robert and Larry McCarn, "Tuffy" Brown, Kenneth Sykes, Clarence "Kissel" Russell, Robert Stewart, Robert and Ronnie Tuttle, "Peanut" Purdue, Sam Murdock, Curtis Rothrock, Wyndell Sifford and many more older boys get into some serious marble games. We just couldn't wait to get to play marbles like those boys played.

The toughest of all was big ole "Buck" Hall. "Buck" was a big boy and seemed to be made of steel. He could take more marbles faster than any of the other older boys. "Buck" was so strong that his shooting marble would burst the other players' marbles when he used his steelie to hit their marbles. "Steelies" were ball bearings that we would find at the dump pile behind the old Packard car dealership on Reynolda Road. We had a lot of steelies, glass marbles and also clay marbles that were made during the war. The clay marbles were perhaps made to save on glass for the war effort.

Some of us young boys wanted to play with the big boys. "Buck" Hall was willing to take on all challengers and teach us a lesson. I didn't hesitate and jumped in for a game along with some of the other younger boys. I had a pocket full of marbles, and I knew that I had to take advantage of getting to play with "Buck" Hall. We had a big circle drawn in the sand and we all put in about ten

marbles apiece in the middle of the circle. The game
started as we took our turn shooting at the other marbles
in the middle of the ring to see how many we could knock
out of the circle. We would shoot until we missed or our
shooter bounced out of the ring. A couple of the boys took
there turn, flipping their shooter steelie across the ring,
and knocked out a few of the marbles. Then came "Buck"
Hall's turn. He was a very tough football player and
nobody messed with him. "Buck" took his shot and his
shooter remained in the ring. He knocked a few more
marbles out of the ring and finally it was my turn to shoot.
All of a sudden the marbles became fewer and fewer in the
ring with nobody knocking the marbles out. We were all
looking at each other, wondering what was happening to
the marbles. Then we looked at big "Buck" Hall. He
always had a joking grin on his face but we hadn't seen
anything out of the ordinary. It appeared that every time
one of us boys would shoot, ole "Buck" would walk across
the ring. He would walk right on top of the marbles. Then
we saw him and we all shouted at one time! "Uh huh, we
caught you!!!" We had caught ole "Buck" stepping on the
pile of marbles and squeezing them between his toes. He
would walk out of the ring then put them in his pocket. We
all yelled at "Buck," "You are cheating." "We saw you pick
up those marbles with your toes." All of the older boys
were laughing at us, and I knew there was nothing that we
could do about "Buck" stealing our marbles. I really
messed up. I went close enough for ole "Buck" to reach out
and grab me as I said, "Give me back my marbles." Boy,
was that the wrong thing to say. Ole "Buck" just grabbed
me around the head in a headlock and began giving me a
knuckle hair rub. He rubbed my head in one spot until I
thought a hole was burned through my skull. In those
days we called it a Chinese hair cut! All of the other young
boys were smart; they ran away as fast as they could so
that ole "Buck" couldn't catch them. "Buck" didn't really try
to hurt me, and later on he let me play some more marbles
with him. Only this time he won my marbles fairly or
busted them to pieces with his strong shot of his "Steelie."
After that I had a real big person friend for life. It really
didn't hurt to have a pretty sister either.

Horseshoes was another game that orphans loved to play. As young boys, we would spend hours watching the older boys play horseshoes. They would challenge each other until there was a clear winner. Sometimes one of us would luck out and get to play a game with one of the big boys. After the big boys got tired of playing, we would jump right in and start playing. It just seemed that there was a long distance between the two pits and the shoes seemed very heavy. After a while I learned how to play the game and enjoyed playing for a long time.

Most all of the older boys were good to us young boys. We learned a lot about being an orphan and had a lot of fun with very little. We learned how to take care of ourselves. I had a lot of heroes to admire, having all of those older boys as brothers. They all played sports that we were able to watch.

I had many girl heroes as well as boy heroes. We cheered for the girls' teams just as we did for the boys' teams. The girls cheerleading squad was a special attraction to us younger boys. I was able to see my sister when we had a ball game because she was a member of the cheerleading squad.

Bobbie, Doris, Voncille, Charlena, Jean, and Toni

Every Easter Monday the Alumni would come back to the Home for homecoming day. All of the Alumni would come back dressed in their finest clothes. The girls and their children would all be dressed in their Easter dresses and everyone looked real pretty. There would be a big dinner prepared at the Central Dining Hall. After dinner the Alumni would challenge the varsity baseball team to a game on the Home field. One year it rained but a game would still be played. They all went to the gymnasium and challenged each other in basketball. The competition was just as fierce as any high school ball game.

The old timers were a tough group. Many of them continued their physical activities in the military or college. There were several of the Boyette brothers that came back every year and they were all my heroes. One of the brothers had lost one arm below the elbow while at the Home. When he was a young boy helping in the laundry, his arm was caught in a steamroller-pressing machine called a mangle. The machine was used to press the many sheets from all of the cottages. Even with this disability, he could still play baseball better than I ever could play. He could hit the baseball as well as many of the other boys. His brother, Bill, played professional baseball after leaving the Home. Many of the other boys made the professional or semi-pro circuits. Many were stars in college. Many became teachers and coaches in schools across the country. I got to know a lot of the older Alumni by them coming back to homecoming each year. I was too young to remember a lot of them since many had left the orphanage before I came, or while I was still in the Baby Cottage. I have heard many stories about many of the Alumni and they too are all my heroes. I always felt proud to be a part of such a big family, and I couldn't wait to grow up and be just like them. Where else could I live and have so many big brothers as my heroes?

It wasn't long before we young boys in the scouts were doing a lot of camping and fishing. I just loved growing up at the Children's Home even though I was smaller than a lot of the boys my age. We even started to wear grown up

clothes. We wore trousers, Roebucks or Bells. Gone were
the days of the bib overalls. The Children's Home got a
new bus one year so we scouts got the old bus for our trips.
We went everywhere in that old Mack bus. The old Mack
used to be the varsity bus. Coach Gibson drove us
everywhere in it. We went to Raven's Knob scout camp, the
Reynolds family's Camp Devotion, Tanglewood Farm, and
one day we stopped by George Southern's place in the
country. When we got there George was digging a well. I
thought to myself that he surely had a lot of dirt to pull up
out of that hole before he ever came upon water. I further
thought that George had better tie a rope to himself just in
case he did make it to water, then he would not sink to the
middle of the earth. George was raised at the Children's
Home and became famous for his talent in making
horseshoes. He traveled all over the country making
horseshoes and shoeing horses.

When we visited Tanglewood Farm, we fished for a
while in the river and pond and ran all over the barnyard.
The men there let us ride the small horses and donkeys.
My first experience riding a donkey was really an exciting
ride. I thought that I had mastered the donkey on which I
was riding until that donkey took off running towards the
barn. The donkey had a mind of its own, and I had no
control and just could barely hold on. As the donkey got
closer to the barn, he suddenly stopped and lowered his
head, and I fell head first into the water trough. That
donkey was thirsty and nothing was going to stop him from
getting a drink of water. All of the boys started laughing,
and after the initial shock of going head first into the water
trough, I started laughing also. Some of the boys were
rolling in the grass with laughter. It was really a good
experience for my first ride with that magnificent steed.

I had a few more real nice teachers during this period
of my life. I had Mrs. Mae Ramsey She was a super person.
She helped me do well in spelling and art. Her guidance
was evident, as I became the spelling champion for my
grade. Everyone in the class liked the way she taught us
geography. She would roll out a long piece of paper and let
us draw and water paint the different countries. In

addition to each country, we would draw the different people and show how they were dressed. We were taught to change the colors of our water paint by adding other colors to the paint. For some reason I never remembered being bored in her class. She had the same pleasant personality that endeared us to Mrs. Sifford. She spoke softly and engaged each student as if she liked everyone. She was more of a motherly figure. Several of us entered the Winston-Salem art contest on our grade level. Our artwork had to win approval by our school first. My watercolor won at our school and that was good enough for me. Mrs. Dinkins, our librarian, carried our school winner's art to the city art show. I lucked out and won a blue ribbon. Mrs. Dinkins hung my painting on the wall in the library. I just knew that I would be famous. I was really proud of that painting.

My next teacher, Mrs. Ogburn, was a very proper and very nice lady. She was also a very pretty lady. She didn't have time for anyone that was lazy or wouldn't do his or her homework. She encouraged us that we all learn, and we all liked her for her persistence in the end. Some days I dreaded going to class when I hadn't done my homework. She wasn't at all bashful in letting the class know that I didn't do my homework. Mrs. Ogburn must have known what she was doing because we all became good students in her class. Her husband, Mr. Tom, was a great fan of the Children's Home's varsity football team. He would follow the team to every game so he could cheer them on.

Mrs. June Dinkins was the librarian at our grammar school. She was a short and slightly stocky woman with lots of energy. Her husband was a giant of a man. He was tall and had a big belly. He always had a big cigar in his mouth. Mrs. Dinkins taught us how books and subject matter were catalogued in the library. She would teach us how to repair damaged books and how to do bookbinding. I would also get a Boy Scout merit badge in bookbinding so that was neat. Mrs. Dinkins also taught English to the seventh and eighth grade classes. English was a subject that I thoroughly despised. It just didn't make any sense to me and was boring. I just didn't take any of it seriously and that attitude would haunt me for the rest of my school days. Each class had some time in the library every day, and reading boring stories was not my idea of a good time in the library. Mrs. Dinkins tried to get all of us interested in a variety of subject matter. She tried to make each of us good readers. I just wasn't going to wear my eyes out on some old book that didn't interest me. I wasn't going to read any sissy books and let the boys find out what I was reading. Every chance that I had, I would look for a science or frontier book or an invention book. Now that kind of literature fascinated me. Little did I know then that reading a few more books with a variety of subject matter and paying attention in English class would make my world much brighter. Even now I cannot remember reading an entire book during all of my school years. I would read a few pages in the front along with the preface and a few pages in the back of the book. Then I would hope that I would not get called upon in class to tell the story of the book. If a book report were required, I would fake the story with what information that I had read. I got by a lot of times, but telling just a little bit of a strange story would often catch me. Many times I would read the classic comic books that were beginning to become popular in those days. But the teacher had a way of knowing if we had read the book.

Mrs. Bodie was our music teacher. I always thought that she was a little bit too sophisticated to be teaching us children at the Home. Most of us had a country background and we worked on the farm. She was good at what she did as a teacher. She was a very proper lady and most of us were just country kids, so there was very little sophistication in any of us. She put out a lot of effort for us to learn a little about music. Mrs. Bodie taught us how to play the harpsichord and flute. She would teach some of the children piano lessons.

One year I received a guitar for Christmas from my Aunt Louella. I really wanted to learn to play that guitar. I asked Mrs. Bodie if she would help me learn to play music with my guitar. She was one of those ladies who thought there was a certain type person that played guitars and that I shouldn't be one of them. She did offer to teach me classical guitar, but she said that I didn't have a classical guitar. She refused to help, but that didn't stop me from trying to learn to play. I started looking at some guitar music books and listening to some old records from the thirties and forties. I started making some noise on that guitar, but somehow it just didn't sound like I thought it should sound. First, I knew nothing about tuning a guitar, and really didn't know that it was necessary. There were some awful sounds coming out of that guitar. One day one of the boys asked me if I had ever had my guitar tuned. I asked him what he was talking about, and he explained to me the best he could what he thought tuning meant. So I went to talk to Mrs. Bodie again in hopes that she might be able to help. She was really not impressed with my guitar, but she did offer to help me tune my guitar, somewhat! She would blow in this little round harmonica and tighten one of the strings and then she would blow on the harmonica again and loosen the string. She would pluck the string and then tighten the string again. I thought I'd never be able to tune my guitar if it took all of that effort. Finally, the guitar did sound a little different after Mrs. Bodie had finished tuning it. I even learned a few chords after a while, but I still had a long way to go before any human could stand being in the same building while I practiced on my guitar. I strummed and blurted out some of the strangest sounds you have ever heard. I was really getting on the nerves of all the boys in my cottage. It came to a point that I even got a black eye for my beautiful singing. I was trying to learn how to play country and bluegrass music and that was just not what the boys my age wanted to hear. I even had my guitar cracked on my head by one of the older boys as we scuffled over my wonderful sounds.

When "Red" Church and "Buddy" Cagle heard about my near success in being a guitar-playing star, they came to my rescue. "Red" and "Buddy" played their music well enough that people actually listened to them and applauded them for their efforts. They would get up early in the morning and go to the radio station in town. There they would play their guitars and sing with George

158

Hamilton IV. George went to high school with "Red" and "Buddy" at R. J. Reynolds. On weekends and after school George would come to the orphanage to practice playing music with them. They would let me come in the room where they were playing their music to watch and listen. When they had a few minutes, they would show me a few chords and show me how to strum a guitar. I was in heaven, being in the company of those guys. After seeing the condition of my old guitar, they agreed to let me have one of their old guitars. I took that old guitar and sanded and sanded and sanded it until the guitar was as slick as silk. I sanded it so much that "Red" told me I was going to sand the sounds right out of it. I went to the carpenter shop and ask my big person friend Ravanelle if he had any of that clear paint to put on my new guitar. He gave me some of the stuff in a jar that he called varnish along with a well-used paintbrush. I put a varnish finish on that guitar and it looked almost new. I had my own guitar, given to me by my heroes. I was one proud young lad with that new guitar, and I carried it everywhere I went.

Now I just knew that I was going to be a star. Grand ole Opry, here I come! I tried to learn what I could from "Red," "Buddy" and George but it was time for "Red" and "Buddy" to leave the orphanage. They were grown and had finished high school so they had to get out of their rooms so another boy could move in. At the orphanage, it was tradition for a boy or girl to leave the next day after graduation from high school. You were on your own! I felt kind of depressed when they left. I finally had someone that cared or at least took the time to help a little boy like me with his guitar efforts and now they were gone. I let my guitar-playing slide after "Red" and "Buddy" graduated and left the Home. Mrs. Gibson at the Central Dining Hall offered to help me after she finished her work at night, but she worked so hard and late that I couldn't accept that offer. There would be one more disastrous event before my career, as a famous guitar singer would end.

Mrs. Bodie, our music teacher, wanted our class to put on a program on the stage in front of the rest of the school. She selected small groups of children to perform a song selection. Each small group would practice together until they were ready to perform on the stage. Mrs. Bodie asked me to play my guitar and sing with a pretty girl named Anita Janes. After a little coaxing I finally agreed to try. I didn't know but one song that Mrs. Bodie suggested we play and sing. I imagine it was a pretty song if I could only play it without ruining it. We practiced a few times, but I never seemed to keep up with the rhythm nor the proper chords. I only knew one set of notes and Anita sang like an angel. It appeared to me as if I were on stage to destroy her beautiful voice. Now that was embarrassing to me.

At that very moment I decided that my guitar-singing career was over unless I got some much needed and serious help. I still wanted to play my guitar but that help never materialized. Oh well, there were other things that young boys should and could be doing. There was playing football, catching crawfish and chasing critters.

Many years later during my military career, I was able to see George, as he and Kitty Wells would be on tour playing for the troops in the Pacific. I was able to visit with them in their dressing room before their performance. That was quite a treat to get to see someone that I knew from home, and especially since they were both famous stars. I told Kitty where I was from, and that George and his friends "Red" and "Buddy" gave me one of their guitars and helped me learn a few chords. I introduced all of my service buddies to George and Kitty and the boys were thrilled to get their autographs. My service buddies thought that I was somebody that night, and we all enjoyed George and Kitty's show.

I had begun playing junior varsity football as football was my favorite sport... along with fishing, hunting, climbing trees, horseshoes, baseball, basketball and just about anything else that us orphan boys did at the Home. Football just seemed to fit me better. I couldn't dribble a basketball very well, and besides, they never made a pair of basketball shorts long enough for me to wear in public. Boys with skinny legs just didn't look very masculine in the kind of short pants that are worn in basketball. I tried basketball and Coach Gibson put me in during a game. I actually made more points while I was in the game than any of my teammates. The only problem was that the points went to the other team. I committed three or four fouls in less than three minutes of my entire basketball career. You might say that I had a "three minute career" in basketball. I just couldn't get over my football habit of knocking someone down. It seemed that when I went to dribble, somebody would try to get in front of me and that was a mistake on his part. I ran over them. I would stop and try to pass the ball to another player, but somebody would try to take the ball from me. That was another mistake on their part, as I would fight to keep the ball. I found it embarrassing when someone would take the ball from me. I would chase him down and take it right back but each time I tried to do something; the referee would blow his whistle and charge me with a foul. I guess I was not supposed to knock people down in this game. Coach Gibson took me out and replaced me with one of the regular players. When I got to the bench, Coach Gibson said to me "Way to hustle Fred," just as he had often said when I played football. I had just given six points for the other team and he said, "Way to hustle!" I guess that's why he's the coach. I'm still waiting for my next turn to go into another game. It didn't happen that year. I guess he didn't want to show every team his secret weapon.

Every summer, just about everyone at the orphanage worked canning food for the coming winter. A lot of the girls would come to the cannery and peel tomato skins.

Charlena, and other kids
peeling tomatoes

Some days we would snap green beans or shell butter beans to be canned. It was hot and itchy work, but at least we were able to see the beautiful older girls working in the cannery. That helped with our morale when we would come in from picking vegetables in the fields. Once in a while I saw my sister and some of her pretty friends working with her. They were older girls but they sure were pretty as a picture, even after sweating all day and with tomato juice staining their cotton dresses. Those good days were few and it was back to the normal grind of working in the fields, but for some reason, it all balanced out. The work and the time we had to play, either playing sports or swimming, seemed to go together to make it easier on us. Don't get me wrong; we worked hard at times but we also played hard. We had plenty to eat and plenty of fresh milk from our dairy.

Coach Gibson was my football coach when I was on the Junior Varsity team. I believe he thought that I would be a great backfield man because he put me in the backfield running and passing the football. This was when the single wing formation was the popular style of play. We would later phase in the "T" formation for part of our plays. I had always played on the line as a blocker and tackler when I played for Coach Edwards. I had a problem switching from blocking for the runner to running away from the tackler. I would always try to run over the tackler instead of running away from him when I was carrying the ball. I was still small which made it almost impossible for me to run over another player, but I wasn't afraid to barrel into other players. Usually I would go backwards after the point of contact. Most of the time when I would try to run over someone, I would be traveling through space soon after the hit, looking at all of the stars. I also had small hands, which made it difficult for me to pass a football. The only thing I had going for me was a lot of determination. After a few times of being knocked out of breath by the football in my chest, I asked Coach Gibson If I could switch to the line so I could block and tackle. I told him that blocking and tackling were a lot more fun than being tackled, and I had some getting even to do. Coach Gibson let me play on the line, and I really enjoyed doing the blocking and tackling. I would still see a few more star shows when I made a good tackle on one of the big boys.

Little did I realize that the man in the backfield that handled the football was also the one that got all of the glory. Everyone cheered for that person, including the most beautiful cheerleaders in the whole world, and I had asked to give up the job that would give me all of the glory and also impress the pretty girls. Then I thought if we lost all of our games because of me, the girls certainly would not be impressed. So I decided to go where the coach wanted me to go and do the best that I could. I held my chest out and stood as tall as I could stretch in hopes that the boy on the other side of the line would be a little bit afraid of me. That didn't work because I was so skinny that no one could even tell that I was sticking my chest out. Most of the time I would end up on my back with several other boys on top of me, and I could hardly get my breath. I kept trying as I loved the game, and I sure did like it when I was lucky enough to help out on a tackle. I would go to the gym and lift a few weights and hold my chest out with my shoulders back while looking in the mirror. I liked my new image as it made me look a little bigger than I really was. I think the pretty girls were impressed with my new image also. I remember one day before church, Coach Gibson walked by and stopped and asked me, "Are you all right?" I told him that I was and he said, "You are standing so stiff that I thought your back was broken." I said, "No, that is the way I stand." I just hoped that the girls didn't think that I was standing so strangely because I was trying hard to impress them. All I had ever heard from adults was, "Stand up straight!" Just how straight they wanted me to stand I never figured out, so I kept standing up straight with my shoulders back. I keep that posture even today, and I seem to breathe better standing in the correct posture. When I went into the military, I was standing just like the drill instructors wanted me to stand.

Sometimes after the sun had gone down, a large group of us would play a game called fox and geese. One boy was selected to be the fox and the rest would be the geese. The geese would be allowed a head start and would take off running all over the Children's Home property. They would run through the pastures and all the way down to where the girls lived. The boy that was picked to be the fox would take off after he had counted to a hundred and the geese would run wide open for several hours trying to stay away from the fox. Surprisingly, the fox could catch many of the geese in the dark. Sometimes with all of the excitement of trying to stay away from the fox, we would forget where all of the clotheslines were at the various cottages. I saw many of the boys run into clotheslines and it was pretty funny to us at that time. We would laugh until we fell to the ground as someone was trying to get up moaning. That was just orphan humor! One night I was running in an attempt to get away from one of the other boys. I was going to jump off of a stone wall at the Anna Hanes cottage. It was very dark, but I could barely see the edge of the wall. I was running as fast as my legs would carry me while trying to get away from the other boy who was chasing me. Suddenly I felt something grab me under my neck and my feet went right up in the air. I flipped head over heels

164

several times, and I could see the stars and then the dark ground each time that I would flip. Then, flop-bam-thud, I hit the ground with ten times as many stars in my eyes, and I couldn't breathe a lick. I didn't know where I was, and I don't remember if I even cared at the time. After I came to, enough to gather my senses, I realized what I had done. The other boys were laughing as hard as they could. I had forgotten where the clothesline was, and when I started to take my leap from the rock wall, the clothesline had snagged me under the chin. All of the laughing that I had done to others had finally caught up with me. I ended up with a stomachache and one heck of a headache as I headed back to my cottage to lie down. Boy, were we ready to sleep after an evening of running like that. Somehow we all survived the potential dangers of the games that we would dream up, but not without some serious knocks and bruises to help refresh our memories of those games. Many times the injuries required stitches or casts but that seemed to be the norm for us boys at the orphanage.

Coach Edwards was my seventh grade teacher and Coach Gibson was my eighth grade teacher. They were both great teachers and great coaches. Coach Edwards became the grammar school principal when Coach Clary was selected to be the assistant superintendent of The Children's Home. Those days brought more distractions to the boys my age. We had to spend all day with a school full of beautiful girls. There was a lot of flirting going on by the boys and some of the girls. Coach Edwards or one of the other teachers would catch us from time to time while we were getting out of hand with our mischief. Sometimes the mischief became dangerous. We would break paper clips in half and use a rubber band to shoot someone in the hinny and laugh when they yelled. Sometimes we would make paper airplanes and sail them across the room and hope that the teacher didn't catch us. It seemed that a lot of our show off pranks were done to impress the girls. I never did see how shooting a girl in the hinny with a paper clip would make her want to like you. We were not even thinking that the paper clips were dangerous and could put someone's eye out. We would put thumbtacks in the girls' seats, then act like we didn't know what had happened when the girl would jump into the air and scream. Whenever we were caught in these mischievous acts, the teacher would punish us. Once in a while the teacher would send us to Coach Edwards, and we would be invited into the supply room. Once in the supply room with Coach Edwards, we would be persuaded to get back on the right path and be good children again. Coach Edwards had a nice hefty paddle tucked away. He used the paddle where it did the most good while we were in the bent over position. I know all about it. If you got a paddling from Coach Edwards, you could believe you deserved it.

Chapter Six

We were living in the Duke cottage at this age. Mrs. Sigmon was our home mother. She was a gentle speaking woman but meant what she said. She would sit and watch television with us and see that we spent our study time doing our homework. She was very supportive of our being in the scouts. We were into a lot of mischief in those years. We were just doing orphan things that were normal for orphans. We had slingshots and slings in our pockets and would go everywhere on and off the Children's Home property. We were living over top of the old gymnasium. Our dormitories were at each end of the cottage with the younger boys sleeping in the dormitory closest to Mrs. Sigmon's room. The shower and locker rooms were on the back of the building. It seemed that we spent very little time inside this cottage since we were always on the go with our Scout program or sporting events. Mrs. Sigmon didn't have to deal with many of our discipline problems because they usually happened away from our cottage.

Back Row: Benny, Gilmer, and Tommy. Front Row:
Charlie, Frank, Jody, Roy. On Floor: Gordon
Mrs. Sigmon sitting with Fred

Next door to the Duke cottage was a new cottage being
built for the junior and senior boys, called the Wrenn
cottage, which would have a modern kitchen in the
basement so we no longer had to bring firewood from the
wood shed for the cook stove. While the contractors were
building the Wrenn cottage, they had started digging a
gigantic hole for the basement kitchen and dining room.
They piled the dirt up on each side of the footings fifteen or
twenty feet high. Well, leave it to the orphans to come up
with another challenging game. All of us boys chose up
sides and started having mud clod battles. As soon as the
construction workers left for the day, the mud clods started
flying through the air. Nobody ever really got hurt (bad),
but a lot of battles were fought for bragging rights. I guess
you could say it was a lot like playing Army. Every time
somebody raised their head, the mud clods started flying in
their direction. When the clods would hit you, they would
just burst apart and wouldn't cause any serious damage
like rocks would do. When someone threw a rock and hit a
boy in the head, there was usually bleeding and stitches
required. If you got caught hitting someone with a rock,

usually your buttocks received a very painful whipping. Rocks just don't feel good when they hit your head; I know!

Sometimes on Saturday or Sunday afternoon, we chose up sides and played tam ball, in earlier years called "town ball," a game just like baseball but played with the soft baseball.   Most of the time there were not enough players to field two teams so perhaps this was why they played the game the way they did. Sometimes if we didn't have enough players, we would rotate the players in the field each time we could get someone out and eventually you would become the batter. Many times we played with any kind of ball we could find. One day we had a fierce game going on and it was my turn at bat. I hit that ball a long way out into the outfield and just knew that I had hit at least a double. I took off running and never slowed down as I ran past first base. I just knew that second base would be easy for me and maybe third so I ran very fast to second base. By the time I reached the base, there was someone there with a ball in his glove standing right in my way. I ran right into the boy with the ball in his glove and everybody shouted, "OUT!" I didn't want to hear the word "out." I was so upset that my temper got the best of me. I reared back and hit that boy smack in the hardest part of his head. He wasn't going to get me out when I was supposed to be safe on second base. I didn't even hurt the boy but my hand sure hurt and began to swell up. The boy that I hit was Monroe (Bill) Heller, a good boy and the fairest sportsman that I ever knew while I was at the orphanage. He always played by the rules and played hard. Monroe played in every sport in school and played well. He, along with a lot of us, would never receive any big hero awards for his playing, but the boys who did wouldn't have if it weren't for the likes of boys like Monroe. He also did well in his studies and was a good friend to everyone. I felt bad about hitting Monroe in the head, but I would pay for it big time. I went back to my cottage and ran water over my hand but the pain became almost unbearable. I deserved every bit of that pain for hitting my friend. I dreaded it, but I had to go back to Miss Smith at the infirmary. I had broken my hand again and Miss Smith would have to carry me back to the Baptist Hospital to have a cast put on my hand. I believe this was my fourth broken bone. My stupidity in learning hard lessons was not getting any better, only more painful!

One day my sister left the Home. Shortly thereafter she married her boyfriend Sam who left about the same time. Sam joined the Air Force. When they were stationed in Greenville, S. C. they would take me on my summer two-week vacation. I enjoyed getting to go to the Air Base where Sam worked. It was nice to be with my sister as a family.

Sam and Charlena

One night two of the boys were talking about running away instead of going to work the next day. The more I heard them talk about running away, the more interesting and exciting it sounded. Were we going to California, Alaska or maybe Africa? I didn't know why anyone would run away or where anybody would go if they ran away, but I asked the boys if I could run away with them to somewhere. The boys agreed to let me come along, probably because I had always bragged about my dad having that dump truck full of money and the fact that I just didn't fear much of anything, "in their eyes." The three of us had made up our minds that we were not going to work on the farm anymore and that we were going to run away the next morning. When morning came we went to breakfast with all of the other boys as usual. After breakfast, when all of the other boys headed to the farm to go to work, we slipped around the back of the cottage and down near the back gate onto Reynolda road. We were going somewhere, maybe to the mountains, but we were not sure how to get anyplace. Nevertheless, we were going there, to someplace. We had no money and we were in our work clothes, but we were brave and going to run away to nowhere or somewhere no matter what. We cut through part of the pasture and through the woods. We ran through some brush behind some houses so nobody could see us running away. We got thirsty and we got hungry. We got lost and we got scared of being lost. The more hungry and thirsty we got the more scared we became of being lost, hungry and thirsty. It began to dawn on me as I thought of all of the other boys that had left the Home and never returned. Then I was terrified and wished I had gone to work with all of the other boys. I never wanted to run away from my Home, ever again. It was all about getting attention and being accepted by the other boys. I believe it was Ted Barnett and "Tink" Reese running away with me. Ted said, "Lets cut through this corn field; I think I know the way." The way to where I didn't understand because none of us had any idea about where we were going or where the way to somewhere was. I soon found out that Ted didn't know his way to somewhere either. As we were walking through the cornfield, we could hear noises in the distance that sounded like a tractor running. That couldn't be our cornfield as we had been running away to nowhere for several hours. As we got closer we could hear voices. We got a little closer and the voices became more familiar. We recognized the voices of the older boys who were cutting silage corn. The way we got our silage corn was by the older boys would cutting the corn stalks using machetes. Then they would load the corn stalks on the hay wagon that was pulled by a tractor. The tractor would pull the wagon back to our dairy farm. The corn stalks were then pushed off the wagon into a machine that would chop the stalks into small pieces. The machine, powered by a wide belt driven from a power wheel on the side of one of our tractors, had a large blower built into it that would blow the pieces up a pipe and into our silos. We had a silo at each barn to provide feed for our cows during the winter months.

"Kissel" and Glenn, with machetes,
cutting corn

When we heard those voices, we took off running
across the field in between the cornrows so that we would
not be caught. We knew that we couldn't get caught so we
kept on running. I thought we were going to pass out from
being so thirsty and hot. I just wanted to stop somewhere
and rest. Suddenly we ran right smack into a group of
older boys working at the edge of the field. The older boys
already had the news that we had run away. I guess they
thought we were really dumb for running directly into
them. We had been running away from home for nearly
five hours. We were starving to death; we were dying of
thirst; we had been scared to death, and had only gone
about three miles. Now we were scared to death of what
trouble we would be in when the older boys would turn us
over to the farm manager. We made it to the other side of
Arbor Road where one of our farm fields was located.
Somehow, even though I knew that I was in trouble, I felt a
bit of relief knowing that I was not lost anymore. I had run
away and found my Home again. I was happy that I

wouldn't have to show how brave I was anymore, and I
knew that we all would get the same punishment for the
trouble we had caused. We knew that we would be beaten
to death for running away and worrying everyone at the
orphanage. The farm manager, Mr. Brady Angell, took his
belt off and gave each of us a few swats on the buttocks.
He then told us to climb up on top of the pile of corn stalks
on the wagon. We did as he said and rode that corn wagon
back to the orphanage farm. We didn't say a word all the
way back to the farm. When we got to the farm yard, Mr.
Angell had us climb into the back of his pickup truck and
he drove us to "Pop" Woosley's house. "Pop" was not
pleased with what we had done. He told Mr. Angell that he
would handle the situation and let Mr. Angell go on back to
the farm. I didn't know what would happen next but he
told us to go to his basement. Then it got real scary. There
was one little light bulb shining down there and it was not
very bright. Then in walked "Pop" and he didn't seem at all
happy with what we had done by running away from home
and skipping out on our assigned work. One at a time he
told us to drop our drawers and bend over. My heart was
pounding out of my chest, as I just knew I was going to die.
You should have seen that paddle that he pulled from a
convenient spot. It was a wooden board about two feet
long and towards the spanking end, there were holes
drilled through the board. I just knew that I was a goner.
When he started to swing that board towards the first boy,
he told us that he loved all of his children but sometimes
some of us need a little more help than the others. When I
heard that paddle pop the first boy on the behind, it
sounded like it hit a piece of raw meat. Boy, was I scared!
That paddle left little dots on that boys buttocks from the
holes in the board but most of his buttocks was red
already. I remember wishing that I had gone first as that
boy continued yelling. It was then my turn and that
spanking was every bit what I thought it was going to be. I
didn't have much meat on my hinny, and I think that
paddle got closer to where the pain begins. I never wanted
to get another spanking like that, and I definitely never
wanted to run away again. I always loved "Pop" Woosley
before my spanking, and I always loved "Pop" after my
spanking. I guess "Pop" was as close to a daddy as I could

173

possibly have. I knew that I deserved that spanking. It was somewhat of a relief that I faced my wrong doings and didn't have to worry about it anymore. I would never receive another spanking from "Pop." I knew that he truly thought that we needed every bit of what we received; however, I always thought that it hurt him more than it hurt us. "Pop" was that kind of man. He was an honest and kind man. He loved all of his children as if they were his own, and he always tried to show us all that affection when he could. We did not know it at the time, but "Pop" would be leaving us to retire in the not too distant future. When that time came, things at the orphanage began to change from the ways to which we were accustomed. For a long time after he retired, I still sensed his presence in my life.

We got what we deserved for the trouble we had caused but it could have been worse. Usually when the boys would cheat and lay out of work, the punishment would be time in the ditch. Some boys who would skip out of work or did some more serious misbehavior were assigned two hours in the ditch after supper every evening for a period of time depending on how bad the infraction was. The ditch, about three to four feet deep, was used for the runoff of everything that was washed down from the cow barn. It stunk and the yellow flies were bad during the hot summer months. The weeds and grass had to be chopped from the banks of the ditch so that the runoff could flow freely. We used swing blades and scythes to cut the grass. Nobody wanted to be put in the ditch. I'll have to say that the ditch was a persuasive instrument for some who were not affected by the spankings. After we became older spankings were almost unheard of.

Some children at the Home were into something all of the time. We worked hard much of the time but we also had free time. We would get into mischief once in a while, but we were boys and there was the whole world in which to explore, to experiment and to experience. We had a lot of fun, and most of the time we all were good boys. We were not shut in but had freedom to roam all over.

One Saturday afternoon, Grady Mitchell and I stopped by the Dr. Pepper bottling plant, which was on the way to the movie theatre in Winston-Salem. We could walk to town Saturday afternoons to go to a movie or to go shopping. Grady and I took our slingshots with us, and on our way, went behind the Dr. Pepper plant to shoot our slingshots. There were a lot of old bottles stacked beside a wall so we got the idea to line them up on the wall and use them for target practice. We had a ball shooting those bottles. We kept score of how many bottles we hit and the competition was getting tough. We shot for a while and were just about to leave when we saw a police car pull up behind us. I was in trouble again, and just knew I was going to get another spanking. The police officers put us in their car and took us straight to Coach Edward's room in the Wrenn Cottage. The police officers knew Coach Edwards and told him what we had been doing. Coach Edwards took our slingshots from the officers and crushed them in one hand. Then he broke the slingshots into little pieces and threw them into the trashcan. I could see that he was mad as a bull and his head turned red all over. I had heard the older boys call him, "Big Bull," but never to his face where he could hear them. I knew right then that I had made the "Bull" mad and that I was in serious trouble. He was real thankful to the police officers for bringing us to him. He then said good-bye to the officers. I knew we were in deep trouble but didn't know what to expect next. He then told us to bend over and touch our toes, and my thoughts were that we would be kicked out of the second floor window. I just knew we would get the old "touch your toes treatment," and it would be over with after a gentle kick in the buttocks. Coach Edwards would just boot us slightly to get our attention. Then came the swift kick with the side of his foot. It was not hard enough to hurt us bad, but he had a way of letting you know he meant business. This time the kick lifted us off of the floor and jarred our senses a bit. The fear of that number nine making contact with my skinny buttocks was much worse than the actual kick. Again, Coach Edwards proved to me he was a "GENTLE GIANT." Then he made us walk back to the Dr. Pepper plant and pick up every piece of glass that we had broken. That was a job and we knew never to break any more bottles.

Another Saturday afternoon Grady and I found an old golf club. We had a few golf balls that we had found around the cottage and decided to learn how to play golf. We went down to the baseball field and began driving the golf balls from one end to the other and back. Then it was my turn to hit the ball. As I started my back swing, my club struck Grady in the forehead. He was standing right behind me, and I didn't know it. I thought that I had killed him with that club as the blood was running all over him. I was so afraid that I had really hurt Grady. It scared me so bad that I put him on my back and gave him a horse back ride all the way to the infirmary. Miss Smith took him to the Baptist Hospital to have his head stitched up. He came back in good condition, as the wound wasn't as bad as it first appeared. It seemed we were getting a lot of attention every time we tried to do something.

At the Duke Cottage we each had a locker to keep all of our belongings, clothes and our private boys' things. We never had a lock to put on our lockers. We had learned early on that taking from another boy would get you into serious trouble. If you were caught stealing from another boy, the home mother would surely whip you. Then she would put you on restriction while all of the other boys were able to go out and play. There was yet another price to pay. If the other boys in the cottage found out that you were a thief, then you would usually get a black eye from one of the boys. There was certain mistrust in anyone that was caught stealing, and it took a long time for the boys to overcome that mistrust.

While we lived at the orphanage, we never had a lock on our room doors or where we would keep our private things. Sometimes we would put what little change we had under our clothes so that no one would see it. We also needed to hide our sling shot from our home mother because we were not allowed to have them. If we would go on a trip, or vacation or move to an older boy's cottage, the home mother usually kept cardboard boxes in the attic for us to use to carry our clothes. We usually didn't have many clothes so a cardboard box was plenty big enough for all of them. If we rode the Greyhound bus to where we were going on vacation, the home mother would tie a piece of string around the box to keep our clothes from falling out.

Most of our time was spent playing, and most of the time we were happy and found something to do. Very seldom would you ever find a boy inside of a cottage during play hours as we took full advantage of all the time we had. When we were not in the fields working, we were into some sort of playing. Sports took a lot of our time. We were either practicing for or playing a game. It may sound like we were into mischief all of the time but in reality we were not. We were pretty good boys most of the time.

Once we were lucky enough to earn a few real money dollars. The orphanage was tearing down the old Tise One and Two cottages. The contractor asked us if we wanted to make some money and we eagerly replied, "YES!" He told us that he would give us a certain amount of money for every hundred bricks that we would clean the old mortar from. You should have seen the orphans stacking up the cleaned bricks. As the contractor tore down the bricks from the cottage walls, we orphans jumped right in and started cleaning bricks. We would use our Boy Scout hatchet or an old hammer to beat the cement off the bricks. Sometimes we would just slide two bricks together real fast and knock the cement off. There were a lot of smashed fingers but it was worth the pain to get a few real dollars. Shucks, if we worked real hard, we could make a whole dollar during a Saturday afternoon's work. We would chip at those old bricks right up until dark. Later on the orphanage would build a church on the site of the old torn down Tise building.

One day "Tink" and I found a bunch of honeybees swarming inside of a hollow tree. The tree was inside the hog pen. We climbed over the fence and investigated the cause of all of those bees gathering in the tree. We came to the conclusion that there had to be some honey inside that tree. We talked it over and remembered that we had always heard that if you would build a fire next to the bees and make it real smoky that the bees would fly off. We went after some matches and found some empty containers. We then built a fire in that tree and put some green leaves on the fire to make it smoke. A lot of the bees left the smoky area, and we finally decided that we would try to get the honey out of that tree. We broke a couple of limbs from a bush and began poking the limbs up into the tree. Sure enough there was some honey in that tree. There were a few bees still in there also. We finally got brave enough to reach our hands up into the tree and began pulling out the honeycombs. We were just like a couple of bear cubs reaching for their favorite treat. Every once in a while one of us would get stung and we would yell and try to find the stinger so we could pull it out. That didn't stop us, as we had to show our bravery. We continued to pull honey out of that tree until all of our containers were full. After we took what honey we could carry, we began walking home eating honey comb just plum full of sweet honey. We chewed the wax comb until there was no more honey in it then we would grab another big piece. We ate until our bellies could hold no more. We took the honey to our cottage and let every one of the boys dig into that sweet treat. Then we started looking after our bee stings as we both had many on our heads and arms. That smoke didn't work as well as I had heard it would. I knew a lot about bees and just about any other varmint in the woods. I knew about every varmint that wasn't smart enough to hide when we orphan boys came to play in their woods. I loved this awesome playground here at the orphanage. Some boys would complain at times for having to live in this awful place, but they just didn't take advantage of all of our friends in the woods. I fussed a little myself, but I knew there was no other place in the world like our playgrounds, and I always thought of my orphanage as a mighty good place to live. There was always something to do in the woods and creeks. The mere excitement of beginning a new friendship with a new creature in the woods was full of wonder, and learning to enjoy the freedom to explore like that was equally exciting.

If there was a critter that didn't bite too hard then I tried to make friends with it.

Some more orphan mischief was about to happen. Several of us boys were helping Mr. Paul Boose in the cannery while he was inspecting some of the cans of vegetables and fruit that had been canned for a while. Wouldn't you know that some of the boys had to check out all of the unusual attractions around the building? Weldon and I found an old corn shelling machine sitting off in the corner. We didn't know how this machine worked, but another boy said that you stick an ear of corn down inside the machine and as you turn the handle, the machine will take all of the kernels off of the cob. We just had to watch this magic one time so I grabbed the crank handle on the side of the machine and turned the handle as fast as I could. A couple of the other boys wanted their time turning the handle so we took turns, and we really wound up that handle so fast that we could really hear the machine roaring inside. One boy told Weldon to put something down into that hole. Weldon put something down that hole and let out a scream as he pulled his hand right back out of that machine faster than he had stuck it in. His hand was bleeding and he was holding onto his hand with the other hand. We hollered to Weldon, "What's wrong, what's wrong?" We had tried to shell Weldon's fingers right off of his hand. I felt really bad as we wrapped a shirt around his hand, and Mr. Booze rushed him to the infirmary in his truck. Miss Smith carried him to the Baptist Hospital as fast as she could. We had shelled off one whole finger and parts of two others from Weldon's hand. We were really worried about Weldon and really felt bad about what had happened. His hand healed very well but it just didn't look the same as it did before the accident. That accident didn't slow Weldon down one bit as he continued to play very well in sports went on to college and later served in the U. S. Air Force. I always thought a lot of Weldon and considered him to be one of my favorite friends. In later years, every time that I saw him carry that football and saw his hand, I thought of just how brave a young boy he really was. I knew that he would make it all right in life. He was an excellent role model with a good personality. I didn't know of a single boy that disliked Weldon. He certainly was like a real brother to me. He didn't have the temper that some of us possessed and rarely did you ever see him in an argument.

During those years, all of the high school children would attend the Centenary Methodist church up town on Fifth Street. The church was the prettiest that I had ever seen. It was gigantic and a lot of pretty dressed up people would go there to worship service on Sunday mornings. There were some of the nicest people there that I ever met in my life. The boys would walk to church and the girls would ride the bus. I guess it was about three miles to church. I remember walking past some of the houses on the way to church and picking some of the sour grass out of the front yards. I always liked the taste of sour grass. Some of the boys would stop at the service station and get a piece of candy if they had any money in their pocket. We always checked out the Plum Granny (Pomegranate) tree in the side yard of the church to see if any fruit was ripe enough to eat. After we became high school age we attended Sunday school and then went to the main chapel for the church service. We would sit in the balcony. The ninth and tenth grade children would sit on one side of the church, and the eleventh and twelfth grade children would sit on the opposite side. Coach Clary and Coach Edwards would sit with us to monitor the girls and boys behavior. Keeping everyone awake was the biggest job. Every year at Christmas, the church would invite all of the little children to a Christmas party in the basement. They would have lots of candy, coloring books and toys. The children would listen to Christmas stories and socialize with the church members. The Centenary Methodist Church people were very good to the Home children.

Children's Home kids
joining Centenary Church

At this age in my life girls were becoming a big part of
my thoughts and interest. During the previous years I had
a crush on at least a dozen of the prettiest girls that you
have ever seen. There was no kissing or anything like
that, but we did trade valentines and say "Hey," at school
or church. I don't believe some of the girls even knew that
I liked them as some had their own sweethearts. Some
were older girls, and I couldn't say "Hey," to them because I
would surely get a black eye from one of the older boys if
they knew that I had a crush on their girlfriend. There
were a lot of girls that I liked. There was: Bonnie, Aurelia,
Irene, Betty, Ann, Dorothy (Dot), Diane, Shelby, Joyce,
Betsy, Doris, Nancy, Gay Nell, Gladys and many more.

The first time that I had a real date, where you sit with
somebody, was with a girl at the Stockton cottage. Mrs.
Hatcher was her home mother. She seemed very nice to us
boys when we would come for a visit on Sunday night. Her
son Rodney was my age and lived in the same cottage that I
did. Mrs. Hatcher had an older daughter named Toni that
was my sister's age. She kept a close eye on us while we
were dating her girls, making sure that we behaved in a
gentlemanly fashion. I remember sitting at the little

children's wading pool, which was in the back yard of the Stockton cottage. In good weather the boys and girls that had dates would sit around the little pool and socialize during their two hour Sunday night date. Other times we would go inside the basement to the game room and watch television or listen to records or just grin at each other. I was really trying to impress my love for life. I would put on some extra hair oil or butch wax and try to get my hair to lie down so I would really be sharp. I'd put on a nice clean shirt, if I had one, and sometimes I would remember to shine my shoes. If I could find a piece of gum, I would carry it with me to give my new friend. I knew that girls chewed gum all the time, and I thought that she might like me just a little more if I brought her a stick of gum. I never liked chewing gum and never chewed it myself. I just felt this girl liked me more than anybody in the world. The next week, I went to the woods and climbed my favorite tree and carved our initials in the bark. I just knew it would last forever or whatever "IT" was, that's what I wanted to happen. Her name was Brenda Jean and she wore glasses. I could see behind those glasses, and I saw the prettiest girl in the world. Not only was she pretty, but also, she had a very pleasant way of talking to me. She was mentally much more mature than I was. Every time that I was near her, my mind went blank, and I couldn't think of the right things to say. A lot of times, I just couldn't think of anything to say. I would just sit there and smile as pretty as I could and she would smile back at me. She would ask me questions; and I would answer the best that I could, but most of the time it was just a "yep" or "no" and then a grin. She was not as shy as I was and she talked very calmly and gently.

Sometimes the boys would tease you if you liked a girl with glasses or if the girl was tall or stout. There were girls at the Home who had few friends, especially boy friends, just because of peer pressure from other children. I look back today and feel bad that we didn't know how to deal with peer pressure. There were other girls who wore glasses and were pretty, but the boys said bad things because they wore glasses. They would say "book worm" or "four eyes." I didn't care what anybody said. I knew that I would love my sweetheart forever. I can remember when we first kissed goodnight while sitting at the little children's wading pool. She had on a white cotton, no sleeve top and her hair was combed real nice. She had real lipstick on her lips, and I thought she was the prettiest thing I had ever seen. She was so pretty that I was afraid I might mess her up. We kissed right straight on the lips. Oh, what a feeling as I was breathless. I had to learn to breathe and kiss at the same time because for a while I thought I was supposed to hold my breath. That was something that we boys didn't talk about, girl things that is. I finally found out what all of that confusion was all about when I was a year or so older. Boys and girls were supposed to sit beside each other for two hours on Sunday night and feel good. That's what it was all about. Boy, when she kissed me I didn't know what to say or do. I got all sorts of feelings. I was totally lost for quite a spell. That was the nicest thing that had happened to me in my whole short life. I could forget about school or the rest of the world from then on. I knew that I just wanted to sit by my special friend for two hours every Sunday night for the rest of my life. We dated for a while, and I was so proud of my girlfriend. It was the happiest time in my life. I was king of the world and the prettiest girl in the world liked me. I smiled all the time. I couldn't wait for Sunday evening to come around so I could just sit beside my girlfriend. Just to hear her gentle voice and feel her hand in mine was like being on a cloud in the heavens. When she kissed me goodnight, I forgot all about everything else in the world. When I would go play in the woods during the week, I would always go by and look at our initials with a plus between them high up in my special tree. I could daydream all day about the next time I would get to see my special friend.

Brenda Jean   Fred
   "Bo"

    I don't know how long we dated, but I never got over
the tragic end. I mentioned before about bowing to peer
pressure and sometimes making the wrong decisions.
Well, I let that peer pressure do me in. One Sunday night
when all of the boys and girls were all spruced up for their
dates, I didn't show up for my date. I just knew my girl
wouldn't mind me not coming for our date because she
loved me so much. She was just the prettiest girl in the
world, and I had more important peer pressure things to
do. I had to climb trees with my good friend and help him
get a baby squirrel for a pet. My absence from our date
gave my sweetheart the opportunity to be with other
friends. She became fond of another young boy who was
smarter, more handsome and certainly a more dependable
young boy. That evening, one of the boys in my cottage
told me that he didn't think I would need to go back
anymore to see the girl of my dreams. My life was crushed,
and I realized that I really did love her. I couldn't show it
around the other boys because I had to play tough. I
always wanted to be the one in her life. Wow! This loving
thing was no fun after all if this was part of the game. I
didn't have a stomachache, black eye or a headache, and
none of my bones were broken but I hurt for some reason.
After a while things didn't hurt as badly but I had strange
feelings. I knew that I loved her because I felt very happy
for her when I saw her happy with someone else. Down
deep I really didn't want to see her with another boy, but
somehow, with her appearing so happy, it strangely made

me feel a little better. I still feel happy for her today knowing that she is secure and happy in her own family. I have strong feelings for all of the Home children and the adults that looked after us. I pray they are safe and happy in this big world. I've seen the bad all around this world, and I often think of how richly I grew up, without worldly things, but with a chance at life with love.

As the days passed, I wondered if my beautiful friend and I would ever have a chance to be together again. To me it seemed certain that this love was a learning experience of how good love feels and how bad love feels. Surely I didn't want any more of the bad. I guess I was just too young to have all of those feelings and not understand how I was supposed to feel. There was no one to talk to about what I felt; and I certainly would not open up and discuss my feelings with the other boys, as it might become another joke to them. I would just go about my orphan life and take things as they came at me. Maybe another cute girl with glasses would make a gesture of some kind to let me know that she would like my company. There was Eva, Shirley, and many other pretty girls. Many of the girls already had boy friends so I had to be careful to not flirt with another boy's girlfriend. There were dozens of other girls there and surely one would let me know they wanted to be my special friend. Having a girl friend just seemed to be a natural thing. Sure enough I had a few more close friends for a while. I gave up on my special tree since I would probably kill the tree climbing it so many times and carving in its bark every time that I changed my special friend. Evidently some of the other boys were having the same difficulty in learning this girl friend thing, as they began climbing my tree and carving their girl friend's and their initials with a plus sign in between on the bark. I really didn't like it much if one of the boys put their initials and a plus with my girl friend's initials. Learning how to manage this girl thing was never something I did very well. I thought that I was not a bad looking boy, but it seemed that I often got dumped. So I guess I wasn't so cool after all. I would have to start all over and learn how to be cool like some of the other guys. Maybe if I paid attention in school and stopped being a dummy might help for a start.

185

Many years after I left the orphanage, I went back to the woods to visit my favorite friendship tree. I was surprised to find that all of my friendship initials were hardly readable. The tree had grown much larger in diameter and was beginning to show signs of stress and old age. When I searched for my friends' initials, the tree's bark had grown to cover much of the writing in new bark. It seemed to me that the tree was trying to tell me that it would hold on to my memories as long as it could, but for me to live my life and cherish the good times for what they were. There were many grown over scars on that tree, and I wondered if the other boys remembered where they wrote their feelings at a special time with a special person.

Every spring we all pitched in and cleaned the manure out of the barns. When we started cleaning the barns the smell from the manure carried through the air all across town. Depending on the direction of the wind, the smell would carry over to the high school when we were in school. Everyone in town including our friends at school knew that the orphans were cleaning their barns. One Saturday morning, when we were starting to clean the manure from the milk barn, I lifted my pitchfork up to jam it into a pile of manure. As I did, the handle hit the joists in the floor of the loft above. When I brought the pitchfork down the tine went right through my foot. It went through my boot and was sharp enough to go all the way through the boot sole. I let out a yell and the boys next to me could see what I had done. I snatched as hard as I could to get that fork out of my foot. One of the men drove me to the infirmary so that Miss Smith could take a look at my foot. Miss Smith washed my foot real good with alcohol and then took a cotton swab on a stick, dipped it into alcohol and pushed the swab as far as she could into my foot. I knew I was dying; it hurt so much. After several attempts at the swabbing, she wrapped my foot. Then she prepared a needle and gave me a tetanus shot. After Miss Smith had finished with her care for me, she said that I could go back to work. I walked back to the dairy farm and jumped right in helping the other boys fork that manure into the manure spreader. We were trying to hurry and fork as much of the manure as we could in order to finish cleaning the milk barn. We knew that we had several other barns, which we had to clean. I raised my pitchfork up, and I felt it strike the overhead of the barn just as it had done about an hour previous. Before I could adjust where my fork was going to land, I felt the pain in my foot again. I had stuck the same foot with that fork a second time in the same day. Now I knew what I would have to face again as once more I rode to the infirmary. Only this time Miss Smith said it would not be quite as bad as the first time. She said at least I wouldn't have to take another shot as she started pushing that swab, with alcohol, into my foot. It was just as bad as the first time. The shot was not even close to the pain of that swab and alcohol treatment.

Soon I was lucky enough to be assigned a job of cutting the grass all over the orphanage with a big reel type-riding mower. I really liked that job, especially when it came time to cut the grass around the girls' cottages. I would take off my shirt to get a tan, but truthfully, I took my shirt off to show the girls how strong I was. I don't think any of the girls were too impressed as I was a mere one hundred and ten pound bag of bones. Nevertheless, I would try to get my hair to lie down, flex my arm muscles and hold my stomach in when I thought any of the girls were looking my way. When I stuck my chest out, I looked like a skeleton but maybe at a distance the girls wouldn't see my ribs. That had to be the greatest job in the world. I would mow all day long on that mower and stop only long enough to eat lunch or gas up. I would mow starting at one end of the Home grounds and when I finished mowing all of the grass, I would start all over again. What a good job to have! I would get to go to town with Mr. Booze to the Brown-Rodgers-Dixon hardware store and to Pleasants Hardware store to buy supplies and seed. Those were fun stores to visit. They had everything that you could think of in the line of tools.

Evidently I did such a good job of mowing grass that Coach Clary assigned me to drive the trash and supply truck with Weldon Brigman. Weldon was a year older than I. We had known each other as long as I could remember.

187

We were in the baby cottage at the same time. We were
good friends, and worked well together. Weldon would let
me drive the truck every chance that he could. I wasn't but
fourteen years of age but that didn't matter on campus at
the Home. As long as you were big enough to do the job,
that was all that mattered. I had already had some truck
driving experience. I had learned to drive a truck under
some very unusual circumstances. Some of the older boys
who got up at four-thirty in the morning to milk the cows
would get me up with them. Sam Murdock, Eugene
Wallace, "Kissel" Russell and Robert and Ronnie Tuttle
would take me to the milk barn with them. After the cows
were milked and the feeding chores were done, Sam and
some of the others would teach me how to drive the dairy
farm truck. They would take me to the pasture around the
Little White Church and teach me to drive and change
gears. I would try to learn how and when to push the
clutch in to shift the transmission into another gear. I
know that I stripped at least a pound of metal from the
gears in that transmission. At least it sounded like I did.
There wasn't much for me to run into out there in the
pasture, and before long, I could handle that dairy farm
truck pretty good.

Robert and Kenneth loading milk truck

I could drive farm tractors, trucks, school buses and
other equipment long before I was old enough to get a
drivers license. Weldon and I would get up around four-
thirty or five o'clock in the morning and walk to the big
farmyard to get the truck. Most mornings we had to push

the truck to get it started. This was often the case, especially in the winter months. We usually parked the truck on a slight hill so that we could get a better running start the next cold morning. The truck was an old forties model International and of the two or two and a half ton size. We tried hard to get the truck started on the first down hill run of the morning. We would push hard to get the truck rolling as fast as we possibly could, then jump in, jam it into second gear, turn the key on, pull the choke and let the clutch out as many times as we could before the truck stopped rolling. We would talk to that engine real nicely in hopes that the engine would burst into life to start a new day.

Sometimes the truck just didn't want to start, and we would have to push that big truck back up the hill as far as we could roll it. Then we would start the pushing and rolling process all over again to try to start the truck. After we finally got the truck running, we began our daily schedule. During the weekdays we would drive to each cottage, pick up their trash and garbage and load it on the truck. Then we would load up the cold ashes from the coal furnaces. We would rake the hot ashes out of the boilers and shovel them into the steel cans so they could be cooling for pickup the next day. Then we would shovel coal and fill the furnace hoppers. We would sweep the cement floor to be sure that there was nothing on the floor to catch fire before we went to the next cottage. We went to each cottage and did the same job.

When we had finished making our rounds to all the cottages, and our truck was loaded, we would drive to the farm and to the dump, or GULLY, as we called it. We would sometimes spread the coal ashes on the farm roads if we saw any ruts in the road. We stopped by the pigpen and built a fire in the slop cooker. Then we would pour the garbage from the kitchens into the cooker and let the slop start cooking. Cooking the slop was supposed to kill any bacteria. We would then drive to the gully and shovel the rest of the trash off of the truck. After we were unloaded sometimes we would burn the trash. We then drove back to the pigpen and shoveled the garbage that had been cooking into the trough for the pigs to eat. We would then shovel some corn from the corn bin to add to the slop in the trough. If there was left over bread, from the bread company in the feed house, we would throw some of that into the trough. Mr. Angell, our farm manager, would drive into town to the bread company periodically and load his pickup truck with out dated bread and cakes. Oftentimes some of the cakes didn't make it to the pig trough. Some of the boys would sample the cakes that were not too moldy. Sometimes Mr. Angell would park his truck loaded with cakes in front of his house overnight. The word got around fast to all of the boy's cottages when he had a load of cakes in front of his house. If he had a load of cakes in front of his house, he would always leave his front porch light on so that he could look out of his window and see if any of the boys were taking some of the cakes. If a cake looked good, it certainly didn't last long. We would pinch a little mold off and carry some cakes back to the cottage. Oh yes, the girls got some of the cakes too! We raised about one hundred pigs each year to provide pork for all of the orphanage children.

On Saturday mornings, the older boys on the dairy milk crews had to go to the mill and grind grain into cattle feed. The boys would grind enough cattle feed to feed all of the cows and pigs for a week. On Saturday morning, Weldon and I would duplicate our weekly job of hauling the trash and garbage. After we were done with that job, we would scrub our truck with soap and hot water in preparation for delivering food supplies and canned goods to all of the kitchens. Mrs. Sue Smith, at the Wrenn cottage, didn't mind us cleaning our truck at her back door after we had finished hauling the trash and garbage. Mrs. Smith's kitchen had a hot water hose connection, which we used while scrubbing our truck bed. After we cleaned the truck we would meet Mr. Simpson, the Children's Home's business manager, at the Cornelius cottage. In the basement of that cottage, Mr. Simpson stored the cottage cleaning supplies and toiletries. He would have the orders filled and in boxes for us to pick up and deliver to the individual cottages. We would load all of the boxes on the truck and drive to the Central Dining Hall to pick up any canned foods and supplies. When the truck was loaded we would make a drive to all of the cottages and drop off what had been ordered for the week. I really liked our delivery stop at the Anna Hanes cottage because Miss Holland always had left over toast and fried eggs warming on that big old wood-burning stove. Sometimes she would have a nice piece of fresh cornbread waiting for us. Needless to say, we gave Miss Holland special attention for we knew her well from the time when we lived in her cottage. After that job was completed, we would make the rounds to all of the cottages again and pick up all of the dirty laundry in large laundry baskets. We would deliver the dirty laundry to the laundry room in the industrial building. This is where some of the girls worked with Miss Flora Styers, Miss Tula Harrelson and Mr. Padgett. The girls worked on Saturday morning just as the boys did. They would take the dirty laundry, and we would load up and deliver the clean laundry that had been dropped off the previous Saturday. We would deliver the laundry to each cottage and when we were finished we would drive our truck back to the farmyard. We then filled the truck with gas and parked it on the hill in its usual spot so that we would be ready to push it off to start it on Monday morning.

I couldn't wait until Monday morning to get to drive the truck again. I just liked driving anything that would move. We had learned to have fun driving when we were small kids driving our wagons and tricycles. Many times I would see Mr. Gray Todd driving the farm bulldozer while plowing a field. I wanted to drive that bulldozer awfully bad. Mr. Todd always had a shiny car, and I think all of the ladies liked him. He was a very strong and tough looking man and was always admired by us young boys who hoped to be like him some day. He had grown up at the orphanage and seemed somewhat like an older brother, but when he told you to do something he meant for you to get it done right now. One day he traded his shiny black Olds for a brand new turquoise and white fifty-five Olds. That was a really nice car, and we all couldn't wait until we were old enough to own a car like that. Not many of the boys go back to visit Mr. Gray, but I go as often as I can. Since I retired from the military, I drop in periodically and let him know how much I appreciate what he meant to us young boys growing up at the orphanage.

All of the girls and boys had free time on Saturday afternoon. That was the one time that the older girls were allowed to walk to town to watch a movie or shop in the stores. Everyone had to be back by five in the afternoon. Some of the boys who had girl friends would walk with them to town to watch a movie. The Children's Home boys and girls could get a show pass from their home mother and get into the movie for nine cents. Sometimes on Saturday afternoons, some of us were able to find a little work in the Buena Vista neighborhood just outside the Children's Home property. This was an upper-class neighborhood with a lot of very nice people living in it. They would call the home mother and let her know how many boys were needed at what address. We would rake leaves or mow their grass all Saturday afternoon and make a couple of dollars. It doesn't sound like much, but that was almost as much as our monthly allowance so it was good for us. Some of us would go play in the pastures and woods. We would always find something to do. A lot of Saturday afternoons, I would work for Mr. Simpson out in the country. He had purchased an old plantation home with property and was fixing the place up for his and his wife's retirement. We cut down overgrown vegetation and large trees so the nice house could get some sunlight. We worked on the old home, replacing rotten wood and painting it to make it look good. I was a small young boy but never backed away from hard work. I could swing an axe as good as any boy my size, and I could keep a crosscut saw moving all day. I had learned to use the lumbering tools while we were clearing land at the Shoffner Farm and, on Saturday mornings, splitting firewood in the wood shed. One day I reared back to take a swing at the limb of a fallen tree. The axe bounced off of the limb and stuck right in the front of my shin. Mr. Simpson really got worried about me getting cut, but I told him not to worry, it didn't hurt much at all. On the way home, he carried me to the Baptist Hospital and had the doctors put some stitches in my leg. Mr. Simpson always paid me generously. Sometimes on a Saturday afternoon he would give me almost two dollars. Mr. Simpson, his wife and two sons lived in a staff home on the orphanage grounds. We all liked his sons, Marshall and David. They played sports for our orphanage team and did well in school.

Some Saturdays I would walk to the movies with Grady, James or Tony. On one occasion two of us were walking along minding our own business when a man pulled up beside us and asked if we wanted a ride to town. We didn't know any better so we accepted the kind man's offer. We jumped into the front seat of his old business coupe. There wasn't enough room on the narrow seat for our legs because of the gearshift in the floor. The back seat was taken up with a horse saddle, so the man suggested that I put one of my legs on his side of the shift. I thought nothing of it, so I put one of my legs on the left side of the floor shift. The roads going into Winston-Salem were very steep and that required a lot of shift changing while going up the hills. All of a sudden the nice man shifted that gear lever back towards my crotch, and just laid his hand on the most private parts of my body. I punched the man just as hard as I could in the face. My friend had opened the door while the car was still going up the hill and we scrambled out of that car. I may have beaten my friend out of the car as everything was happening so fast. Why do I have to learn all of life's lessons the hard way? All rides are not subject to a kind offer.

Some days Grady and I would stop by his mother's house coming back from town, and she would give us a piece of cake and something to drink. Mrs. Mitchell sure was a nice lady, and she loved not only her sons, but also all of the orphan boys.

Sometimes Miss Whitson would ask me to wash her car for her. I would take her car to the dairy barn and hook a hose to the spigot at the calves' trough. I found a can of Ajax and a scrub brush and washed her car real good. There wasn't a spot of dirt on that car anywhere. It was the first time that anybody had asked me to wash their car for them. I really didn't know how to wash it, but I guessed that they wanted it clean, so I cleaned it real good.

Mr. Hamilton heard about the fine job that I had done with Miss Whitson's car and he ask me to wash his. I told him that I would clean every bit of the dirt from his car. I went into the cottage and found some Ajax and a brush, and I put Ajax all over that car and really rubbed it hard to get it clean. Mr. Hamilton's car was a brand new black and white Plymouth. It was real bright and shinny. I rubbed and rubbed on that paint to make it clean. I scrubbed the tires and got the whitewalls real white. I rinsed the powder off of the car and dried the car off. I called Mr. Hamilton out to look at his newly washed car. He walked out of the house and looked at that car, and I was just a grinning with pride on what a good job I had done. Everywhere that I had rubbed his new paint, with Ajax, you could see the glitter of the sunlight. There were circles all over that new car where that Ajax and hard rubbing had worked into the paint. He was not at all impressed with all of the hard work that I had done. He ask me what I had washed the car with, and I told him that I used Ajax and rubbed real hard to get it clean. He told me that using the Ajax ruined his new car's paint job, and that he would have to take it to the dealer and have the paint buffed to get the scratches out. I felt real bad about cleaning his car too good, but he said he would go ahead and pay me since I didn't know not to wash the car with Ajax. I was always learning hard lessons about everything, but it seemed the harder I tried the more I learned, in most cases, the hard way.

Some days we would just go piddling around the dump and gravel pit. There was some shallow water left from a recent rain and we would float an old cement-mixing box in the water. It was built like a flat bottom boat but very short. We tried to get in the box and float into the middle of the water pool. Every time we would get in we would have to bail the water out because the box had so many holes in the bottom that it would sink. We would drag it to the side of the water hole and start all over after we had tried to patch some of the holes with pine rosin. We got tired of sinking our boat so we became interested in catching some of the many tadpoles. It was a lot of fun seeing how many we could catch and taking them back to our cottage and showing the other boys. It was always a good feeling to do something that the other boys thought was interesting.

One afternoon when I was walking back to my cottage I spotted an older boy stooped down next to a vent under the old school building. I thought to myself, "What is that boy doing looking into that open vent hole?" I hid and waited for the older boy to leave the area, and I went to investigate. I looked into the hole and didn't see anything so I took another look to see if there were any black widow spiders. It looked clear to me so I reached my hand inside the open vent hole and felt along the wooden floor beam. My hand bumped into something, and I pulled it out. Golly, what a shocking sight! I had pulled out a whole stack of playing cards with naked women on them. Every single one of those cards had a different woman on the face of the card. They all were wearing bathing suits. Those bathing suits were not covering much of what ever they were supposed to cover. In those days a picture of a woman in a bathing suit meant that they were naked or semi naked, so I thought. I can understand why, today, American children get themselves into so much trouble by being stimulated by all of the soft porn and sexual explicit music that our leaders and parents allow them to view and to hear. As a young boy, even those playing cards with women in bathing suits gave me a strong sense of attraction. I always thought girls were attractive to me even in their cotton dresses and brown shoes.

I knew if I got caught with a deck of cards with naked women on them, that I would surely get a spanking. I knew that if the older boy caught me with his playing cards that I would surely get a big fat shiner. I just put the cards back where I found them and went on about my business. I thought, "Boy, I know a secret about one of the big boys. He has a deck of cards with naked women on them." It was always hard to find a place where you could hide something from the large group of boys, living at the Home. I bet that older boy thought that he was the only one who knew where he had hidden those playing cards. There probably are items still hidden all over the orphanage that boys forgot about or forgot to pick up when they left the

Home.

We continued playing in the woods and pastures when we were not in school or working. Sometimes we would walk through the pastures and see a big square block of mineral salt that "Dad" Shaver had put out for the cows to lick while they were grazing. One day I decided to break off a piece of the mineral salt and taste it. I figured if that salt would help those cows grow big and strong that it might make me a big strong man. I bit down on that hard salt and began chewing it up and swallowing it. It tasted awful, but adults always told me that sometimes things that tasted awful were good for you, so I kept chewing and swallowing. All of a sudden I became deathly ill and began throwing up. I felt just as I did when I swallowed a piece of tobacco when I was younger. Only this time I was really getting sick. One of the other boys helped me as we went to see Miss Smith at the infirmary. I was so sick that she put me to bed for a day. I vowed that I would not try that salt block again. I then thought that it was meant to stunt a boy's growth instead of making him a giant of a man. I was beginning to have a real knowledge of things not to try. I sincerely wished that the other orphan boys knew what I had already suffered through.

Chapter Seven

    I was living in a new building named in honor of Cicero Tise, the man whose money made possible the old Tise building, which had been torn down to make room for the church. I shared a room with another boy and our room was at the back door of the cottage. I liked where my room was located. I could go in and out easily with out having the home mother know every move I made. The first home mother, when I moved in, was Mrs. Cole. She was a very nice lady but she soon moved to the Baby Cottage to be the home mother there. We got along just fine as long as I kept my room clean. Mrs. Mull took her place and became our next home mother. She wouldn't stay at the cottage very long either. We then got Mrs. Shellabarger. She was full of humor, but she could get our attention when she thought it necessary to correct one of us for misbehaving. She was tall and very physically built. We knew to pay attention when she said something. Many of us were a little "smarty" to her from time to time, but usually we were corrected in some way. You could only get by with so much or you risked having to go visit with Coach Clary in

197

his office. That is something we did not want to do.

Many of us boys had pet squirrels that we would raise
until it was time to turn them loose. I tried to keep my
squirrel in my room while it was small. We would feed our
pets with milk while they were little. We used a baby doll
bottle for the milk, and it worked well for feeding our baby
squirrels. I decided to keep my pet squirrel in my dresser
drawer located inside of my closet. My roommate shared
the closet and a chest of drawers with me. I made a nest
for my pet with a towel and placed the nest and squirrel
inside the top drawer. The towel gave my squirrel a place
to sleep. Sometimes I would take my squirrel to school
with me. I would tuck it inside my shirt, and the little
squirrel would sleep most of the day. Often it would crawl
around inside my shirt. One day I decided to leave my pet
squirrel in the drawer while I was at school. I left the
drawer cracked a little bit so my pet could get some air. I
went off to school thinking that everything would be all
right. When I returned to my cottage after school, I met
Mrs. Shellabarger as I walked into the cottage. She was
mad about something, and I knew exactly what it was. She
had been to each boy's room to inspect the rooms. When
she got to mine, she opened the closet door and got the
shock of her life. There was a baby squirrel sitting up on
top of my dresser. She took the baby squirrel outside and
turned it loose. When she went back to my room, there
was another surprise awaiting her. She looked in my closet
and saw a bunch of shavings in front of the dresser. She
looked closer and saw a hole in the front of the top drawer.
My pet wasn't going to stay in that little drawer so it did
what it was supposed to do. It gnawed on that wood. Boy,
she was mad. She told me to NEVER bring another
squirrel into that cottage. She also told me that I would
have to fix that dresser drawer. I was a little bit mad about
her turning my pet squirrel loose outside. I knew that
what I had done was wrong, but I didn't like her getting
into my things. I thought to myself, "I'll fix that problem,"
and I began to plan a strategy to protect my "stuff." I tied a
shoestring to the top of my closet door, and on the other
end, I tied a railroad spike. When I would leave my room I
would put the railroad spike on the top shelf of the closet.

I went off to school one day shortly after I had gotten myself into that bit of trouble. When school was over and I came home to my cottage, I knew right away that I was in trouble again. Mrs. Shellabarger was mad as a wet hen. I just knew that she had opened my closet door and that my trap had worked. She began to scream at me and said, "You could have broken my glasses or put out my eye." She also said that Coach Clary would deal me with. I really began to worry. I knew that Coach Clary would settle the score with me, and that I would be punished severely. Usually when you did something bad enough for Coach Clary to get involved, you had gotten yourself into a heap of trouble. I knew that I had done just that. I worried the rest of that afternoon, as Coach Clary didn't come to our cottage until after supper. When he came to the cottage, Mrs. Shellabarger handed him a Rickrack paddle. That was a thin paddle that you would bounce a ball tied to a rubber string. It occurred to me that if he used the Rickrack paddle, it would not hurt and everything would be all right. He drew back and popped my behind with that paddle. On the second blow, the paddle broke in half. He never slowed down one second as he threw the handle to the paddle out of the way. He said, "That's not good enough for you," and punched me right in the gut. Then he let me have it with one more punch to the gut as I fell back across the bed. I was trying to catch my breath when he began shaking me and shouting, "You had better NEVER do a stupid thing like that again." When he left my room, I knew that he felt he had left a good enough message. The message of course, was that I would never do anything like that again. I had asked for the punishment that I received, and I sure got what I asked for. I was lucky not to have been kicked out of the orphanage or sent to a detention camp or training school for troubled youth. I guess at that age some of us boys just didn't think of what the result of our actions would be. We were just plain mischievous and into something all of the time. Most of the time it wasn't bad things, but it seemed we had to be doing something all of the time. I guess if it were today, they would just drug us and make us plum mellow. On the other hand, there were boys who never got into mischief, but I just wasn't one of those types. I wasn't book smart but I could get by without doing my homework just by listening in class. I have always wished that I had put forth more effort, but the dreaming of adventure overruled that prospect. I was very lucky to get to stay at the Home and have someone care for my well-being. I think the home mothers; teachers and other faculty members knew that we boys would try their patience at every chance. A lot of us were stubborn, but the adults really were understanding and cared about our need for a chance at a good future. Maybe they knew the difference between a really bad boy and a boy just plum full of mischief. Everything was a learning experience.

We attended R.J. Reynolds high school off campus, but we had our own high school sports program at the orphanage. The Children's Home was well known in that part of the country for its athletic teams. We never had as many players as the teams we played, but we loved the sport no matter what the game was. I loved football and tried to play the other sports as well, but football was my favorite. Our varsity football coach was Coach Clary and he was all business. He took his sports program very seriously. If you didn't pay attention, you would find yourself running laps around the field until you thought you were going to drop. Coach Clary knew that our football team was much smaller than any of the teams we would play. Some schools that we played had ten to fifteen times as many students as we had. That didn't faze Coach Clary in the least. He just made up for it in conditioning, quickness, stamina and strength. He would run us until we thought we would drop and didn't believe in drinking a whole lot of water during our hot practices. We hardly ever had water at practice. Most of us were already in good shape when the practice season began because we had worked all summer on the farm. We did all kinds of exercises in intensity. We would rock on our stomachs, do push-ups, sit-ups, knee bends, and stretches and run around the field. When the hitting started, we had better be in shape. Coach Clary demanded intense hitting while blocking and tackling our opponent. I just knew that I was ready. Coach Clary would use us younger boys as the defense for his older boys to practice against. I wanted to play right in the middle of things, so Coach Clary let me play defensive guard and/or tackle. I had a tough go of it for a while as the older boys out weighed me by forty to fifty pounds. I wasn't going to give up because I loved the game. I tried my best to hang tough, but I got knocked out of breath ever now and then. Coach Clary thought I should try a little harder. He told his big tackle nicknamed, "Gorilla," to hit me harder and make me tough. "Gorilla" wasn't the real name that WE called him, but I'll just use the name "Gorilla" for my story. Compared to me, this "Gorilla" guy was big and tough and he took the coach's word to try to make me tough. The first team, with all of the older and heavier boys, was smashing right through us young boys on defense. The weight and size difference was enormous to us. Every time "Ole Gorilla" caught me on the bottom of the pile, after a play, he would growl, smack me in the face two or three times with his fist and grunt some more. I would get up for the next play and, wham, on the bottom of the pile I would go and "Ole Gorilla" would beat my face again. I tried my best to stand my ground against "Gorilla," but he was getting the best of me and Coach Clary was shouting, "Hit 'em harder, hit 'em harder." Finally, after one more face pounding on the bottom of that pile, I made up my mind that "Ole Gorilla" could out do me man to man in a football struggle because of his mere size, but he was not going to beat my face anymore. After all, I was supposed to be on his team. In one thirty-minute struggle, he had caused both of my eyes to be nearly closed; he had split my lips, and I had blood running down my jersey from my lips and nose. I got up off the ground and charged after him. Tanner was going to get him. I didn't know what I could do to him but that didn't matter at the moment. I didn't care how big he was. I tried to hit him but that was useless. He had his whole face covered with a plastic shield that was built onto his helmet. No wonder he was so brave to use his fist on other people. Coach Clary grabbed me and asked me what the problem was. I told Coach Clary that "Gorilla" was getting me on the bottom of the pile after the play ended and was beating my face with his fist. He looked at my face and could see my swollen eyes and the blood running down onto my jersey. Coach said, "Get back in there and be tough." I got

201

back in there for another play and again he busted my face after the whistle had blown. I got up out of the pile and told coach, if he wanted "Gorilla" to do that to me, then I'll just quit. He calmly said, "Turn in your gear and report to work on the farm tomorrow during practice." The next day and for the remainder of that week I worked on the farm. The team pictures were taken, and I wouldn't be in them for that year. As I was working, I could see from a distance the team scrimmaging and preparing for their first football game. All of the team was getting their picture taken in their uniform, and I would not be with them that year. I didn't look good in my uniform anyhow as my legs were awful skinny and a football player is supposed to have big legs. Everyday the pressure would build as I would think, "Why isn't GORILLA working at the farm and me playing football?" The next day was the same. I shouldn't be the one working at the farm; I should be playing football. The following Monday I went to Coach Clary and told him that I was going to play football. I had made up my mind that no one was going to run me off of that football field. Besides that, historically, all Children's Home boys played football. I went back to the football field more determined than ever. I took a lot of abuse, but I began to give some back. Anytime that I had a clean shot at "Gorilla" he had better look out. I would try to hit him as hard as I could, but a lot of the times I almost knocked myself out. Some of the others on the team began to see just what kind of person he really was, and things got a little better for me. I didn't fear him and he knew it. I would take my hits and hurt for a while, but he knew that I would hit back a little harder each time. Maybe this was what Coach Clary was trying to get me to do, learn to take the abuse and keep on trying to overcome my opponent. Slap, #*# Bam,#*# Whap! Boy, what a way to be having fun! It was fun part of the time; I think. I wanted to play no matter what. Well, that strategy fell apart as mere size dictated the outcome of every encounter that I had with "Ole Gorilla."

Another day "Gorilla" was with a group of boys in the cornfield up on Arbor Road. They were cutting silage corn with machetes and loading the corn on trailers and trucks. I had finished my normal duties driving the trash truck, and Coach Clary told me to go to the cornfield and haul silage back to the farm for the rest of the day. I drove to the field and began stacking corn stalks on my truck. Suddenly "Ole Gorilla" jumped up on that truck bed and said that I was going to cut corn and wasn't going to drive that truck any more. I told him that I was responsible for the truck and that Coach Clary had told me to drive the truck. About that time, he hit me right between the eyes and knocked me off of the truck. He then jumped on top of me and busted my face up real good. Some of the other boys pulled him off. When the truck was loaded with corn, one of the boys drove me to the infirmary to let Miss Smith see if I needed stitches. Miss Smith wanted to know who had done this to my face. I told her that Coach Clary had told "Gorilla" to make me tough on the football field and ever since that time "Gorilla" has been bullying and beating on me every chance that he got. Miss Smith called Coach Clary to the infirmary to show him what "Gorilla" had done to my face. He told her that he didn't realize that "Ole Gorilla" had carried it that far and said that he would take care of the situation. I thought this would stop the bullying but that didn't stop him from pushing his weight around. His bullying continued until he left the orphanage. It seemed every time that an adult wasn't around; "Ole Gorilla" would do his meanness.

Evidently Coach Clary didn't leave a good enough message to "Ole Gorilla" about beating and bullying me. On one other occasion, I was but one more fist in the face from taking my opportunity to get my revenge. I was supposed to take the trash truck to the local Shell service station to get the oil changed and serviced. I was going to drop the truck off on my way to Reynolds High School and pick the truck up on my way home from school. "Ole Gorilla" tried to take the keys away so that he and some other boys would have a ride part way to school. When I was all cleaned up from my chores and walking to the truck, he stopped me, grabbed me by the front of the shirt and shoved me into the side of the truck door. I had made up my mind that he was not going to get his way even if I had to take another beating. At that time, some of the other boys walked by and he left me alone. He left and began walking to school with the other boys. I went back inside the cottage and washed up a little and tried to settle myself down. My heart was beating out of my chest from standing up to the bully. I was afraid to fight him, but I was determined to fight even if it killed me. I was frightened to death but I was going to fight back. I jumped into the truck and started driving towards the service station. Along the way, I passed the boys walking to school. They were walking on the road since we had no sidewalks. I was just about to pass a group of boys that included "Ole Gorilla." He heard the truck approaching and all of a sudden he jumped out into the road a little bit as if to try to frighten me. What he didn't realize was that I had no intention of putting on the brakes or turning the wheel. Instead, I just pushed in on the clutch, throttled up the engine and continued straight for him. I believe my actions startled "Ole Gorilla" as he jumped back out of the way as fast as he could. To this day I am not sure if I would have stopped that truck to avoid hitting him. The hatred was there; and I believe that one more ounce of abuse from him towards me could have caused both of our lives to be ruined forever. I am happy that this didn't happen to either of us. I hated him for what he did, but he was one of my orphan brothers. Always before, when I had gotten into a fight with one of the other boys, there seemed to be a short time between fighting and being friends again. This situation was different since he was older, much larger and stronger than I. It just seemed that at every opportunity he had to take advantage of me, he did just that. None of the other boys would call him on his actions, fearing perhaps that they would become victims also. When it was time for "Gorilla" to graduate from high school I was very happy to see him leave the orphanage. There seemed to be a feeling of peacefulness within me.

Every time I see a bully today, it brings back memories of how much I hated being beaten by that one individual. I feel for the children today that act out violent behavior from the abuse they have suffered in the presence of older, bully type people. Believe me, the hate builds up slowly; but the hate is genuine. There comes a time, during this mistreatment, when serious thought of how to neutralize this threat becomes reality. I became a very bitter young boy; and I realize now that had I not experienced such abuse, my life may have been much more pleasant living in the orphanage in those years.

I really liked baseball even though I wasn't a super player. I practiced with the team for the entire practice season and was able to play during practice. As the season began, I thought that if I warmed the bench and cheered the team on that the coach would put me in the game to play an inning or two once in a while. I waited and waited with anticipation to get to play in a real game. That was just not going to happen. I never was asked to go in and play one inning or even to get up and bat in any real game in my first varsity year in high school, so I got the message. I thought that was a good enough message for me so I gave it up. I still supported our team though by chasing foul balls, picking up bats and handing out clean towels and fresh jocks. Coach Clary was a super baseball coach and we were fortunate enough to have plenty of other good players on our baseball team.

We still had high school to attend and all of the life that goes with it. I really liked most of the Reynolds High School students with whom I came in contact. Some were a little snobbish, probably because they didn't know us from grammar school, but most were very friendly to us kids from the Children's Home. Most of them came from wealthy and middle class working families and treated us very well. I made a lot of friends at school. I remember some of the Reynolds High girls that I sat near in school. I recall Ginger Simmons. I enjoyed helping her with drawing in Mr. McClain's class. I remember Cleve Fletcher and Sally Glenn were always nice to me in the ninth grade. I used to tease Sally about her dad being a grease monkey, who he wasn't, but teasing was kind of like flirting. Get my drift! Her dad was with Quality Oil Company. Bobby McMillan was a friend of mine until he was killed, along with three other Reynolds students, in a car wreck while driving through the mountains. Bobby's dad was a heart surgeon at Baptist Hospital. Dick Voorhees was always friendly to us Home boys. Butch Edwards was another who showed us special kindness. There were too many boys and girls to mention them all who were our friends at Reynolds High School.

Very seldom did you hear of a student that was a deliberate troublemaker and especially not a Children's Home boy. We would be in serious trouble if we did not mind our manners while at school. Mr. John Tandy, the assistant principal, biology teacher and coach would not tolerate any troublemakers. I really liked him as a teacher in biology, and he always spoke to us in the hall. I had only one scuffle after I went to high school. A boy laughed at me when he deliberately threw ice cream on my chest. The boy was a lot taller but he found out that I was a whole lot bigger than I looked to him.

One day when everyone was coming back from lunch, several of us boys were waiting outside of my English teacher, Mrs. Margie Stevenson's, classroom door. We would always be there on time because she was strict about being ready to start class soon after the bell rang. We used to run all the way back to the Children's Home to have our lunch, and then run all the way back to Reynolds to get there in time for class to start. The Home gave us lunch money the next year so we could buy something in the school cafeteria. Having lunch money we would not have to come home everyday.

On this particular day, I was standing there as I usually did with my arms crossed leaning back against the wall. I had always stood straight with my shoulders back like I was told very early in my life to do. Mr. Tandy walked by and said to me, "You report to my office." I was completely shocked. He had a very gruff voice, and he definitely sounded like he was upset about something. I walked into his office a little bit frightened since I had never been in the Reynolds High School office before. I thought that if I have done something so bad, Coach Clary would surely hear about it back at the Children's Home and then I would be in more serious trouble. Mr. Tandy walked in and closed the door behind him rather roughly. I was standing in front of his desk almost like I was at attention. The first thing out of his mouth was, "You think you are pretty tough, don't you?" As I tried to get out of my mouth, "No sir," he started shouting that I stood out there in the hall every day with my long sleeves rolled up and my arms crossed like I was looking for a fight. I tried to explain to him why my sleeves were rolled up, but I guess he thought that I was trying to be smart alecky. Before I could get my explanation out of my mouth, he shouted, "Roll down those sleeves, and don't let me catch you with them rolled up again." So I rolled down my sleeves as far as they would reach. They were about three or four inches short of where the sleeves should extend. He said, "Boy, those sleeves are a little bit short." I explained to him that a lot of my shirts sleeves were a little short as I have long arms. I explained to him that the reason I always rolled up my shirt sleeves was that I didn't want anybody to see me with my sleeves too short, so short that I couldn't even button them. I explained to him that my shirts were issued to me at the Children's Home clothing room, and that whatever is handed down from the older boys is what they give me to wear. He turned around in his chair and bowed his head. There was a long silence. When he turned to face me, it seemed as though he was trying to regain his composure. He didn't realize that I was one of the Children's Home boys. He lowered his head for a moment, and when he looked up, I saw his eyes were glazed with moisture. Then he spoke and said, "So you are one of the Home boys. I guess you know Herman Bryson, one of our teachers and coaches." I told him that I knew Mr. Bryson and that I see him often at our annual Homecomings. I also told him that Coach Bryson was one of our heroes. Mr. Tandy then apologized for forming the wrong impression of me. He then asked me if I could bring him some cow manure from our dairy farm. I told him that I would ask Coach Clary if it would be all right. He then shook my hand and told me to go on back to class and that he was really sorry. Later on I carried a load of cow manure to Mr. Tandy's house. After carrying the load of manure to Mr. Tandy, he gave me some money, which Coach Clary allowed me to keep. From then on, Mr. Tandy was always nice to me. He would pass where we were standing in the hall, and sometimes he would stop and talk to us Home boys. Mr. Tandy once mentioned to me that he thought being a Navy Chief would be the best job in the world. He said that if he were not teaching that he wished he had stayed in the Navy and become a Navy Chief. Many years later I would stop in for a visit with Mr. Tandy at Holden's Beach where he had retired and dealt in real estate. I told him that I was a Coast Guard Chief. He began to tell me how he had requested help from the Coast Guard in his efforts to rid his community of the drug traffic that plagued his boating and vacation community. I told him that I was part of the patrolling of his area by searching from the air. At that time I think he was the Mayor. We had a nice visit, and that was the last time that I saw Mr. Tandy. Even though there was an initial misunderstanding of my demeanor, I thought highly of Mr. Tandy. His integrity and the moral values that he espoused were demonstrated to us on a daily basis at school.

I went on back to my English class. I always had difficulty with English. I didn't understand why grown men were supposed to talk like they were a little feminine. I found it difficult speaking in front of the class, and I also had a country dialect that I thought wasn't compatible with the English literature. I despised the background in literature that was being used to teach English. I thought that there should be more emphasis on American literature and studies. Mrs. Stevenson thought that I should spend part of my summer changing my attitude towards English. My attitude would never change, and that it almost caused me not to get to play my favorite sport. With constant failing marks in English, all of my other grades would have to be good in order to qualify to play football. I remember one year I needed one point in geometry to be able to play football. I went to Miss Gladstone, soon to be Mrs. Craver, as fast as I could and told her that if I didn't get a passing grade that I would not be able to play football. I told her that I would do anything that she wanted me do to if she would let me have that point. She agreed, and I didn't have any grade problems the rest of the year.

I found that my studies were a struggle for me, but I

also knew that I was able to get passing marks on my grades if I really wanted to. I just didn't study unless it was absolutely necessary. Schoolwork seemed to be so dragged out and boring. It seemed to take forever to cover a simple subject, and I really became bored. I was so involved with life away from schoolwork that I made my schoolwork last on my list of priorities. When it came down to the last minute I really struggled to try to pass. Sometimes within a day of having a test I would try to read as much as I could just to get by. So much of my other world was more interesting to me, and there was so much pressure to do more and more with my time.

When my study time came around, I was so tired that I could not concentrate on my homework. I would dream of some adventure I wanted to do the next day or in the future. If I could have just written about all of my dreams and adventures, I probably would have impressed my English teacher enough for her to throw away that Shakespearean literature. "NAA," There's no way she would be interested in inventions, insects, Daniel Boone, Huck Finn, flying and the Great Western Frontier. She was too proper a lady for such boyish notions. I would struggle, but I knew the struggle was of my own making. This kind of mind set would bring some unnecessary embarrassing feelings to me. I felt, at times, that there would be no other chance to prove myself. I knew I had the ability to score as high as any one of my classmates, but I never arranged my priorities to do my best in school. I wish I could tell every kid in school today just how important balancing studies with other activities really is. To fulfill all of one's dreams you must build a strong foundation of learning, so when the dreams become real, you will be able to function and live within those dreams. Reading one more book can make a difference in a dream becoming a wish or a reality.

Every year when the temperature dropped cold enough during the winter, we would process our hogs. We raised about one hundred hogs every year. Every one of the older farm boys would help with the many stages of processing. Mr. Angell would shoot the hogs, bleed them, and we would carry them to the processing room. There was a tub full of

209

boiling hot water in which we would put the hogs. That made it easier to get the hair off of them. The men would do the carving and we would assist when they needed us. Some of us would chop the fat and skin into chunks. Then we would cook the chunks in a big round cooking pot which had a fire built under it. After the chunks were cooked for a while, we would take the chunks out of the pot and put them in a squeezing press to squeeze all of the fat grease out of the meat. The fat grease was run off into a five-gallon bucket and as it cooled, it turned into white lard, which would be saved for each cottage to use in their cooking. Some times we would be a little mischievous and cut a piece of loin from the meat table. We would push the piece of loin down to the bottom of the cooking pot and let it cook. The men couldn't see our piece of meat cooking on the bottom of the pot. It was our job to keep the fat chunks stirred with a large paddle, so it was easy to hide the meat. After the meat was cooked and we had finished working for the day, we carried our piece of meat up to the gully where we dumped our trash. There we would build a fire and roast that piece of meat over the fire with a coat hanger. That had to be the tastiest piece of pork that I had ever eaten.

Junior, Mr. Hege, Walter and Mr. Gray Todd
preparing meat in curing house

The older men at the processing room would cut and shape the hams. We would then help them salt the hams and put brown sugar on them. Most of the other meat was processed into bacon and other special cuts and carried to the smoke house or around to the different cottages. We always had chunks of ham in our beans and other vegetables as seasoning. We loved getting into that brown sugar. When the fat was pressed out of the chunks of meat, the remaining product was called "cracklings." We loved getting into those crackling cakes. Some people call them "pork rinds" or "pork skins." They were delicious and sometimes we would eat so many that our throats would get sore. We could now see that some of the hard work that we did had its rewards. Every job we did, we learned a little more about life all around us.

One day seemed to be the worst day of my life at the orphanage. My home mother told us that "Pop" Woosley had died and that we could go to his funeral. That really upset me since "Pop" was not supposed to die. "Pop" was as close to being a father as many of us would ever know. He was the one that brought me to "My Home." He had retired but he was not supposed to die. I walked to the Centenary church in Winston-Salem to say good-bye to "Pop." It was a sad walk, and I really didn't want for my walk to end. I had a feeling that I would not want to see what was waiting for me on the other end of that walk. I tried to be brave, but it was hard for me to keep from crying when I saw "Pop" lying in that big box. I loved "Pop" but I couldn't get to close to that box. I was afraid of what I saw and afraid of a dead man. I had never been to a funeral before, and I never wanted to come back to another one. As I walked into the church many of the other orphan children were already there. There were a lot of big people there also as "Pop" had a lot of big people friends. A lot of the girls and boys were crying, as it was the saddest occasion that I had ever had to experience.

My walk home was equally as rough. Seeing "Pop" like that gave me some very strange feelings. It seemed to me that I felt a little dizzy and couldn't clear my head for some time. I walked home by myself, as I didn't want anybody to see me crying. I walked home using the back roads so people driving by would not see me. We all wore our Sunday suits to the funeral and all of the boys walked over to Centenary Church and back. I didn't feel good for several days after the funeral. I thought of "Pop" often, and I knew that I would never again feel his gentle touch rubbing my head and saying that I was one of his children. He had become feeble and his hands were shaky before he retired from the orphanage. We had a new Superintendent named Mr. Lambeth who had taken "Pop's" place when he retired. Although this new man was looking after the children, he didn't seem to have that magical touch in showing us children we were "his" children. Nobody could take "Pop's" place that didn't show a loving feeling for all four hundred of us. I hardly ever saw "Pop" without his arm around one of us children. He had a gentle smile on his face, as he would talk to each of us. Mr. Lambeth was a very proper, nice and soft-spoken man, but there was something missing. "Pop" was the one that we had all grown up with and the man we thought of as our real "Pop." I didn't feel good for several days, and I knew that I never wanted to see anyone else ever die.

I was in Mrs. Stevenson's English class when she brought in a colored girl one day and introduced her to the class as Gwendolyn Bailey. She said, "Gwendolyn will be attending our class for the remainder of the year." She sat Gwendolyn down in the desk next to me. There had never been any colored folks that had attended this school before. Some of the kids in class grunted out loud as if to make some sort of gesture. I had played in the pasture with colored boys, but I was not familiar with colored girls. I had no reason to be unkind to the girl, and I introduced myself. I asked her if she knew Alvin and some of the other colored boys that we played with in the woods and fields. That was not a popular thing to do, and I sensed some dirty looks on my way out of the classroom. I didn't fear any threats, as there were several orphan boys in my class with me. Then we looked out the windows of our school and saw grownups coming down the driveway in cars and shouting all sorts of epithets about black folks coming to our school. Some were painting slogans on the auditorium walls and the flagpole. The police came in cars and restrained the crowd of parents. The police were there when we left the school building and some escorted the black children away from the school. As days passed, things cooled off and the colored children were a normal sight in our school. I thought as school went on, "Did Mrs. Stevenson put Gwendolyn next to me because I was the dumbest in my class?" Ah! That couldn't be the reason. Gwendolyn made straight A's on every test that year. I didn't fair so well with my Ds and Fs.

There was much farm work to be done during the summers. Summertime meant that a lot of work would be expected of us. There were a variety of jobs around the Home. The boys as well as the girls spent many hours of the day helping prepare for the upcoming winter. The boys worked on the big farm or dairy farm all day and sometimes into the night harvesting grain, taking care of the corn fields, filling the hay barns, straw barns and filling the silos with Milo or chopped corn stalks called silage. Mr. Angell, our farm manager, would combine wheat, barley or oats until dark. It was a very dusty job working on that combine. The boy who tied the string around the top of the grain sack would wear a rag around his face to help keep the dust out of his throat. One of the boys would work with Mr. Angell on the combine. His job was to catch the grain as it came out of the chute. The chute had a double outlet that was controlled with a lever. As one bag was filled the boy would switch the lever to the other outlet while he was tying a string at the top of the full bag of grain. After the string was tied to the full bag of grain then another bag was fastened to that chute. Then the full bag was pushed down a slide chute onto the ground. All of that grain was lying in the field in grain sacks and had to be picked up before the dew or rain could get it wet.

Mr. Angell combining wheat

Gray Todd and Mr. Angell
cutting hay

When the hay was cut and dried in the field, sometimes it was picked up the old way, with pitchforks. In later years, the hay was baled with a hay baler and the bales were dropped on the ground in the field. Mr. Gray Todd or Mr. Angell usually did this hay cutting and baling job. That hay also had to be picked up before it could get wet. If the hay got wet it would mold or start a fire in the barn from combustion. Several nights during the summer we would finish picking up the grain or hay around nine or ten o'clock.

The swimming pool was always kept open for us no matter how late we worked. We were allowed to swim for an hour after work. Coach Clary always saw to that. Always too tired and hot to eat, I would drink a pitcher of ice-cold milk and head to the pool to cool off. After we came home from the pool, we would just pass out into our beds and find ourselves awakening to another day of the same. It was hard work, but there was something about getting that last load of grain or hay loaded and riding on the back of the truck, in the cooler air, on the way back to the orphanage from our other farms. I loved the sound of that truck loaded to the max and in first gear climbing the hill coming into the Home entrance. Sometimes I would be driving, and I loved driving a fully loaded truck and getting to change those gears. That was as much fun as playing in the sandbox when we were a little younger, and driving our trucks through the sand.

Hauling hay on wagon

Working around the farm had its hazards that we all had to deal with and Bill, a boy just slightly older than most of us, always seemed to take a few bruises from time to time. One day we were gathering hay the old fashion way. After the hay was cut and dried in the field, a tractor pulling a hay rake would rake the hay into rows. Another tractor pulling a large hay wagon would pull along side the rows of hay, as boys with pitchforks would scoop up the hay and toss it up onto the wagon. When the wagon was loaded, it was then pulled back to the barn to be unloaded in the hayloft. At the barn there was a rig called a spider that would lift the hay up from the wagon into the loft. The spider was pulled up by a rope from the track in the top of the barn. There was a set of large doors at the top of the barn that could open to let the hay be carried inside the loft. The overhead track allowed the spider to roll down the entire length of the barn. A tractor, pulling from the other end of the barn, was used to pull the rope that lifted the spider and carried it down the track in the barn. When the spider reached the spot where we wanted the hay to be dropped, we would pull a trip rope that was attached to the spider. This caused the spider to open and release its hold on the hay. Bill's job that day was to set the spider jaws into the hay on the wagon. When he had the spider set, another boy would signal the tractor driver on the other end of the barn to begin pulling. When the spider started up with a load of hay, Bill still had his hand on the spider. Suddenly there was a whole lot of shouting. Bill's hand was hung in the jaws of that spider. His fingers were lifting him up into the barn. He was screaming, "Stop the tractor! Stop the tractor!" Finally, the tractor was stopped and backed up so that Bill could free his hand. He was lucky that day to have only a few fingers mashed.

Unloading hay into the barn loft

He wasn't so lucky another day while hauling baled hay. He was riding on the back of a truck, and the hay was tied on with ropes. Bill's foot got tangled in one of the ropes as he slipped and fell from the back of the truck. He was dragged for some distance over the sandstone road. It seemed that orphans could always take a bruising and somehow get over it. He recovered well and the injuries never slowed him down. On still another day while we were again hauling hay, my friend Frank was giving directions to the hay truck driver. He was motioning to the driver to come on back. He had his hand on the back of the truck as the truck bed made contact with the barn door. Frank's hand was smashed and was badly damaged. He was in a lot of pain as he was carried to the Baptist Hospital for surgery. After quite a bit of surgery and a lot of therapy, Frank's hand was back to near normal. Frank was still able to do well in sports, and he never let his

injuries stop him from doing what he enjoyed. He became
a star baseball pitcher in high school.

One day we were hauling hay from the Shoffner Farm,
about six miles away from the Home, on Peace Haven road.
We had been picking up hay bales from a field that had a
very poor quality of hay. We were driving all over the field
trying to get a full load. We would go back and forth across
the terraces and the hay that we had stacked on the truck
bed would loosen up and not be packed tight like most of
the hay that we would load. When we got the truck loaded
and headed out from the farm onto the paved highway we
ran into another nearly disastrous event. We had a large
number of boys getting in hay that particular day. The
only way the boys could get back home from the Shoffner
farm was to ride on the truck so all of the boys were riding
on top of the hay bales that were stacked on the back of
the truck. The hay was not stacked as well as most of the
good alfalfa hay that we normally carried. It was very light
with a lot of grass mixed into it. We had no ropes to tie the
hay securely to the truck. In addition, we had an unusual
number of boys riding on top of the hay that day. None of
us felt very secure about riding on top of the hay. We had
the truck stacked with as much hay as we could get on it.
We slowed down for telephone lines crossing the road, and
lifted the lines over the top of the hay bales and us until
the truck passed under the lines. There were about five of
us sitting on the top front of the haystack. My friend Allen
was sitting at the front on the right outside corner. He was
very afraid as the hay bales would shift at the least
movement of the truck, and there was no rope to hold the
hay onto the truck or for one to grasp for support. Allen
asked me if I would swap places with him. I said "Sure,"
with a trace of nervousness in my voice. Then I moved to
the outside position. At that age we all had to prove how
brave we were. We probably drove no further than a half
mile on Peace Haven road. We were going through a steep
leaning curve. When we started into the curve, I could feel
the hay beginning to separate and everyone yelled, "It's
falling off; look out; hold on!" All of the boys scrambled to
protect themselves, but there was nothing to hold on to.
The hay bales were bouncing in every direction. As the hay

separated, I dropped straight down to the edge of the truck bed and grabbed the first thing I could feel to hang onto. Mr. Finney, the driver, gradually stopped the truck and jumped out to see if anyone was hurt. There were boys scattered everywhere, covered in hay bales. It just so happened that the spot that I had switched with Allen went inward as the hay bales separated. Allen went straight down to the bed of the truck and bounced off the bed and down to the pavement. He was hidden under all of that hay along with a number of the other boys. Several of the boys were hurt as we uncovered everybody, but Allen was hurt badly. His head was lying in front of the rear truck tire. The driver had stopped just in time to not run over Allen. The rear tire had made contact with Allen's head and pushed on his face hard enough to do structural damage to his face. The ambulances were coming with the sirens screaming, and everybody was trying to help. All of the local residents turned out to help. They put the injured boys on the bank of the road and tried to comfort the boys. It was the first time in my life that I felt like I was in shock. I had a very strange feeling. It was not a good feeling along with being nauseated. I suppose in those days, people just didn't look for someone who was in shock. Allen was carried to the hospital in an ambulance along with several other boys, but Allen had to stay. We were all worried about one of our brothers. We didn't hear anything for a long while, and then finally we heard that after a little surgery, Allen would be coming home. Of course he wouldn't have all of his teeth and he would never breathe the same way as before the accident. It was still a great relief to me, as I felt bad that he was hurt, and that I had switched places with him on the truck. Allen recovered enough from his injuries and was able to play sports in a reasonably short time.

Don, Glenn, Mr. Finney, Bob, Bill, and Brock
loading baled hay

Sometimes the hazards were from just being around a
bunch of orphans with their usual Orphan Humor trickery.
Every time we would go to another one of our farms called
Salem Bottoms to hoe the cornfields we played a certain
trick on all of those who were unaware. After a long day of
hoeing corn in the fields, everyone was tired and ready to
go home. All of the boys would jump up on the truck and
sit down with their legs dangling off the sides. The truck
had a metal band all the way around the bed to hold the
planks together and to hold the sideboards when they were
used. We always parked in the shade next to an electric
fence. When everyone had a drink of water from the large
milk can, we would put the can and our hoes up on the
truck. Leave it up to a few of the mischievous orphans to
hang one of the hoes from the bed of the truck down to the
electric fence. When no one was looking the boys would
pour the left over water onto the hoe and let it run down
the hoe handle to the electric fence. As soon as that water
hit that electric fence, everybody on the truck would jump
right up into the air and shout, "Oh," grab their buttocks,
and look around to see who had done that dirty trick.
There were a lot of grins from the boys that had been
tricked before, but no one would 'fess up to the prank.

We were getting in hay bales late in the afternoon at

220

the Shoffner farm one day when the Orphan Humor and trickery just had to continue. Carl and Jody were stacking the hay on the truck as we threw the hay bales up to them. The hay bales had to be stacked high on the truck and some of them were pretty heavy. A few of us on the ground would grab hold of the bed of the truck, and the truck would drag us to where another bale of hay was waiting to be picked up and tossed onto the truck. By now you know boys and the tricks they will play on each other if and when the opportunity presents itself. Orphan Humor! As I was dragging along behind the truck, I heard a big thud and felt the most terrible pain in my knee that I had ever experienced. Carl and Jody had thrown a heavy bale of hay down from the truck and it landed on the back of my legs. I let go of my handhold on the truck bed and just lay there. I couldn't move. The truck kept going as if nothing ever happened. I tried to get up, but my leg was in so much pain that I was just stuck there. All the boys were laughing and thought that I was faking being hurt. Orphan Humor You Know! I lay there as I watched the truck roll over the hill and out of sight. I thought for sure that they would stop for me but they didn't. I was in a lot of pain, and I couldn't move my leg. It was getting late, and I knew that I was going to be left in that field all night. Suddenly, one of the boys came back to check on me. When the boy saw how much pain I was in, he took off over the hill screaming for help. It wasn't long before the farm manager drove up in his pickup truck. He and the other boy picked me up and took off in the pickup truck, driving me back to the Home infirmary. Coach Gibson came running over from his house next door and drove me to the Baptist Hospital. When the hay bale had struck the back of my leg, it separated and tore the tendons in my knee. When the doctors finished treating me, they put a cast on my leg that went from my ankle to my upper thigh. I just knew that I would not get to play football when the season started. Playing football was more important to me than eating. I just had to hurry up and get well. Learning to climb stairs with crutches and a cast like that was quite a challenge. I fell backwards several times, but after many tries, I eventually became successful at it.

I got my cast off in time for football season but my leg was mighty skinny and weak. I had skinny legs anyway and the cast had made one even smaller. I worked out pretty hard and by the time our games started I was strong enough to play. We had a good season in football that year. It was a lot of fun playing for Coach Gibson. We all had close ties to him from school, from the Boy Scouts and from his being our coach when we were younger. He ran us hard and was serious about the game, but he let us enjoy the contests and we wanted to play to win. He always built you up with praises of accomplishment and showed you how to be better. We all gave him our best all of the time. Coach Gibson had some big shoes to fill; he had taken over the varsity football-coaching job from Coach Clary. He not only filled the shoes of Coach Clary, but also did the job while building up a super team in just a few years. The Children's Home had had a lot of glory years in football in years past, but none in recent years. The winning cycle seemed to be returning again, but this time Coach Gibson would be at the helm. I could feel the spirit and desire that permeated the entire squad. I could just feel the speed and the strength growing within my teammates. With every practice and every game we got better and more confident. We played as a team, hit hard and played the game with true sportsmanship. Every player was important to Coach Gibson. He made us feel that we could accomplish anything even though we were outweighed in most of our conference contests. We played down to the last second of every game and sometimes that would win the game for us.

Coach Gibson continued to be a big part of the boys' lives while he was the leader in many areas. He was concerned about our health and our physical well-being. He was a good moral leader with a sense of humor and friendship with all of his boys. If we ever had a coach that felt to us like real family, it was Coach Gibson. All of our coaches were great but Coach Gibson and Coach Edwards grew up there at the Home. No doubt this gave them something extra in their coaching. I call it the "personal touch."

Chapter Eight

Well, what do you know? I finally made it to the senior boys' cottage. This was a new cottage named after John W. Hanes, and the place where I would spend my last two years at the Children's Home. We boys thought we were something, finally getting to live in a cottage where the oldest boys lived. I had lived in the Baby Cottage and every boy's cottage at the orphanage. We had quite a bit more freedom than anywhere else we had lived. I first shared a room with a boy named Talmadge. Talmadge was one of those very quiet boys that liked art and studied a lot. I never knew of a time that Talmadge ever got a spanking while he was growing up at the Home. He was just a good boy but he never tattled on us more mischievous types. If I had studied just a little more, like Talmadge, then I probably would have graduated with honors. My life was just too filled with being all boy and getting into all boy kinds of mischief. Talmadge also had a half brother named Jimmy Summers that lived at the Home. They were both well-behaved boys.

There was a small roadside market, called the Robin Hood Curb Market, just outside the Home property that we boys would frequent often at night to get a snack. If I had a little money, I would always get a box of vanilla wafers and an orange juice drink. That was my favorite snack. The market had a fence around it to keep people from walking in and taking things after hours and it would stay open until about eleven at night. I would hear from time to time about some of the boys that would raid the market. They said they would spread the chain link fence and go inside and take some things. That really bothered me because the man that ran the market would give us a piece of candy or something once in a while. He was always good to me. He knew we were Home boys and we didn't have much. I didn't think much of the boys that would do that to a man so kind to us. If I had said anything about it, I would surely have gotten another black eye. If I told on them to an adult, I would be hated and beaten up for sure. One thing you didn't want to happen to you while living at the orphanage was to be hated by the other boys in your cottage. Living as an orphan was tough enough but living there and being picked on all of the time, as some were, was extremely depressing and pure hell. Having friends to play with was the only thing worth living for while we were growing up. Getting into mischief is one thing most all of us boys did, but stealing from another person was a terrible thing to do. We would take a few old cakes from that Mr. Angell was going to feed to the hogs, but that was more mischievous behavior that we had learned from the older boys.

One of the most enjoyable events that we orphans had every year was a trip to Hanging Rock State Park during the summer. We had a one-day event about every year that I can remember. As we became older we were able to participate in more activities at the park. When I was younger I had wanted to be able to row a boat out into the lake by myself like the big boys did. Now I was a big boy, and I could row for a pretty girl just as big boys had done in the past. I took all of the girls and some of the home mothers for a ride. I was proud to take my home mothers for a ride to show them what a big boy I had become. I

224

never got tired of rowing that boat. We were able to climb to the top of the Hanging Rock Mountain. It was quite a hike to the top, but the scenery was beautiful and worth the long hike. Some of the boys would walk their girlfriends to the top on a romantic journey. We would have our picnic lunch there and swim when we got hot. The water was always nice and cool. When the day ended, everyone was tired as we crawled into the back of the grain trucks and buses and headed home. When we reached Reynolda Road and turned into the orphanage, we all sang "The Children's Home Song." We could hear the singing from the vehicle in front of us, and we all joined in with our song. We sang it each time we returned from a trip and started up the entrance of our Children's Home. Someone would start off and the rest would join in with the song we loved so much.

The Children's Home Song

We're the girls and boys from the Children's Home And a merry band are we. We work and we play and we're hap-py all the day. As girls and boys should be. I am proud of my home, Is my home proud of me. What she needs is girls and boys trained in loyalty. When we work, When we play, With our fel-low men, Good cit-i-zens we will be For I am Proud I am proud of the Children's Home And I'll make her proud of me.

We all had a good time going to high school and playing sports. Some of the boys were dating girls from the high school who lived in town. Sometimes they would have to walk a great distance to the girl's house. They would have a date on Friday or Saturday night instead of the Children's Home way where we could only have a date on Sunday night from seven till nine. Sometimes if they were a little late coming in, we would cover for them by telling the home mother that they were in the bathroom when she came around to check.

Mrs. Davidson was our home mother. She had three sons to grow up in the Home. Big Jim was several years ahead of us in school. Then there was Bill who was a year ahead of us and Bob who was a year behind us. They were all good boys. Mrs. Davidson was a nice lady, and we really didn't mean to cause her any grief, but we were a bunch of boys who always had to make up some sort of fun to keep us occupied and entertained. That was just the way it seemed to be. Some of us would do things just to be accepted or to prove we were not afraid to do what ever it was. Anything we did to prove to the other boys that we were brave or strong would win us some credibility and friendships or so we thought. Sometimes we would get into trouble or things would backfire, and we would really make a fool of ourselves.

Mrs. Davidson's middle son Bill survived a nasty accident while milking the cows early one morning. We had two milk crews and we would rotate everyday with the milking chores. We would get up about four thirty or five in the morning. Just about everyone of our milk cows would become very gentle soon after we would begin to milk them for their first time. As the cows got older and used to being around us, several of the cows would let you lay across their backs as we would walk them up from the lower pasture to bring them into the milking room. Most of the time it was completely dark, but the cows had a sense of who we were, and they were not afraid of us. We knew every one of the seventy or so cows by name. Most would be easy to lead to the stanchions where we would lock their heads while we milked them. We would bring so many into the milk room and then close a wooden gate to keep the cows inside the room. We could walk all around the cows and they would never spook. On one particular morning, Bill was walking behind a new cow that had just started being milked regularly. Evidently something spooked this young cow. That cow kicked Bill right in the face with both feet. Bill went through the air and was thrown through the wooden gate. "Big Stew," Bill's milk crew leader saw what the young cow had done to Bill and ran to help care for him. The boys picked Bill up and drove him to the infirmary in the milk truck. Bill was in an awful shape. That cow had kicked several of his teeth out and had broken bones in his face. After "Stew" got back to the milk barn, he said, "That cow will never hurt another one of my boys." He smacked that cow, and he did a few other things, nearly knocking that bovine to the ground. The cow was not suitable to work around without danger to one of the boys, so Dad Shaver decided to put the cow in the beef barn until the appropriate time to make beef. The cows never hurt the boys intentionally, but from time to time, one of those big bovines would lean towards you and step on your bare feet while you were trying to milk her. We would always push our head into their side; just in front of their rear leg and usually that would keep the cow from kicking the milk bucket or creeping over to step on someone's foot. We would wash the cow's bag and utters with a little warm water and disinfectant and begin the milking process. If the cow had good milk that could be put in with other cow's milk, then we would use our central milk vacuum on those cows. The milk vacuum system would milk the cows down to a certain point. Then we would hand milk the cows until not another drop would come out. We called that "stripping." If we didn't do the "stripping" the cows milk glands would become clogged with mastitis. If that happened we would have to milk all of the milk out by hand until the mastitis cleared up. Most of our cows gave several gallons of milk twice a day. We had close to a hundred cows, but an average of about fifty were ready to be milked twice a day.

We always would be working at the farm or dairy barn so you can imagine the smell from the clothes of twenty five to thirty hard working boys. We would try to keep our rooms clean the best we could. We would try to get a couple of days wear out of a pair of work trousers before we would wash them in our laundry room. We then hung the trousers up on a hook in our closet. You just couldn't get rid of that dairy barn smell unless you stripped yourself of all of your clothes outside of the cottage. We didn't want to leave our work boots out in the rain so they had to go into the closet. In the John W. Hanes cottage, most of us washed our own clothes in a couple of washing machines in our laundry room. We all learned how to iron our own shirts that we wore to high school without burning them. Even today I help my wife by ironing my shirts. I learned so well how to do this chore at the Home.

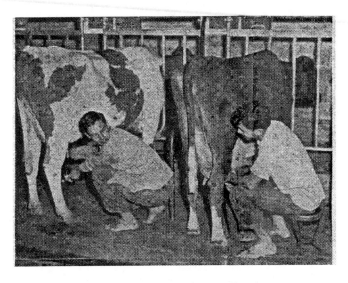

Lyndon and Robert milking

At one time or another most of us were on a milk crew. If you were on the milk crew you would get up early and go to the barn and milk an average of fifty cows. We would frequently run to the barn barefooted and slip on a pair of rubber boots, if we could find a left and a right that would fit. A lot of times we just wouldn't wear any boots. If a cow stepped on top of your foot while barefooted, it hurt just as bad as if you were wearing boots. Each cow weighed over a thousand pounds so you can imagine that sharp hoof standing on the top of your foot. The more you would push on the cow's side to get it off of your foot, the more the cow would lean that much harder in your direction. There were probably many boys with broken bones in their feet as often their foot would swell and turn blue. After the swelling went down, we would go about our playing and working as usual.

Once in a while I would grab a turnip out of the turnip patch to nibble on while I was walking to the milk barn. I would rub the dirt off of the turnip and break off the leaves. The turnips seemed to get real sweet in the fall when the night air turned a little colder.

If the snow hadn't turned to ice, we sometimes ran barefooted to the barn with snow on the ground. We ran as fast as we could so that we would not have to stink up our work boots. That just shows you how smart and brave we adolescent boys were.

Eddie Newsome told me, when I was a little younger, that if I stepped in every fresh cow pie that I saw on the ground that I would grow just as tall as he was. He said to be sure that the cow pies squeeze between my toes and that would fertilize me. I noticed over the years that I hadn't grown anywhere near his seven foot tall stature, but I continued to step in those cow pies as I ran across the barn yard barefooted in the cold weather. The cow pies may not have helped me grow up to be a big man, but I remembered that they were warm.

Sometimes the barn cats and their kittens would come into the milking room in hopes that we would squeeze the cow's "teat," and squirt some milk in their direction. The cats would stand up on their hind legs and try to catch the milk that we would squirt towards them. We became pretty good at directing the cow's milk to the cats. It was funny to watch, as the cats would sometimes fall over backwards while trying to catch the milk.

Sometimes we would milk a cow that had just had a calf. That cow would take an extra amount of time to milk. Any cow that had a calf recently would not produce clear white milk for a while, so that cow's milk had to be kept separate from the other cow's milk. When the calves were separated from their mother and put into the calf barn, they would still need to have special care for a while. These younger calves were still fed milk; at first through a large nipple bottle and then they would start drinking from a bucket. There were usually four or five baby calves in the calf barn at any one time. They were the favorite attraction when young children came to visit the dairy.

Almost as good as mama's milk

We would always try to finish milking early enough to get back to our cottage and take a hot shower before breakfast. We would really scrub ourselves good so that none of the barnyard smell would linger and be noticed when we were in class sitting next to a pretty girl. Some of the boys were very sensitive. They did not want the city girls knowing where they lived. I was always proud to be from the orphanage, and the girls knowing that didn't bother me, but I surely didn't want that barnyard smell on me when I went to school and sat next to them in class.

One evening after a heavy snowstorm I thought of another mischievous boy thing to do. "Dad" Shaver, our dairy manager, had a daughter named Edie who was in the same grade as I. We had been good friends for as long as I had known her. Edie was dating another boy at our cottage named Walter. I thought that I would go up to her house after dark and build a snowman in her front yard. I wanted to see if Edie would say anything about a snowman suddenly appearing in her yard. When I got to their house and began trying to roll up a ball of snow, the snow wouldn't roll. The snow had frozen solid. I tried several times to scrape up enough snow but I was wasting my time. I walked around to the back yard to try to scrape up some snow but the snow was frozen there also. I kicked and kicked the top of the snow to see if I could break the top cover of snow loose. All of a sudden out of the corner of my eye, I saw Edie's Dad looking out of the window. I bet he thought, "What kind of an idiot is that?" I thought to myself, "Boy, I am in trouble if Dad Shaver finds out who the idiot is." I just walked on back to my cottage, and as I looked around behind me, I could see Edie's Dad following my tracks in the snow. I knew that he was going to catch me so I hurried on into the cottage. I never heard a single word about my snowman adventure.

When springtime came, Coach Gibson asked me if I would like to coach the young boys ball team. I told him that Coach Clary had asked me to be an umpire for the junior boys in the city league. He mentioned that I could work my umpire schedule around our boys' games. I told him that I would like to coach the junior boys. This would be an experience of a lifetime. I remembered when I was a junior boy that Coach Gibson was my coach. I thought that was a big deal. I began to coach the young boys and really tried to give them the experience that had been imparted to me. I would make them run laps just like Coach Clary did to us big boys for being late, but I didn't have the influence that our grown coaches had and that just didn't work. The boys just didn't want to run the laps. I continued to do my best at coaching the boys. We would play some of the other schools in the city and the city schools would come to play against us. Some days I would have to go to another school and umpire a game that they were playing. When our team played another school in town, I would drive our team there in the bus. One particular day, I drove to a school with our team and found that the city umpire manager had scheduled both team's coaches to be umpires for their own game. I didn't know how this would work if there were a dispute between one umpire and the other team. I talked with the other team's coach, and he thought that we could get through the game without incident. I agreed and we let the game begin. The boys on both teams were playing a good game and everything was going along just fine. The score was very close and the game came down to the last inning. Their team was able to get a runner on first, but we were ahead by one run. There were two outs and the runner on first was the tying run. The batter hit the ball and the ball was thrown to the second baseman. The second baseman was a few feet off of his bag and the runner ran right into his glove and he tagged the runner out. I was the bases umpire, and I shouted, "Out." The plate umpire, who also was coach for the other team, came running out to second base and shouted "Safe." The other coach and I were in the same class at high school. We had never had a disagreement, but this would be one to remember. The shouting became louder and louder. Our team didn't have any spectators like the parents on the other team, but I wouldn't back down from my call. The runner was out and that was all there was to it. Our boys won a fair and well played game, and I called a fair game, so I wasn't backing down for anyone. After the screaming subsided, I got the boys on the bus and headed for home. I thought to myself about the times that I had seen both Coach Clary and Coach Gibson take a stand when they thought their boys were right. Our boys were proud of their coach for his bravery and not letting someone take their win away. I sure hope that I was right. Maybe this would win me some points when we got back to our practice and made one of them run around the field for being late. Nope! Didn't work!

Every time that we had the opportunity we would go to the pasture and woods to play. We would walk along the creek and look at the minnows and crawfish scurrying as we passed by them. Sometimes we would try to catch a crawfish and put it in a tin can. The crawfish were not real big but the little claws on the female really hurt when they would pinch your finger. The females had red color on their claws, just like a girls fingernail polish. Sometimes we would carry a piece of string and a strait pin and try to catch some of the minnows. We would bend the pin to look like a fishhook. Sometimes we would be lucky enough to catch a few of the minnows. We would stop at the spring, stoop down on our knees and cup our hands into the spring water to dip up a nice cool drink. We would try to catch a dragonfly or a butterfly as we walked towards the woods. There was a cave dug into the hillside of the pasture that much older boys had dug many years before our time. The cave wasn't very far inside. Gray Todd and Coach Gibson said they had dug in the cave when they lived at the orphanage as boys. That was a well-known landmark to remember by many of the boys who lived at the orphanage.

Some days we would walk down the creek and through a culvert under Reynolda Road. We continued down the creek and passed under two more culverts under Robin Hood Road and Buena Vista Road. We would end up on the Hanes property, where we would be in a bamboo thicket. We chose a nice stalk of bamboo and cut it down. We made a vaulting pole, about twelve feet long, from the stalk. After backtracking up the creek we reached our pasture. We then used our bamboo pole to vault back and forth across the creek. We would run real fast and jam our pole into the creek bank and fly across the creek. We really had a good time. We went higher and higher as we felt more secure holding on to our long pole. Some days we would take bamboo poles to the football field where we had a jumping pit full of sawdust. We dug a little hole on the edge of the pit so that our vaulting poles would not slip when we placed them on the ground. Then we sailed into the air. We would run as fast as we could and vault ourselves into the air. Each time we tried we would get a little higher. Each time I vaulted a little higher, I got a few more stars in my head when I landed and felt like I had broken my teeth. That sawdust had been in the pit all year and had packed down very hard.

My thoughts went back several years to when I was much younger. At that time I heard that George Holland and Fred Walton were planning to vault over the goal post on the football field. I had remembered seeing them with their bamboo poles when I was a very young boy. Now I thought that they were really brave big boys for attempting something like that. I decided that I would try to make a few runs at the goal post. I practiced for a while, getting a little higher each time, until I could grab the cross bar and hold myself up with my pole. That was stimulating enough but then I thought about what would happen if I make that daring vault over the goal post. I thought of all the glory I would get when the boys realized that I was brave enough to vault over the goal post. Then I thought of all the stars I had seen when I landed in that sawdust pit. If I made that famous vault, I would probably kill myself when I landed on that hard ground. I rationalized further that if I were dead then it wouldn't matter much if all of my teeth were broken out. I decided that I didn't want to feel the pain from falling on the ground, so I gave up any idea of vaulting over the goal post. However, we would continue to play with our vaulting poles. The next year, Coach Gibson arranged for all of us boys to go a few miles up Reynolda Road to Wake Forest University where the Wake Forest boys had agreed to show us a few nuances about track and field events. It was really a treat to have real college boys show us how to do things. Coach Gibson had bought an aluminum-vaulting pole that was much lighter and had much more spring in it. I joined in with the vaulting team and listened to what the college boys had to say. We listened as they explained and demonstrated how to drop the pole in the hole and begin the lift upward. I thought, "I can do that," and I really believed that I could vault nearly as high as those college boys. When I started practice at home, I would run for the pit and drop my pole in the hole and really get into the air. Each time Coach Gibson would say, "Fault." I asked him what I was doing wrong. He said that I would have to hold my top hand in place instead of dropping my top hand down to my bottom hand. All of those years of vaulting across the creeks with my bamboo pole, I would always drop my top hand down to the bottom hand. It just felt more natural, and besides, what difference did that make? Those were the rules, and I never could break that bad habit.

Sometimes Coach Gibson would take us to Hanes Park where the Reynolds High School boy's track team practiced. They had a regulation running track and at times there would be a real track meet going on that we could watch. At that time the track was made of packed sand and gravel, which seemed to slow us down when we would run against each other. I was used to running on grass or hard packed roadbeds. A lot of the running that I was used to was when we ran through the woods and open pastures in our work boots, nothing like runners have today. Tennis shoes were thin soled and felt flat on our feet. In fact, some people said if we wore them very long we would become flatfooted. I never liked running around a track. I loved to run in the woods where I could jump over a log or a ditch. Jumping over a creek bed without getting wet was an everyday challenging thrill.

One day while I was walking through the pasture on the way to the woods behind Little White Church, I noticed a wild dog walking towards a pile of stumps. I ducked down so the dog could not see me. I saw the dog stop and look around to see if anything were watching it. Then the dog crawled into the pile of stumps. Very cautiously, I crept up close to the stump pile to see what was going on. As I got closer I could hear what sounded like puppies crying. I slowly eased back away from the stump pile and ran back home to my cottage. There I found some of my orphan buddies watching television. I told them what I had found and asked them if they wanted a puppy. We were not allowed to have pet dogs, but I figured if we kept them in the woods that none of the adults would know about it. I created some real excitement in that bunch of boys. They all agreed to go to the pasture with me to get a puppy. I didn't want to go back by myself because that dog might decide to attack me. I should have learned from my earlier years that if you mess with a dog, that dog is likely to get mad and bite you. I wanted to see what those puppies looked like so I ventured on with my plan to check things out. When we got back to that pile of stumps, we were not sure if the big dog had left the den or not, so we made some noise and began shaking a stick down into the entrance of the den. We didn't hear any growling so I cautiously went head first down into the den to see if I could pull out the puppies. I would move a few feet into the stumps and then make some more noise and then move a little further inside. It was frightening the whole way into the den, but I finally made it to the puppies. I couldn't see what I was grabbing, but I would grab one ball of fur at a time and crawl all the way back out of the den. Then back in I would go. When I had pulled the last puppy out of the den,

the total number reached eleven. No two of them were the
same color. We picked up the puppies and carried them
back to our cottage. We put them in the boiler room for the
night and brought them some milk and food from our
supper table. The next day we went into the woods behind
our cottage and built our pets a pen and puppy house.
They were a lot of fun to play with as the pups had a lot of
energy. A few of the pups were very shy at first, but soon
began to play with the others. Most of the boys had
already picked the pet that they wanted. I picked a little fat
puppy with red fur so thick that it looked like just a ball of
fur. We would take the puppies out of the pen and let
them play on our grassy lawn. They were really funny to
watch as they would run and play until they would drop.
Then they would just fall asleep in the warm sun. It wasn't
long before our home mother heard about the puppies that
we had in the woods behind our cottage. She was
somewhat alarmed because we were not allowed to have
the pups. She was also concerned about the possibility of
one of them having rabies. She contacted Coach Clary and
it became evident that we were going to have to get rid of all
the pups. Then Coach Clary and Mr. Lambeth, the
orphanage superintendent, seeing that we were attached to
the pups decided to let us pick one puppy out of the litter
to keep. All of the boys decided that since I was the one
who found the pups, I should keep my pet. That was the
first time we were allowed to have a pet dog at any of the
orphanage cottages. Dr. Lorber was a local veterinarian
and provided our pet with a free rabies shot. Dr. Lorber
was a very kind man and seemed to like all of the orphan
children. He cared for all of our farm animals. Our dog
was named "Red," and he became popular with all of the
children at the orphanage. "Red" liked everybody and
especially anybody who had something to feed him.   He
liked to chase squirrels and he ran all over the Home
grounds looking for someone to play with or to just chase a
squirrel.

I built a doghouse for "Red" and placed it just outside
of my window. My room was the lowest to the ground of all
the rooms in my cottage. Sometimes on a stormy or a very
cold night I would push my screen out and let my friend

"Red" into my room to stay for the night. That didn't work so well. The soil outside my window was pure red dirt, and when it rained, the soil was pure red mud. I let "Red" in through the window and he jumped onto the foot of my bed to sleep. The next morning when I awoke, I was in for a big shock. "Red's" footprints were all over my bed. To avoid being in deep trouble, I got "Red" out of the window, then I took my bed covers to the laundry room and washed them before Mrs. Davidson, our home mother, could catch me with the mud on them. "Red" made more friends every day. All of the ladies that cooked our meals liked him. They would try to leave him scraps at their kitchen door. "Red" loved to run with the boys through the woods and pastures. He loved to play with all of the boys anywhere they would run. He trusted everyone as his friend and would let the little children pet him and rub him as long as they wished to do so. "Red" came home one day all beaten up. He must have met up with a big bad dog that crossed his path. We carried "Red" to Dr. Lorber to see what he could do for him. Dr. Lorber stitched him up in several places and told us to look after "Red." He told us to keep him in a warm place, and to be sure that he ate and drank water. He didn't charge us anything for looking after our best friend. That was so good of Dr. Lorber. "Red" was really hurting, and we all felt bad about the way he was hurting. All we could do was try to keep him comfortable. "Red" finally began to feel better and before long he was back running with all of the boys. His fur was growing back and it looked nearly as good as new. One day "Red" just disappeared and we never saw him again. I looked everywhere for him. I walked through the pastures and woods but just couldn't find him. I asked several of the girls if they had seen "Red" on their end of the Home grounds. No one had seen him. I really missed "Red," and I thought of all the good times running with him through the woods and fields. "Red" was family to a lot of the orphan children and he was loved by everyone.

It was quite some time later that one of my orphan brothers told me what he had heard about what happened to "Red." I was really upset with what I heard. It seemed that a couple of the boys had taken "Red" to the pasture to play with them. "Red" really liked these boys and would do anything with them. These boys had a .22 rifle hidden in the woods, and they were playing with it. One of the boys just decided that he would shoot "Red." So he raised the rifle, pulled the trigger and shot "Red" dead. These boys would never tell me what they did. There was nothing that I could do for "Red" now; I was left with only a memory of how good a friend that I had in "Red" and a sadder memory of how some kids can cause a lot of hurt by making very bad decisions. I hope that the boys always remember what they did to a helpless loving animal that trusted them and loved being with them until the very minute of his death.

Some of us would have a BB gun hidden away in some real safe place. For a while I had one that I kept in the boiler room of the old school house. I knew some good hiding places because I was very familiar with all of the boiler rooms in all of the buildings. I used to tend to the furnaces a few years earlier. Once in a while we carried our BB guns to the pasture with us. It was fun shooting at targets like a real cowboy. We would go to the dump and shoot tin cans. Sometimes we would shoot at a tadpole in the gravel pit. Our BB guns disappeared soon after we got them. No matter how good we thought we had them hidden, somehow they would just disappear.

In my last season of football playing for Coach Gibson, we ended the season with a record of eight wins and two losses. It was my most enjoyable year of playing football ever. We were happy to have had a good season, but I was not happy for the season to be my last. Even though I ended my career without being one of those who made all of the points, I knew that it took the whole team to win the games. The sports writers seemed to always forget all but the ones in the limelight but the team didn't forget. That year our football team and coach selected Jim McKnight and myself as the Unsung Heroes to represent our team with all the other Unsung Heroes of other teams in Forsyth County. I really didn't know how to say thanks to all of my teammates, but maybe they could sense my pleasure in my smile. I thought all of us should have gotten that award, but it did make me feel good, as I had never received any mention of outstanding playing in football my entire life. I always remembered my very first day of playing football for Coach Edwards. I remembered when I was trying on my first uniform. I remembered my first kick in the buttocks in my learning experience to be a great football player. There was no other place on earth that I would have preferred to play the game of football than at and for the Children's Home. Along with the playing was a certain spirit that consumed our emotions with pride, and being part of a long-standing tradition replete with memorable heroes, was equally exhilarating.

Fred's "last year of football"

During my senior year, I had an English teacher that didn't care for my being in her class. This all came to light when she was calling the roll at the beginning of the year. She was calling the roll and telling each student where she

240

wanted him or her to sit. She called Roy, then Rodney and Allen then a few of the girls. She then called my name and asked me if I had a sister that went to this school about five years previously. I said, "Yes," and it was like I had insulted her from her facial expression. I was all happy and thought that she might say something nice to me about my sister. She acted like a very proper lady with certain stiffness about her. All of a sudden she said that I would not be staying in her classroom, and that I would have to go to the office and be reassigned to another English class. I was dumbfounded. I knew that I had done nothing wrong but I gathered my books and walked to the office. I told the office lady that Miss Edwards had said that she didn't want me in her class, and for me to get reassigned to another class. The lady in the office said that it was her job to assign classes and not Miss Edward's. She then went in to the principal's office to ask him what to do. The principal called Miss Edwards from her classroom, and she and the principal had a long discussion. After Miss Edwards left the room, the principal called me in and told me that if I would go back to Miss Edwards' class, not cause any trouble, and did my work all year that at the end of the year he would let me graduate with my class. That was what I had in mind. Home boys would always get into trouble with Coach Clary if they caused trouble at the high school. I told the principal that I would do as he asked.

In the spring of my last year at the orphanage, all of us seniors would go to the Baptist Hospital for a physical. The orphanage wanted to see that we were all in good health before they turned us out into the great big world to be on our own. My senior year really began to set the stage to future events, strange feelings and uneasiness. Our days were numbered since graduation night would be the last night that we would have a place to sleep or eat at our orphanage home. All of the years of calling this "my home" would be ended by the necessity to give another child a chance at the same love and care that was offered me. Even though I knew how to work hard and felt that I could survive somehow when I left, I really began to wonder what was going to happen to me. This had been my home for as long as I could remember.

As the school year finally came to an end, all of the seniors prepared for graduation. The roll was called and each student was told how he or she would file in on graduation night. My name was NOT called so I went to the principal's office to see why my name was not on the roster. The principal told me that he could not embarrass Miss Edwards by letting me walk across the stage on graduation night. I asked him about our agreement and he said that he was sorry. He told me to come in on Monday morning and he would give me my diploma. Wow! Four years in high school, and I wouldn't be able to walk across the stage with all of my friends. I guess it was mostly my fault for not doing my best in everything all of the time.

Graduation night was a very difficult night for me but somehow I managed to get through it. The next morning as other boys were moving into our cottage, I knew one would be taking my bed. I had my clothes packed in a cardboard box and an old suitcase that I had found somewhere. I was ready to leave the Home, but had no idea where I was going. As the other boys were waiting for someone in their family to pick them up to carry them back to their hometown, I would say good-bye for the last time to some of them and would never see them or hear from them again. I put my clothes by the front door and watched as they left one by one. A couple of the boys were together and seemed to know where they were going. I asked them where they were going. They said that they were going to the Y.M.C.A. I had never heard of people going to the Y.M.C.A. to live, but I asked, "Would you mind if I rode with you to this place?" I knew they were going to have jobs in Winston-Salem just as I had been offered a job. I asked if they could help me get a room at this place and they said, "Sure." I felt a little relieved at that point. They helped put my things in the trunk of the car that would take us to the Y.M.C.A., and we rode to the administration building. We went inside and Miss Taylor, the Home's secretary/cashier presented us with our savings earned over the entire time that we were at the orphanage. Each of the boys got his, and I got mine. I thought it was the most money that I had ever seen in my entire life. I was rich. I had received a lump sum of One Hundred and Sixty-Five Dollars. I thought WOW! I can buy me a car. I can buy me some clothes to look good in when I start work. I thought, BOY ole BOY, I'll be somebody. All that money sort of gave me the feeling that everything was going to be all right. The other boys and I jumped back into the car, and the man drove us to the Y.M.C.A. in town. We got our belongings and the man in the car drove off. The other boys said, "Come on in and register at the desk." I walked up to the desk and asked the man for a place to stay. The man gave me a few minutes introduction to the rules and told me how much I owed him. As I was standing there, I turned around from the desk and saw a very large sitting room full of men. I felt very uneasy. Every one of them seemed to be looking at me as if I didn't belong there. It was a very strange feeling to be in their presence. I just told myself that being this was a place for Christian men to live that everything would be all right. I thought that they were just Christians looking to do good for an orphan boy just as they had done for me all of my life. Those were mostly the only kind of people that I had ever known. The man behind the desk gave me my room key and told me that I would be sharing a room with one of the other boys whom I had grown up with. I grabbed my cardboard box and suitcase and headed toward the stairs. I politely nodded to several of the Christian gentlemen on my way up the stairs. My room was several floors up, and I finally made it to the room carrying all my belongings. I opened the door and my roommate said, "You can have that bed." The room wasn't large at all, but we each had a dresser and closet. I put my things away and asked him where our bathroom was. He said that the whole floor had to share a common bath halfway down the hall. I had lived all my life sharing a common bathroom with boys, but I was very shy about sharing a common bathroom with all of those older Christian men.

We decided to go out and get something to eat. I asked, "Where do we go to eat?" He said, "We go to the K&W Cafeteria and go through the lunch line." When I had previously come to town I had only stopped to get a drink and hotdog so everything was very new to me on how to live on my own. He showed me how to go through the line at the cafeteria. This wasn't hard at all, but I was very nervous eating with all of these strange people. The cooks behind the line asked me what I wanted, and I pointed. Then I came to a big man with a very large piece of meat. He asked if I wanted a slice of it. I said, "Yes sir," and he cut me a very large slice of the reddest meat that I had seen since we killed pigs back at the orphanage. I've seen them get well when they were not hurt any worse than that. He put juice all over the top of it and handed me the plate. I was so nervous, and I didn't know how to ask for a slice of meat that was cooked. I thought all meat was cooked. I just knew that I was going to get sick. I took my tray on through the line and paid for my meal. I sat down with several of the boys in the midst of all of those strangers. I was frightened to be sitting there and afraid about minding my manners as I had always been taught. I could only remember going to a place like this with my nice sponsors from High Point when I was little, but even then, I was very uncomfortable. I tried to eat a little and every time I took a bite, while looking at that red meat, the more nauseous I became. I got so scared of getting sick that I just got up and walked out. It was some time before I would try again to eat in a big place like that with all of those people around.

Many tough learning experiences would shock me in this strange new world that I had entered. Oh, I was physically brave and in real good shape from all of the physical work that I had grown up doing, but there were a lot of strange scary things happening that I really didn't want to experience. I got back to my room; and it dawned on me that I had not been gone from the home that I grew up in but half a day, and I had already been relieved of quite a bit of my life's savings. I started thinking. I could not eat in a place like that cafeteria and have three meals a day. I have to pay my weekly rent, and I knew I wouldn't get paid for my job until I worked for a month. I'll be "dog gone; I wasn't rich after all.

The first day that I started my job, I walked from town to my high school principal's office to get my diploma and then to the company for whom I would be working. It was quite a walk, and I was anxious as a young boy waiting for his first kiss from his favorite girl friend. One of the boys that went to another city high school offered me a ride the next day. He said that it wasn't out of his way. His name was Jimmy Saylor who went to Gray High School. I had played football against Jimmy but never remembered many of his team's players. Only "Big Tony" who smashed me several times when we played them. Jimmy helped me for some time getting to and from work. Jimmy's brother would marry a very good friend of mine, Bonnie, who I had grown up with at the Home. Jimmy, Donald Weir and I would ride to work nearly every day throughout the summer.

When I walked through town, I would walk by several car lots. I dreamed of the day when I would be able to buy a car. I finally worked up enough nerve to ask the man at the car lot how much it cost me to get a car. He wanted to know how old I was. I told him that I was eighteen. He said that I couldn't get a car until I was twenty-one unless I had someone to sign for the title. I was shocked one more time with another learning experience. He suggested that I bring my parents in, and he could sell me a car. I thanked him then informed him that I didn't have any parents. Here I was, eighteen years old, living on my own, and I couldn't vote, and I couldn't own a car; so I started thinking about joining the US Army. I called my sister Charlena, who was living in South Carolina, and asked her if she would help me get a car. I told her that I was not old enough to own one here in North Carolina. She and her husband Sam said they would look for a car for me to drive. I boarded a bus and rode to Greenville, South Carolina, where I bought a car, but had to keep it in my sister's name until I was twenty-one years old.

The learning experiences kept coming at me from all sides, and I began to realize just how wonderful a home I had had at the orphanage. It seemed strange at the Y.M.C.A., Every time I would leave my room to go to the shower room, several other men would come out of their rooms at the same time. They seemed to be the same men.

245

After several visits to the shower, they seemed to follow me into the room as I turned on the shower. Each time, they made conversation with me, and I thought they were just trying to be good Christian men. Then they began to get overly friendly and asked if I would I go to the gym with them or if I would come to visit them in their rooms. I hurried to finish my shower and got out of there each time as fast as I could. Finally things came to a very serious point. One of the men standing at the adjacent shower told me that I had the prettiest velvet skin. At the same time he reached over and put his hand on my back. I became so mad that my mind returned to my childhood when another man tried to force himself on me. I exploded with hatred. I turned toward the man and swung as hard as I could, hoping that I would deck him with the first blow of my fist. I knocked the man to the floor when I hit him right between the eyes. I was blind with hatred for the man, and I glanced toward the others in the shower as they cowered and retreated. I would have fought to the death if one of them had made a move towards me. I was shaking all over with fear. I ran out of the shower room and back to my room as fast as I could. At that time, I began to fear living at the Y.M.C.A. This place was not a place for Christian men, as I had thought. It appeared to be a haven for sick men with filthy intentions to prey on young men and lay with each other. Boy, when will these learning experiences end? This event only brought back sad memories from a previous attempt by an older man to make unwanted advances on me. That first attempt happened when I was thirteen. A young man that I knew tried to force himself on me with sexual intent. I wouldn't dare tell anyone about it because of the fear and embarrassment of people knowing of it. It took fifty years for me to speak of this horrible day because I was frightened to death at the time that it happened.

From then on these men seemed to not come out of their rooms as often when I went to the shower. On one other occasion a different man came up to me while I was standing at the sink and put his hand on my shoulder to rub it. I flew hot again and had to punch him as hard as I could to get him away from me. What was wrong with those people? Why did they call it a Christian place when it was a front for all of those men? That was the last straw, because I was getting out of that filthy pit of perverts. It was disgusting, but in our country everyone has protection unless you violate other's freedoms. I felt strongly that my freedoms were being violated. They should at least stay among their own kind and not prey on others. In later years, I felt I understood why some men are driven to kill this type of men who prey on children and other unsuspecting young men. It takes many years for a young boy to release the information that some adult abused or attempted to abuse him as a young person. In our society today, this type of behavior is the most abusive, vile, sanctioned behavior of all crimes against the unwilling and helpless young boys. A trail of invisible tears will drown our very existence as an honorable people on this earth if the parents and adults don't make a major change in accepting responsibility for the decline in morality of our great nation.

I didn't have time to get out of that Y.M.C.A. before I faced another learning experience. I went to the shower one day and when I came back to my room, my wallet was missing. I had locked the door as always but the wallet was gone. I had just gotten my pay and now I had no money, no driver's license, and no other identification and shocked to the point that I wondered what possibly could happen next. How could all of this be happening to me? Was all of this supposed to be part of my learning how to live on my own and how to trust people? A few days later my roommate brought my wallet to me. He said he found it on the roof outside a hallway window, but my payday money had been taken. What could possibly happen next? I would sleep with one eye open for the remainder of the time that I had to live in that awful place. I wished that I could find a home as nice as the orphanage that I had to leave. I would have to work hard, and in time, I would make my own happy home. I hoped it would be as comfortable as the orphanage, and I could find the time to be all boy again. For now I had to be all man like the Children's Home taught me to be. Many years later I found the Y.M.C.A. in our neighborhood to be a real clean and decent place to visit. There were no rooms for rent in this facility. Maybe the one I lived in has been cleaned up. I sure hope so for the sake of all young boys.

I couldn't wait until the following football season so I could watch the boys that I had played with have a chance to prove themselves. I just knew they would have a special team. They were growing in size and ability. Many of them had proven they had what it took to be winners. They would end up with a perfect regular season record. I was so proud of that team and proud that they represented my Home.

Jack Hartness, an older boy who attended Hanes High School, took me under his wing when I went to work for Western Electric. He got me started playing sports after hours for the company team. He knew about the orphanage where I had grown up, and he knew many of the older boys that had lived there. Jack had served in the Navy as a "Frog Man" and was very active in sports. He gave me all the advice he could about my new life in the real world. He and his wife Dianne gave me support and friendship until I left the area on my thirty year Coast Guard venture around the world. Where are all of the real men like Jack, "Pop" Woosley, Coach Gibson, Coach Edwards, Coach Clary, Coach Tandy and Gray Todd in our society today?

There was one other man, named Robards that I met at work. He had been reared at the Barium Springs Orphanage and knew what I was facing in my new world. He and Jack made special efforts to show me their kindness, and I will never forget their friendship.

I would go through the rest of my life telling people where I was from and how proud I was of the Children's Home. People in many foreign countries that I visited during my military career could not escape the story about where and how I grew up. Some could not understand my language, but they understood that "something" made me proud and happy about "something."

I eventually found my "Happy Home" by volunteering to serve my country in the U.S. Armed Forces. I started with the Army by serving 4 years and then served thirty years in the U. S. Coast Guard. The Coast Guard became my home because I loved helping others in need, assisting in our national security, saving lives and working many missions of different types. My reward was the shear excitement of performing my duty. I was fortunate to have a wife that understood our separation while performing my missions and the importance of those missions. My wife, Wanda, and I have settled down in retirement on the bank of a river. We watch the waterfowl floating by and the fish jumping out of the water. We watch the sun settle into a glowing sunset across the water and then, at night, we are blessed with the Carolina Moon glittering across the water and shining beautifully upon us. I'm still an orphan at heart and enjoy playing pranks at times. That was a big part in making my boyhood home the Happy Home in which I was fortunate enough to have been reared. My wife Wanda tells everyone that she had to take over where the orphanage home mothers left off. She works hard at trying to take The Children's Home boy out of me, but she knows that that would be like making a city slicker out of Huckleberry Finn.

Wanda and Fred

My heart is full of warmth and gratitude to all of those
who helped give me a chance at a decent life. My heartfelt
thanks go out to all of the children who put their pennies
and nickels into their Sunday school offering plate so that I
would have a warm place to sleep at night. My heartfelt
thanks to all the parents who gave and explained to their
children how important their thoughtful gifts were to so
many needy children. Many successful men and women,
through their thoughtful planning and giving, provided us
with a safe and comfortable home, The Children's Home, in
which to live as we grew in stature and in our learning to
be able to provide for our own futures. What amazed me
most in my experience, growing up at the orphanage, were
the many adults who gave up a promising chance at a
successful career of their own in exchange for giving their
entire adult lives to the care of children such as my sister

and me. I, along with many others, had no other place to live and to have a home like The Children's Home was surely a blessing from God. Today, my Home is in my heart no matter where I travel, and no matter how many changes are made to the Home. It wasn't perfect, but I found out it was the best place in the world for me. My suggestion to the many, many problems with immature parents and troubled children is to look at the only alternative. Make the best of what you have and what is offered. It's time for parents and adults to take charge of America and take America back from the evils that have caused the decays in our society. I certainly was no angel growing up, but I am able to recognize what is destroying our great country from within and it directly relates to our immoral culture destroying our children.

THE FREEDOMS OF ADULTS, KEEP WITH ADULTS. THE BLESSING OF HAVING A CHILD SHOULD ALWAYS BE A PROTECTED BLESSING.

After I left the orphanage, I returned to the mountains to visit from time to time over the years with what remaining family I had. There were uncles and aunts and lots of cousins that I had never met. I saw Uncle Roy and Aunt Lizzy. I became familiar with my first cousins, Charles, Edward, Thelma, Blonde and Ora Mae. I got to know my Uncle Winslow King and Aunt Sally. Sally was my dad's sister. She always told me how proud she was of me serving my country. She would always say, "I sure am proud of you for serving your sentence." I wasn't sure if she got me mixed up with some other family member that may have gotten caught for moonshining and "served his sentence". Uncle Winslow was a fiddle maker and people from all over came to him for repairs on their fiddles or to have him construct a new fiddle to their liking. He also was a good recipe maker. Moonshine that is! Aunt Sally has a twin sister Mae whom I've still not visited with. I would visit with Mr. and Mrs. McGlamery. Mrs. McGlamery was the daughter of Doctor Killian who found The Children's Home and convinced "Pop" Woosley to take my sister and me there to live, grow and have a better chance in this world. I couldn't thank them enough for their kindness and caring.

The End

Gilmer and Graham

My brother-in-law, Sam Murdock, has a set of identical twin brothers, Gilmer and Graham, that are a year or so younger than I. We used to play in the woods and pastures and they did most of the same things that us older boys did. A year or two older meant that you were a big boy there at the Home. They both had a pair of slingshots that they carried into the woods with them, and they would climb big trees just as we did. They would both end up joining the U.S. Marines together when they grew

252

older. Each of them told a couple of stories of things that happened to them as they were growing up at the orphanage, and I agreed to pass the stories on through my memoirs. Orphan humor was what made us happy at times when there was no other happiness.

Graham's Story

There are times when ingenuity must be displayed. A kid has the awesome responsibility to invent ways to improve upon the ordinary sliding board.

It was a cold day by North Carolina standards but Miss Harbour had still allowed all the kids at the baby cottage to go out and play. We were playing on the different yard toys and thought there might be a better and faster way to go down the sliding board. That's when we spotted a cardboard box. It looked just small enough to fit on the sliding board and large enough to hold one person inside.

Neither Gilmer, Walter Greer nor I wanted to try our hand at it, so we unanimously elected Sue. It took a bit of persuading to convince her to get into the box at the top of the sliding board, which to us looked like a hundred feet up in the air.

Sue finally fit herself into the box and Gilmer and I shoved the box to get it started down the slide. This was the first but not the last time I would hear the word "OOPS!" This is not a word one spoke lightly. It usually meant something had gone wrong and this was indeed the case. Instead of Sue sliding down the board, she started end-over-end rolling down the sliding board in that cardboard box. Each roll elicited a yell. Before she hit the ground Walter and I were off that sliding board and running into the crowd. Gilmer was still on top of the sliding board looking in amazement at Sue in a pathetic, unstoppable roll.

It was too late. Miss Harbour had spotted the tragic heap at the bottom of the sliding board and simultaneously saw Gilmer, the culprit, at the top. She ran over to Sue and saw that she was indeed still alive, though not the same person as she had been moments before the slide of her life began.

In a flash, Gilmer was marched off to stand in the corner. After a few minutes Gilmer motioned me over to take his place. Being identical twins did have its benefits as we could trade punishment and cut the ordeal in half. Little did anyone know.

At just the right moment, I darted over to take his place and he darted into the rush of other games. Less than a minute had gone by when Miss Harbour appeared with a paddle and said, "Now I am going to give you that spanking I promised you."

You can bet that it was the end of "trading places" as I took a spanking for my twin brother. I think Sue finally forgave us but it probably was years before she ever trusted a boy again. Sue, if you ever read this...Walter Greer put us up to it.

Graham H. Murdock
CH Resident 1946-1959

Gilmer's Tales

It was a hot summer Saturday afternoon at the Home. That was almost always the case in the summertime, especially if you were hoeing corn or practicing for the upcoming football season. Indeed there was a feeling of excitement around the football field about an impending football game—a game of flag football. Not just an ordinary game...this time the girls would be playing with the boys. That meant only one thing, the chance to prove that Judy Dusenberry was not faster than all of the boys. This was a matter of pride. In fact, we thought there was a law against girls being better than boys at anything, except, of course, ironing and laundry. A comment like that heard by any of the girls would mean the certain, "You'll never get your hands through that Sunday starched shirt." The girls ruled the laundry and any boy who was in a beef with them could wind up in a starched shirt that would almost break if you dropped it. They could starch a shirt so stiff that it would rub your neck raw before Sunday school was over.

Teams were chosen, with a certain slant toward those who were out to prove boys were superior beings selected for the team opposing Judy Dusenberry.

Battle had hardly begun when they gave her the ball. It was time to prove, once and for all, our superiority. Off she darted toward the left side of the field. All the boys on the defensive team were fast after her. Winfred Hope and Walter Greer were within a step of catching her when she suddenly turned and darted back behind them. Our two best were grabbing air. Graham and I were the next closest to her and ran smack dab into each other as she hurtled between us. Wilbur James and Lynwood Satterwhite had slowed a bit because they thought we had her. Then, whoosh... she scored. What humiliation! It was time for a change in tactics. We would form a circle around her the next time she received the ball and there would be no escape. After about twenty minutes of play and a few good tricks of our own the score was evened to one touchdown each. It was their ball. Here it came, the handoff to Judy, the freckled wonder. Our plan was put into action. She was zigging and zagging so fast that we were just able to stay up with her. Just as Grady Mitchell was reaching for the flag she zigged instead of zagging and slipped down, just as the circle was closing. Down went Judy and Grady. A pile-up ensued with me on top of Judy and Grady, and into the pile comes Graham, Wilbur, Winfred, Mike, Lynwood and Hilda Smith. Hilda later said she was pulling the boys off of Judy.

From the bottom of the pile I saw my chance to inflict a bit of justice. There across Grady's back and right in front of my mouth was Judy's arm. It said very loudly, "Bite Me." I did.

The scream was not only deafening by those on the pile but heard by Mrs. Reynolds and Miss Tula Harrelson, who was sneaking a smoke, and Miss Little. They ran onto the field and into the fray. Miss Tula was hurling boys off of the heap when she came upon Judy. Judy was playing the pain to the hilt, screaming and crying as though a mad dog had bitten her. When asked, what was wrong; how was she hurt; she displayed her arm with the double teeth marks. It was as though a cloud of cold rain had swept over everyone. Miss Tula peered around to see who had the guilt of Cain on his face. None moved a muscle or outwardly showed any emotion. Inside we all wanted to run. Judy could not identify who had bitten her. Miss Tula deployed the famous "line-up." This was the customary thing to do when investigating a dastardly deed by one of the boys. This was somewhat routine and we all knew to fall in line.

Then came the cunning investigative techniques only Miss Tula could deploy...matching teeth with the bite marks. I saw a sound whopping coming, or worse yet, the "I'll put you in a mattress sack and mop the floor up with you" threat from Miss Tula. Every boy feared this threat, though I can't say that I ever witnessed it. It was legend and no one doubted it or wanted to experience it first hand.

There was a second Christmas for me that year. My identical twin brother Graham had gotten in line just ahead of me or should I say I had gotten in line behind Graham. Being twins did have its good points.

The matching of teeth was quite simple. Miss Tula made each boy put his teeth over the bite on Judy's arm. Miss Little, Mrs. Reynolds and Miss Tula would then verify a possible match. This is where being twins come in. Graham's teeth were an exact match with mine. I didn't want him to get in trouble as he was in line ahead of me, but...

One by one the boys had to put their teeth over the bite marks, Wilbur, no...Grady, no...Mike, no...Bill, no...Lynwood, no...Walter, no...Winfred, Yes! What happened? How could it be? Winfred's teeth were a perfect match! No question. Justice was swift and immediate. The last time we saw or heard Winfred that day was when Miss Tula had him by one ear with his feet barely touching the ground, on his way to parts unknown denying, denying, denying!

We had just missed a certain and sure punishment worse than the infamous ditch or Coach Clary's paddle. We had been spared a fate worse than having a pair of our underwear show up on the girls' end of the orphanage (another story).

To this day we have never told anyone this story, and

certainly not Winfred. If anyone tells Winfred, we'll deny, deny, deny!

Another story is about some things a boy, or at least boys under twelve just don't do. It is an unwritten law that boys do not hug girls, are never seen near the girls bathroom, and never ever do anything that would bring shame down on their buddies or—at the risk of offending Miss Tula Harrelson, the goddess of threatened punishment—bring embarrassment upon the home mothers.

That's all well and good unless you are "Tinker" Reese, "Tink" for short. "Tink" didn't adhere to any code of conduct, much less one that involved girls or etiquette. At that age, "Tink" thought girls didn't exist and had no clue of proper etiquette, or improper etiquette for that matter.

It was Sponsor Day at the Home. Each church group sponsoring one of the boys or girls from the Home had an opportunity to visit the Home and meet their sponsored boy or girl in their natural setting. Sounds like a zoo; truth is there were days... It gave the sponsors the opportunity to see the cottages and meet the home mothers. Days were spent preparing for this special event. Care was taken to see that the cottages were clean and the orphanage was neat and orderly. Each boy and girl was to put his or her "best foot forward." (Never did understand that saying! I thought for years that most people were born with a gimp foot and could only show their good one. Oh well!)

As was the rule, several of us boys decided that since we didn't have to work on the farm that day, we'd sneak off to pick blackberries. This was a favorite pastime as it allowed us to venture beyond the campus and into the unknown world. Usually that was just over the hill of the upper pasture near the Little White Church

We had a particularly good berry-picking day. "Tink" had picked his box of black berries near the gully, the Children's Home dumpsite, and we had our tin cans completely full in no time. With our bellies full and the hot sun beating down on us, we decided to head towards home where all the activities were going on. As we approached the football field, we noticed that all the sponsors and many of the boys and girls were enjoying a picnic style lunch. All I could think of was Miss Holland's fried chicken and potato salad. My mention of that hastened everyone's pace.

"Tink" Reese was leading the pack of shirtless, tanned boys as we came onto the football field. As we got closer we noticed that the crowd was getting quieter. "Tink" was still popping the blackberries into his mouth from the box that he had just filled. Just then from out of nowhere came Miss Tula.... Snatch!!...The box of blackberries was gone and an instant knot was visited upon "Tink's" head. A moment or two passed before the silence was broken with Coach Clary announcing that they were going to cut the watermelons.

It wasn't until a bit later that we learned that the blackberries hadn't been confiscated because we weren't allowed to have them. It was the fact that the box the berries were in was a Kotex box and "Tink" was seen eating out of a Kotex box by all of the sponsors—a mortal sin for any boy for sure, but far, far worse for establishing poor demeanor for pure Christian children. But then "Tink" wasn't into demeanor. In fact, 'Tink" was a boy's boy and had Tom Sawyer and Huck Finn beat...by a long shot... certainly by a Kotex box.

Normally it would be a while before any boy lived that down, but it was only shortly after that that "Tink" was in the thick of it again. That's another story.

Gilmer Murdock
CH Resident 1946-1956

Epilogue

Perry Lefeavers grew up at the Children's Home and when he graduated he served as an officer in the U. S. Navy during WWII and Korean wars. After his service to our country he became a teacher and coach. Following his retirement from teaching he researched and wrote a book on the history of this orphanage where I grew up. I am amazed at the work that went into Dr. Perry Lefeavers's book.

Dr Perry Lefeavers

For a fully pictured documentary history of The Children's Home (First Seventy-Five Years), you can order the professionally prepared book written by Dr. Perry Lefeavers. At present time this beautiful, hardbound book can be obtained for a cost of Thirty-Seven Dollars and Ten Cents plus $5.00 shipping, a total of $42.10. To order, send check or money order to:

> The Methodist Children's Home
> Alumni Association % Mr. John Ammons
> 1001 Reynolda Road
> Winston-Salem, NC 27104

Note From Dr. Lefeavers:

    "Orphan Freddy" received the Distinguished Alumni Award presented by The Children's Home Alumni Association at the 2001 homecoming. His outstanding career in the Coast Guard and untiring efforts through volunteer work with Special Olympics, which earned him the Governor's North Carolina Volunteer award, were cited in the presentation. Then in May 2002, Fred was elected president of The Children's Home Alumni Association for a period of two years (2003-2004).

ISBN 1-41205387-0